a handbook for
FOLLOWERS
OF JESUS

a handbook for FOLLOWERS OF JESUS

Winkie Pratney

BETHANY FELLOWSHIP, INC.
Minneapolis, Minnesota

The Scripture quotations used in this book are adaptations from either the King James version or from an English translation that used a minimum of basic English words.

Copyright © 1977
Bethany Fellowship, Inc.
All rights reserved

Published by Bethany Fellowship, Inc.
6820 Auto Club Road, Minneapolis, Minnesota 55438

Printed in the United States of America

Library of Congress Cataloging in Publication Data:

Pratney, Winkie, 1944-
    A handbook for followers of Jesus.

    Bibliography: p.
    Includes indexes.
    1. Youth—Religious life. I. Title
BV4531.2.P7   248'.83   76-44385
ISBN 0-87123-378-9

Table of Contents

About the Author

WINKIE PRATNEY is a speaker and author who travels extensively throughout the world. He addresses many seminars, conferences, and campus audiences on the truths of Scripture and the claims of Christ. He has written two earlier books, *Youth Aflame* and *Doorways to Discipleship.*

When not travelling, he and his wife make their home in Lindale, Texas, at the headquarters facilities of AGAPEFORCE, an organization bringing the gospel to street people across America.

Mr. Pratney's own background in organic chemistry, and his pre-conversion experience in the youth music culture combine to make him particularly effective as a communicator to the young.

Section I
The Disciple's
SALVATION

1

Welcome to the Family

A LETTER FROM THE LORD

The Word of God,
Heaven's Channel
Eternity, Year One

Don't be afraid anymore, My child,
From now on, I will be with you always;
    I am your God, for you have asked Me to control your life,
    And I will give you the strength you will need to live it for
       Me;
    You can count on this strength always, no matter what faces
       you;
    I will always hold you up with My strong hand of perfect
       goodness.

Yes, I know,
    I know how little you are beside the vast powers that move
       My heavens;
    You are just like a worm—blind to the fullness of My power,
    With a very definite liking for the old, safe dirt—
    Afraid to go out into the sunlight of My Presence.

But, I am in control of all this universe;
    I give breath to all people on the earth,
    And I have called you in goodness and mercy.
    I promise you I will go with you and keep you if you stay
       close to Me;
    None of them will ever be turned away.

I give such rich gifts to My children!
    The gift of *peace* is one of them;
    All the world cannot give you this;
    You don't have to worry anymore, nor be afraid.

In the house of My Father I have made a home for you;
It will be there, waiting for you, when you fall asleep in My
arms.

The most priceless gift I give you is the gift of living forever!
The *real you* will *never die,*
Nor will any man ever be able to pull you from the shelter
of My hand;
The God of Forever will be your safe hiding place,
And underneath you are the strong arms that hold you up
and never let go.

You are like a little lamb, newborn, and I am your Good Shepherd.
From now on you can learn to recognize My voice;
You will know Me someday just as I know you now,
And now you can learn what I want you to do for Me.
If you REALLY love Me, promise Me you will do what I ask;
The tasks I give you will never be too big or too hard.

Read what I have said in My Book;
It is given to you to make you fit and right in all matters
of life.
You will discover its hidden riches now that you can spiritually
see.
Every word I have spoken is full of living power;
It will help you to decide differences
Between My will and the way you used to walk;
It will stab right down deeper into hearts than a switchblade,
Showing what is really going on inside them.
I have caused it to be written so that you will trust Me more
and more,
And that through trusting, you and all others you meet might
have the life that I want you to have.

Talk with Me all the time.
Never let yourself get into the place where you can't pray.
It will help you keep a brave, trusting heart in all places,
at all times—
Yes, even when the way is difficult and hard.
From now on you can expect trouble from the world around
you;
You don't belong to the enemy's world anymore, but to Mine.

So, whenever you are hurt for Me in any way by the world,
You can have a secret cause to be glad:
You are doing it for My sake, so you can be happy about
it;
It is one sure proof that your life is now truly different.

Work for My wages;
> I don't pay My friends in the same evil way the world usually does.
> Every unselfish act you do for Me lays up treasure for you in our unearthly palace,
> So don't let the world around you squeeze you into its own mold.

Don't worry over material things like food, drink or clothes to wear;
> Only people without Me as their Friend have cause to do that!
> No, always look for what you can do for *God and His* world first
> (Remember, He is the spring of goodness, and He knows your real need).
> And I promise you—I give you My word—
> Every single *one* of these things will be taken care of.

I want you to tell others about Me too,
> Just as My Father and I shared that someone called *you* was down there, lost—
> Someone I was willing to die for because I loved and valued you so much.

So, tell your friends—everybody you meet in the whole, wide world
> That there is Someone in heaven who longs to love them
> Back into the great family of God . . .
> That if *any one* of them is really sorry enough to give up his sin,
> Call on My name, ask Me to rule in his heart,
> I will save him and make him powerful to become a son of God,
> Just as simply and wonderfully as I changed you.

Be careful, child; beware of your enemy, the devil;
> He walks your earth like a raging lion;
> He searches for those he can tear and kill;
> He comes for one purpose:
> To steal and kill and destroy.

So—watch and pray in case you feel like toying with temptation.
> Never doubt Me in anything I tell you!
> I would never, ever lie to you; I want you to remember that,
> For doubt will break the contact between us,
> And you will again feel lost and afraid.

Here is a tremendous fact:
> *I give you all power* over any of the devil's forces of darkness and evil.

If you solidly resist him *in My strength*, he will run in fright
from you.
You can do anything I tell you to in My power;
If GOD is working with you, nothing will be impossible!
What I give you to do will never be impossible!

Don't forget to meet with others who also belong to Me.
If you are really walking in the light of My life,
You will want this friendship to share the glorious thing My
Father and I are doing in your life.
Then you will learn just what it means to know that My blood
can clean you utterly from sin.

If you slip, if you fall, and an old habit catches you off guard,
Don't cover it or pretend;
Tell Me about it; bring it all out in the open.
I promise to forgive you and clean you up again,
No matter how much you have hurt Me;
I promise to put it all behind My back and get you started
again.

My child, above all else, *love me*!
With all your heart, all your soul, all your mind, and all your
strength—
More than houses, lands, careers, families, friends, children.
Not until you begin to do this will you really be able to love
others
Just like I love you.

—The Lord Jesus

2

How to Become God's Child

The Facts

1. *God loves you!* He made you. He knows how you feel. He understands all your problems. He knows your background. He knows your name. And God *loves* you and wants you to have the best for your life.

Everything God does, He does out of *love*. His love is not just a good feeling about His universe, but an unselfish choice to will our highest good. "Herein is love, not that we loved God, but that He loved us, and sent His Son to be the propitiation for our sins [the way through which we could be forgiven and come back to Him]" (1 John 4:10).

2. *Sin has come between you and God.* Sin is really selfishness, a "me first" attitude of heart and life. It is denying God's right to be God in your life. It is breaking His laws and scorning His guidelines for happiness. It is putting yourself first above everyone else, living first of all to serve and please yourself instead of God, and refusing to treat all others according to their rightful place and value in the universe. "And this is the condemnation, that light is come into the world, and men loved darkness rather than light, because their deeds were evil" (John 3:19). "All have sinned, and come short of the glory of God" (Rom. 3:23).

3. *God hates sin because it costs so much.* Sin is the cause of all the heartache in our world. God didn't plan sin. He never plans unhappiness. He wants man to be happy and free. Sin is the reason why there is pain, misery and death in our land. Sin enslaves us to our feelings instead of allowing us to do what is right and reasonable. Sin makes us feel guilty and afraid and alone.

4. *Sin is the most expensive thing in the universe.* It cost God His only Son; it cost Jesus Christ His life. God, who must be just, *never* can allow sin to go unpunished, or the universe would

begin to collapse in evil. When God's infinitely important law of love for happiness is broken, the law-breaker *must* pay the penalty. A law without a penalty is only advice. The penalty must be as important as the law it is designed to protect. For such a terribly important law as God's law, made to direct and protect His intelligent, moral creatures, God set a penalty as high as possible—endless death, or separation forever from His universe and from all the rights and privileges of living and growing in it through eternity. The soul that sins shall die, for "the wages of sin is death" (Rom. 6:23).

5. *You, as a sinner, deserve to be punished.* You know that deep inside. By rights, you should pay the penalty of your sin. You knew what was right, but you did not do it. You have made a mess of your life. If you are really honest, you know you have no excuses to make. Nothing you could say to God could possibly justify the choices you have made to please yourself. "Knowing that a man is not justified by the works of law ... for by the works of the law shall no flesh be justified" (Gal. 2:16). "If we say that we have not sinned, we make Him a liar, and His word is not in us" (1 John 1:10).

But in His great love and wisdom, God found a way to forgive you, and still be just, *if* you are willing to meet the conditions.

The Conditions

The Lord Jesus humbled himself and became man. He lived a perfect life and never broke His Father's law of love. He offered His own perfect life as a sacrifice to provide a substitute for the penalty of *your* sin. His death on the cross shows at once how much God loves you and how much He hates your sin. You can choose one of two things: pay the penalty for your sin, or resolve to turn your back on the past and give your life to God, letting the Lord Jesus be your substitute.

God cannot forgive you unless you are willing to stop fighting Him and make Him your "boss." His Holy Spirit makes you willing to change, as He draws you now by his love. He wants to help you to make a life-changing decision *now.* Jesus said, "I am the way, the truth, and the life: no man cometh to the Father, but by Me" (John 14:6). "He that trusts his life wholly to the Son is experiencing eternal life; he that does not believe on the Son of God shall not see life; but the anger of God abides on him" (John 3:36).

Salvation is God's plan to restore man to a holy, happy relationship with Him. All problems of sin, doubt, failure and lack of victory or God's power can be conquered by the following steps:

1. *Rethink*—stop running away from the voice of God and look at your life. We do not naturally want to obey God; only if we let the Holy Spirit show us our sin as GOD sees it will we realize just how bad we have been.

To do this, you MUST be *totally honest*! Don't pretend. Don't "play down" your sin. Stop making excuses! Admit from your *heart*, "God, I am all wrong!" If necessary, get paper and pencil and WRITE DOWN the things that have come between you and God and have stopped you from serving Him as you ought.

2. *Repent*—turn your back on your old way of life. Be WILLING to lose any habit, any plan, any friend that you have been living your life for. This is not easy, but Jesus said if we want to follow Him we must first count the cost (Luke 14:25-33). Salvation is like a marriage. Two people promise themselves to each other, pledge their love to each other before a watching world, and give up all their old dates. This is what God wants you to do to know His love.

3. *Renounce*—give up all rights to your own life. If you are going to be a part of God's world-changing family, you cannot be your own boss any longer. You must *DIE* to your own plans, dreams and ambitions, and be willing to do whatever God wants you to do. He knows EXACTLY what will make you most happy. It may hurt to surrender everything at first, but God knows best, and will *never* ask you to do anything that you will regret in the end. A true Christian has nothing of his own—time, talents, money, possessions, friends, career and future. All must be surrendered for his King's service wherever and whenever He wants them.

4. *Replan*—be prepared to make many changes in your life! The very moment you make this heart-choice for God, the old "you" will die, and a new person inside you will begin to live. If the Holy Spirit is speaking to you about getting something right with someone, you must be willing to do it. God will help you. Wherever you need to confess wrong, or restore or repay something to someone, the Lord Jesus will give you the courage and the words to say. Becoming a Christian implies the willingness, as far as humanly possible, to *right all known wrong* (Prov. 28:13). If you have written out a list of things that have come between you and God, ask His forgiveness *now* for those things against Him; plan to make right all other things with people you know you have wronged and feel guilty about. The circle of *confession* must fit the circle of *committal* of sin. Those against God, confess only to Him; those against one person, to that *person alone*; those against a group, to the group.

5. *Receive*—the Lord Jesus Christ by faith (a loyalty of love to the Word of God) to rule in your heart as King. He must be your absolute "boss" from now on! This act of faith is neither an idea nor a mere feeling but an act, a choice of your will, made intelligently and carefully. Give Him your doubts, your weakness and your loneliness. Your heart will never have peace, your doubts will never clear up, you will never die to the world until you trust, surrender, believe from your heart! *Be totally honest with Him.* Receive Christ into your life as your Lord and Master to live for Him from this moment on, forever (Rom. 10:9, 10).

Are you willing to trust His love? Will you choose His life, or turn your back on His love and choose a future without Christ, without hope and without an end? Will you be very honest with Him right now? Talk to God before the touch of His Holy Spirit lifts off your life. Tell Him in your own words something like this:

God, I'm sorry I've been selfish and rebellious so long. I'm sick of my old life and I want to change. Please forgive my sin and give me the power to live my life from this moment on for You. I give You my heart; take over everything I have and am, and be my Lord and King. Amen.

3

The Marks of a True Disciple

"The one who says he abides in him, ought himself to walk even as he walked" (1 John 2:6).

If you have given your life to the Lord Jesus, you have entered an exciting new world. Things should be different for you. Your life will feel fresh and new. If God has really taken the throne of your heart, you will see these changes in your life.

1. *A desire for scripture.* "Man shall not live by bread alone, but by every word that comes from the mouth of God." As a true disciple, you will want to find out in His Word what God wants you to do. The Bible is your spiritual bread. It is your weapon to defeat the devil. It is a manual to show you how to live. True disciples are people of the Bible (Job 23:12; Jer. 15:16; Deut. 6:5-7; Rom. 10:17; 1 Pet. 2:2).

Make a solemn vow to God to spend a certain amount of time or read a certain number of chapters a day in God's Word (Eccles. 5:4-6). God will take you at your word on any promise you make to Him. Decide sensibly how much time you can spend with your King each day in training. Make your vow and stick to it!

2. *A difference in standards.* "If any man be in Christ, he is a new creation; old things are passed away; behold all things are become new" (2 Cor. 5:17). A real disciple is different in habits, actions and purpose; is different in word, thought and standards. No person really belongs to Jesus who is not trying and trusting to live like his Lord!

Becoming a Christian is like learning to drive on the other side of the road. You must be careful for a while until you learn to think and act *by habit* in this new way. It will take time and discipline to develop the right habit patterns. Beware of the crisis! In times of stress and sudden temptation you may strongly feel like going back to your old way of life. This is especially true if past habits have taken deep root in your memory. But "there is no temptation taken you but such as is common to man; *God is faithful*, who will not allow you to be tempted above that which you are able, but with the temptation will also make a way to escape, that you may be able to bear it" (1 Cor. 10:13).

3. *A discipline of self.* "But the fruit of the Spirit is love, joy, peace, patience, kindness, goodness, faithfulness, gentleness, *self-control*" (Gal. 5:22, 23). If you are a true child of God, you will begin to tighten up old areas where you used to let yourself "hang loose." You will look at food and drink (in both quality and amount) more carefully so that you won't go on either a gluttonous or macrebiotic trip. You will stay away from all drugs and harmful stimulants. You will lose your desire to show off by the way you live and the way you dress. God will begin to deal with your late nights and late mornings! The Holy Spirit will begin to clear the decks in your life.

Your life will show constant changes for the better each day. God will show you the things He wants changed. The disciple of Jesus will be twelve months closer to God a year from now. He will keep on growing—growing in knowledge of his own weakness, and growing in his knowledge of Christ's power. He will learn how wide are God's arms, how high His standards, how deep His compassion and care, how great His strength. He will learn that God is very easy to *please*, but hard to *satisfy*. The Father never gives up halfway! Once the disciple of Jesus has asked Him to take his life, He will do it. And He will keep dealing with him until his life is like that of His Son. "Every man that has this hope in Him purifies himself, even as He is pure" (1 John 3:3; see also Matt. 16:24; Luke 3:11; 1 Cor. 9:25-27).

4. *A despising by society.* Jesus said, "Because you are not of this world the world hates you. . . . If they have persecuted Me, they will persecute you" (John 15:19, 20). A real disciple will have trouble from the world. This trouble will come from those who do not understand your new life and those who are afraid to understand; from those who are angry because you don't belong to their selfish crowd anymore; and from lukewarm, backslidden church members who are being shown up for their formality and deadness by the light of your new life.

Real Christians are the only truly sane persons in a mad, selfish world. The disciple of Jesus is the only person who can be truly called wise; he is not a slave to his lusts and does not live in sin. His life is like a light in the dark pits of the world. When this light shines on selfish lives, sinners caught in it can do only one of three things: run from it, try to put it out or destroy it, or surrender to it and give their lives to God. Make no mistake—

if you will live for God, you can expect real trouble from the world around you. "All that will live godly in Christ Jesus shall suffer persecution" (2 Tim. 3:12). "Blessed are you when men shall revile you, and persecute you, and shall say all kinds of evil against you falsely, on account of Me. Rejoice, and be exceeding glad, for great is your reward in Heaven" (Matt. 5:10-12; see also 2 Tim. 2:12; John 15:18-21; Rom. 8:18; 12:20-21; 1 Pet. 2:20-21).

5. *A seeking of other disciples.* "By this shall all men know that you are My disciples; if you have *love* one to another." Find a true church with true faith. That and only that which saves from sin and exalts (loves, talks a lot about) the Savior, the Lord Jesus, is true faith. All else is false religion and will slowly wipe out your new-found joy and love in Christ Jesus. Just as live coals stay aflame in fire, so spending time with others on fire for God will help keep you aflame for Christ. Go where you feel at home, where you feel the love of God, where truth is preached with compassion, then *work with* the disciples there for the Lord Jesus. Don't just trip out on listening to services on radio or TV—hang in there yourself. And remember, your aim is to *be like Jesus.* He is your standard. He is your example. Keep your eyes on Him. Never lower His standards to try to "fit in" with the crowd, whether that crowd claims to be disciples of Jesus or not. You cannot please Christ and the crowd too (Rom. 15:5-6; Acts 2:42; Eph. 3:17-19; Heb. 10:25; 1 Pet. 1:22; 1 John 1:2, 7; 7:7-13).

6. *A serving of the Lord.* "For me to live is Christ, and to die is gain!" said Paul, a mighty love-slave of Jesus his Lord. A true Christian is a witness! The task of world evangelism is not given only as a lifetime work to the preacher or evangelist; it is given to each of Christ's true disciples as a lifetime work. We have a responsibility regarding the souls of men and women, boys and girls, who pass into eternity around us each day. We must consecrate all we have and are to this task and ask God for His power to carry it out. Jesus said, "You shall receive power after that the Holy Ghost is come upon you; and you shall be witnesses unto Me both in Jerusalem (at home), and in all Judea (in the immediate neighborhood) and in Samaria (among the outcasts of society), and even to the uttermost part of the earth" (Acts 1:8). Every Christian is a missionary; every sinner is a mission field. One of your fellow disciples may cross the world and you may only cross the street, but all of us have a call to serve the Lord and help Him reach His world (1 John 3:16-24; 1 Pet. 2:21; 2 Cor. 9:6-7; Phil. 1:21; Matt. 10:32; John 14:12).

7. *A sticking to the task.* God hasn't planned a continuous up-and-down life for any of His children. You are not expected

to be infallible, but you are expected to keep going on with Him. God has promised to keep you safe and protected from all outer dangers; the world, the flesh and the devil will have no power over you as long as you stay close to the Lord Jesus, but you must go on, and not look back (Luke 9:62).

A true disciple of Jesus must be determined to stay true to Christ. The express teaching of the Bible is that we live a life of habitual victory over sin out of love to God (Matt. 5:13-18; 7:12-27; Mark 12:28-34; John 15:8-14; Rom. 13:9-11; 1 John 3:3-11). No other life is truly Christian. All of us will be confronted each day with temptation, weakness and possible failure; but by God's grace we can make overcoming a habit. Nowhere does the Bible present forgiveness as automatic as long as sin is practiced. A lot of people who have claimed the name of Jesus but have lived filthy lives are going to get shocked on the day of judgment. *Stick to it, saint!* God will uphold you. Paul said, "One thing *I do*: forgetting what *lies* behind and reaching forward to what *lies* ahead, I press on toward the goal for the prize of the upward call of God in Christ Jesus" (Phil. 3:13, 14; 1 John 1-4; Ps. 37:23-24; Rom. 6:1-14; 2 Pet. 1:1-10; John 5:37-39).

4

You Are Important to the Lord

"The Father himself loves you, because you have loved me, and have believed that I came out from God" (John 16:27).

You are important to the Lord Jesus! One marvelous thing about being a disciple of Jesus is that you never get lost in the crowd. God's amazing knowledge covers every tiny detail of His universe. He knows all about you. Not one thing that happens to you is overlooked. If you comb your hair and lose some of it, God's recorders go "minus 22" ("the very hairs of your head are all numbered"—Matt. 10:30). Nothing happens in this universe without God knowing it. He comes to the funeral of every tiny bird (Matt. 10:29-31). He is the *totally aware One*, experiencing everything from the vibration of the smallest meson to the pulsation of the greatest star. And this same God says, "Can a woman forget her sucking child, that she should not have compassion on the son of her womb? yes, they may forget, but I will not forget you. See, I have graven you on the palms of My hands" (Isa. 49:15-16).

Have you ever read those "telephone directories" in the Bible? You know, those lists of people with strange names who never seemed to do anything more than take up a lot of Bible space? Remember reading lines like " . . . of the sons of Issachar after their families: of Tola, the family of the Tolaites; of Pua, the family of the Punites; of Jashub, the family of the Jashubites . . ." (Num. 26:23, 24)? If you ever set out to read the whole Bible right through, you probably wondered why on earth God put in all these genealogies. (The only thing I could think of to do with names like Zelophehad, Jahleel and Izrahiah was to play Bible scrabble: double points on a Bible proper name; one of these on a triple square would "wipe the board" in one move!) The Bible has all sorts of long lists that seem to be a waste of ink. Maybe you have thought, "Why didn't God fill this space with something like Psalm 23 or John 3:16?"

But we can learn from these lists. First, they are lists of ancestors—*my* ancestors, *your* ancestors. The Bible is a history book; what it records actually happened in time and space. It is not a set of fairy tales. It records stories of real people, and their stories are part of my story. These people really didn't do anything special except to have families with names that are hard to pronounce. And yet God knew them. He knew *each one*.

They never did anything that the world would call important. They probably didn't get their names even once in their local newspaper. No one wrote them up in sports or dramatics, much less in politics, crime or war. Yet God cared enough about them to record them in His Book that will last forever. This is the God that you serve. You are important to Him. To Jesus you are worth more than all the world.

Disciples of Jesus do not have to protest against being treated as nothings. They know that with their Lord, no one is ever lost in the machine. They know they are made in God's image, and that God has now put them into His royal forever family. He has pulled them from the gutters and made them clean. He has clothed them in royal robes, crowned them as princes and princesses in His kingdom (Ps. 113:7, 8). Our Father is the King of all kings. We can hold our heads high. To be a true disciple is the greatest privilege in the universe. God has called us into His *very own family!* We are special subjects of His love. Anyone who messes with us touches the "apple of his eye."

So what if you are different? So what if you don't look as far out as your friend next door or don't have the talents of your brother? None of these things matter to the Father. You matter because you are important to Him, exactly as you are. The Bible tells us that man is important, that he is of great value. He is not a nothing. He was made to share in God's happiness. For this reason, disciples of Jesus love all people—from proud prince or president to filthy wino or burned-out street hooker. And He who humbles kings and honors beggars *knows our names.*

You can relax in God's love. You don't have to "prove yourself" to anyone. You don't have to struggle to be someone you know you can never be. You can be content that Jesus loves you as a special person, exactly as you are. Look at yourself. God never mass produces. Your finger prints are different. Your voice is different. Your brain wave channel is different from that of anyone else in the world. Even the hair on your head is not quite the same as that of your blood brother or sister. If God took all this trouble to make you so unique, will you be content to let Him use you to do a job no one else can fill quite as well as you? He has work for you. And as you walk among the crowds, in the streets, at school, at work, remember this: God knows your name. You are important to the Lord.

Section II
The Disciple's SAVIOR

5
What Is God Like?

"Let not the wise man glory in his wisdom, neither let the mighty man glory in his might; let not the rich man glory in his riches; but let him that glories glory in *this*, that he understands and knows *me*, that I am the Lord that exercises lovingkindness, judgment, and righteousness in the earth; for in these things I delight, says the Lord" (Jer. 9:23-24).

Before going on, read these verses again—slowly. Try to think of what they are really saying. If this were the only source of information that you had about God, what would you know about Him? List everything these verses tell you about God:

1. God Is Real

When disciples of Jesus talk about God, who are they talking about? Anybody can make up some "god" and say, "I worship this." "God" can be a vague, plastic nothing that will let you live any way you like. But the God of the Bible made us in His image, and since He knows and loves us best, He has sole right to our worship. Is *your* God the real God? We change to become like the "god" of our hearts. If our "god" is false and plastic, we will be plastic too. To know what the true God is like, we must not only meet Him but must also study His book.

2. God Is Forever

The Bible tells us that even before earth and time began, God was *already here*. This is something that should bring wonder to our hearts. No one made God. He has always been. The Bible does not try to explain this; it just says it. This is hard for us to understand because everything we know or see was made at one time by something or someone. When we go back to the start of all this we come to a place where everything had to begin. But the Bible does not say our universe started with nothing;

it says it started with God (Gen. 1:1). It tells us that "He is before all things, and by him all things consist [hold together]" (Col. 1:17). Before time began, God already was. No one, nothing else in or beyond our universe is like God. He is unmade, uncreated. He has always been. And because He has no beginning, He also has no end. He is forever! God lives in endless time that the Bible calls eternity.

3. God Is Unity and Diversity

We find another area of wonder in our pursuit of who God is. Scripture tells us another truth that we would never have thought of in ourselves. The God of the Bible is a single, unified friendship of three awesomely holy Persons in one. These wonderfully great Beings are *not* each other, but they are one in nature, essence and agreement. The Bible calls them the Father, the Son and the Holy Spirit. The Bible name for this friendship is "the Godhead" (Acts 17:29).

Don't let the strangeness of this truth hassle you. It gives us a basic understanding for some of life's most puzzling relationships. For instance, there are patterns of like in unlike, sameness in difference, unity in diversity right through our universe. Is the river you crossed today the same one that you crossed yesterday? Yes and no. It is the same, but it is different too. Some religions and philosophies give reasons for the sameness of things around us, but have no real answer for the differences. Others give reasons for the differences, but have none for the sameness.

Eastern pantheists believe all the world is an expression of God and in essence *is* God. They can account for the unity of the universe but are bothered about the differences and distinctions in it. Western rationalists, on the other hand, talk of all differences and distinctions coming from chance and chaos. But they have no explanation for the order and pattern of our world.

The Bible at its beginning gives us a full answer regarding creation and who God is. It tells us that our Creator's life-style is unity in diversity, that things are the way they are because that is the way *He* is. Think, for instance, of our limited idea of time. Time can be described as past, present or future. We know that past is not present, and present is not future, nor is future the past. Yet all three together *as a unit* are what we call time. Here is this sameness yet distinctness, unity in diversity. Put this idea into numbers and you could write it $1 \times 1 \times 1 \times 1$ equals 1. Furthermore, just as past, present and future are all equally time, so the Father, Son and Holy Spirit are all equally

God. And just as past, present and future cannot exist without each other and have no reality by themselves, so the Godhead must be known and loved as they are—three distinct Persons in one divine essence.

If this still doesn't explain Him too well, don't worry. God has said that this is where *He* is at, and you can stake your life on it. He knows what He is talking about. Our minds are too little now to span all that is true about Him, but we have all eternity to learn more about Him. The Bible is full of verses explaining what God is like (Gen. 1:26; 3:22; 11:7; Deut. 4:35, 39; Isa. 46:5-11; 45:5, 21; Matt. 3:16-17; 28:19; 1 Cor. 12:4-6; 1 Pet. 1:2). It is important for you to know what God is like. Every false religious trip in the world began by men messing with what God said about himself because it didn't fit into their own ideas.

Here are the references to some verses which give specific information about God. Look up each one in your Bible now, and read it carefully. Without copying the exact words, write down on a sheet of paper what you feel each verse tells you about God. Genesis 1:26; Deuteronomy 4:39; Isaiah 46:5-11; Matthew 3:16, 17; 28:19; John 17:11; 1 Corinthians 12:4-6; 1 Peter 1:2.

What unanswered questions do you have about God right now? Write them down before you read on. Some of these questions will probably be answered as you continue reading this chapter.

4. God Is Love

Not only is God eternal and is He three but one, but the Scriptures also tell us that God loves. The Father loved the Son, the Son loved the Father, the Holy Spirit loved and was loved by both the Father and the Son. Love is not alien to the universe. Behind the earth, the sky and the stars there is love—real love and friendship.

We can look into the vastness of space and, knowing this, not feel a cosmic lostness. We don't have to be afraid of our littleness and its bigness because behind it all is a Friendship, a God, a real Person who cares about us on our lonely little planet that is marked "special."

Honor all three members of the Godhead because they are all important. Dishonor any one of them and you dishonor all that is God. And if you put down God, you put down the very basis of love; something will happen to *your* love. People who reject the Bible picture of the Godhead get cold and hard. God will not honor religious zeal that violates what He says about himself.

This Divine Friendship also tells us that God is not selfish. If the Godhead had each other before the universe was made, God couldn't have made us because He was lonely. He did not need us. Therefore He could not have made us for selfish reasons. If we understand that the God of the Bible was not lonely, we are left with only one possible answer for our creation: God made us to *give* to us. He made us just so we could share in His happiness. And that is the most wonderful revelation about God in the Bible. He really is loving. He really does live without selfishness. He really does care about you and me (Jer. 31:3; Zeph. 3:17; John 3:16; 17:24-26; Rom. 5:5, 8; Eph. 2:4; 3:19; 1 John 4:7-12, 16).

One of the best ways of allowing the Bible to speak to you is to personalize it. You can do this by substituting your own name in certain places in a verse whenever it fits appropriately.

Look up Jeremiah 31:3 and copy the verse word for word— except for one major change. Wherever the word *you* occurs, write your own name instead. Then try the same thing with Zephaniah 3:17. Do it again with Romans 5:5, putting your name in place of *us* and *our*. Read John 3:16, putting your name in place of the word *whosoever*.

As you look back over these verses, how would you summarize the feelings that the Godhead has for you?

Look carefully at John 17:24-26, then ask yourself these questions: Who is the speaker? Who is "the Father"? What characterizes the relationship between the Father and the Son? How long has this relationship been going on? Who is the speaker talking about? What is his request of the Father concerning them?

God unselfishly chooses the highest good for all, and invites us who are made in His image to share in His happiness and joy. What is your response to God's love for you?

Look at verses 20 and 21. Are you one of those who has believed in Jesus through the word of those first eleven disciples? What is Jesus' request to the Father concerning you?

On the basis of your personal investigation and research in these verses, how will you now answer the question, "What is God like?" Try to describe Him in one paragraph.

6

East, West, and the True God

There Is One God

The God of the whole earth, the God of the Bible, is not the God only of the West. As a matter of fact, people in the West have not usually had a true picture of God because they have not read and obeyed the Bible. And the God of the Bible is not like man's idea of Him in either the West or the East.

The God of the Scriptures is the God of the whole universe. He is beyond all barriers of nation, race, country or people. He is "the God of the spirits of all flesh" (Num. 16:22). The Bible does not say, "God so loved the western world..." It does not say, "Christ Jesus came into the eastern world to save sinners..." All men under heaven have sinned the same. They will be judged the same, and can be saved the same way by coming back to the God who made all men of one blood and one race.

He Is the God of the Bible

Why, then, are there so many different ideas of what God is like? Sometimes people do not know enough about the true God. We can find out some things about what He is like by looking at the work of His hands in creation, or by thinking about ourselves and the wonderful way God made us. But if we use only these standards for finding out what God is like, we are left wondering which parts of nature and man show us God, and which parts show us something else. This is why God gave us the Bible. It tells us exactly what He is like. It is the divine standard to correct our strange ideas about Him.

He Is Not a God Made by Man

If ignorance were the only reason that people worship different gods, we could conclude that most people really love and serve

Him, even though they don't know much about Him. They just use different names for Him. But ignorance is not the real problem. The Bible tells us that the reason that people do not know more about God is *sin*. We are made to know God. All men know some things about Him. But we also know that He wants us to live right. If men want to find God without being willing to live right, God must hide himself from them. Then what will a person do if he is empty inside but does not want to change his selfish ways in order to find God? He will do what people in both the East the West have been doing—create his own god to serve.

What will a god created by man look like? It will be just like he himself really wants to be deep inside. When a man refuses to serve the true God and creates his own, that god will reflect his own sick mind. It will be his own lusts turned into a picture or a statue, a creed or a religion. The Bible tells us that when people "knew God, they did not give Him glory as God, but became proud in their thinking, and . . . worshipped and served created things rather than the Creator, who is blessed forever" (Rom. 1:21, 25).

The western man's gods were just like him, only a bit bigger. They were thought of as real persons, but had all of the same sins as man did. The gods got drunk, were bitter with each other, lived immoral lives. Also, the western gods were not infinite. They could do little more than humans. No western god was big enough or wise enough to take care of everyone. So the West invented whole families of gods, each one in charge of a different department of heaven or earth. These gods were feared or toasted, respected or resented, but never really loved.

No western civilization ever created a god which came up to the Bible picture of God—the wonderful, unselfishly loving, infinite Creator. No, the West did not have the right picture of God. Even modern western man who says that he believes in only one god has a poor picture of the Lord of lords. To many men and women of the West, God is a "grandaddy god in a rocking chair" who is smiling worriedly and feebly over what his naughty children are doing. No man who has ever been in the awesome presence of the holy God can call the western god the God of the universe.

Long ago the East saw the foolishness of the West. God must be far bigger than these feeble human excuses for a god. In some places, such as India, the idea of "families" of gods got so big it became ridiculous. They had as many as thirty million gods to worship! Everytime a new discovery, problem or idea came up people would make up another god to be in charge of it.

The eastern man also reacted to the western humanizing of God and went completely the other way. God became the "Infinite

Everything, the Cosmic Ultimate, the Oneness of All." God was in everything and was everything. He was in the sky, the sun, the trees, the grass, the birds. God was in man. God *was* man! God was the earth, the heavens, the universe itself. He was beyond understanding, beyond feeling, beyond human limits. The East pictured God as free from human problems. Unfortunately they also took away His personality. The God of the East has no face. He is beyond understanding because there is nothing in His being that we can relate to. We can only surrender to Him. But to say God has no feelings, thought or choices is to take away His love also, and to invent yet another god who is alien to the true God of the Bible.

It is true that God upholds all things. It is true that He is infinite and that He fills all time and space. But it is not true that He *is* all things. He and His creation are distinct. The God that the Scriptures reveal to us made this universe outside himself. And it is not true that He is unable to feel, to think and to share with us. The God of the Bible is a person, someone we can speak to face to face, like a friend. He is not the finite, selfish tribe of western gods. He is not the impersonal, ultimate force of eastern ideas. He is an infinite Person, infinite in power but truly a person. And He is big enough both to take care of the universe and to love us.

It is not shameful to have questions about what God is like. He is big enough to handle any question you can throw at Him. One of the most complete descriptions of God is in Isaiah 40:9-31. Notice the phrase in verse 9, "Behold your God!" God wants you to see Him, to "take Him on." He's saying, "All you have to do is look at Me, if you have questions." Read these verses. How well can you answer His question in verse 12? verse 13? verse 14? verse 18? verse 25?

In the light of this passage, what would you like to say to God? Why don't you just "talk" to Him on paper for a few minutes?

7

How to Tell What Is False in Religious Groups

"The Spirit expressly warns us that in the latter times some will revolt from the faith; they will listen to spirits of error and to doctrines that demons teach . . . be on your guard as to yourself and your teaching; if you do that, you will save both yourself and those that hear you" (Tim. 4:1, 16).

You can get very confused listening to religious men today. So many people talk as if they were the only ones that are right. While real Christians all agree on some basic things, we can agree to disagree on other things that are not so central in being a Christian.

There is an amazing unity across the world among the followers of Jesus. However, every year hundreds of new ideas about God and religion happen all over. If we believe in right and wrong, these ideas cannot all be true. Different groups often say opposite things. To point out what ideas and movements are wrong, we don't need to call any groups by name. That's a great relief because we could never put down in any one book all the titles of funny religious ideas that mixed-up people can think up each month. When we want to know what is right and real, we should go back to the Bible. All we have to do is read it carefully and prayerfully. God has told us the signs of false faith, the marks of wrong religious thinking. No one ever begins a wrong idea about God without first throwing out something true that God has shown us clearly in His Word. And all strange religious trips, no matter how different or how many, will have the same marks about them. Here are six signs that you can spot if you get close enough to see:

1. Desire for Money or Merchandise

People living by false religions always *want* things. They are coveteous at heart. They use their religion for making money off other people or for getting their belongings from them. False religious teachers are greedy for other people's things. They are money-centered. They have the "love of money" which is the root of all evil. God says, "Woe to you . . . hypocrites! for you devour widows' houses, and for a pretense make long prayer; therefore you shall receive the greater damnation" (Matt. 23:14). "And through covetousness shall they with feigned words make merchandise of you, whose judgment for a long time does not linger, and their damnation does not sleep" (2 Pet. 2:3).

2. Drive for Power

One key mark of a person presenting false faith is some form of "power trip." These people try to build up their own kingdom in the name of building up God's kingdom or in the name of bringing freedom to others. The true disciple is not power hungry. He knows that all power belongs to Jesus (Matt. 28:18). He knows that the earth is the Lord's and all that is in it (1 Cor. 10:26). He understands that God has chosen the foolish things of this world to confound the wise, and the weak to confound the mighty, that no flesh should show off in His presence (1 Cor. 1:27-29).

But the man or woman who is building a human religion is power hungry. This power may be social, sexual or "spiritual."

Social. He may want power over people. His "trip" may be to have lots of people listen to him and obey his orders. He may use religion to build his status. In his church, a crowd is his real creed and he is its self-appointed god.

Sexual. Some religions or religious teachings have as a key offer the promise of unlimited sex without guilt. Forms of sexual sin have been used before and will be used again in false teaching or worship. If people will not bring their sexual lives up to God's standards, they will try to bring God's standards down to their own perverted levels. The Bible marks this teaching as from hell. Leaders in this false faith lure people in by appealing to the lusts of the flesh. They promise freedom when they themselves are the slaves of sin (2 Pet. 2:10, 14; Jude 17-18; John 8:34).

"Spiritual." People from other false religions offer their devotees superior "spiritual" power or positions to get them to join. Serving in this false religion is presented as having the power to place your throne right beside God's. The selfishness and pride that lies underneath this is not hard to see. A man can join and yet never give up his sinful and selfish ways. He just baptizes them and makes them look religious. Jesus said, "If any man will do his [God's] will, he shall know of the doctrine, whether it be of God, or whether I speak of myself; he that speaks of *himself* seeks his *own* glory; but he that seeks the glory of him

that sent him, the same is true, and no unrighteousness is in him" (John 7:17, 18).

3. Denial of Absolutes

One key mark of religious deception is the rejection of right and wrong as revealed in the Bible. Such religions teach that truth constantly changes, or that truth evolves, or that what we once held as true from God must now be changed as man has advanced in knowledge.

The denial of real rights and wrongs extends into many areas, such as denying any authority or government other than their own; discrediting any existing systems of control or direction, often with bitterness and anger; denying any outside source of correction, including that of the properly understood Bible taken as a whole. (Often false religions quote large parts of the Bible, but ignore that which points out their own wrongs.) They may deny that Christ is truly God, or that the Father or the Holy Spirit is God. Sometimes this denial of truth results in a mystic "feelings only" faith where clear thinking is avoided and everything practical is made symbolic, complicated and strange. Other times it leads to rejecting responsibility for sin and the need for Jesus' death and bodily resurrection. The Bible warns us about men who despise authority, often betraying deep hurt and bitterness toward God (Jude 8-10; 2 Pet. 2:10-12; 2 Tim. 3:1-5).

We must be people who accept God's word at face value. We must do what Jesus tells us to do if we are going to be true Jesus people (John 8:31-32; 14:15, 21, 23; 15:10).

4. Deception of Onlookers

The man in a false faith is always a hypocrite at heart. No one ever gets into a wrong religious trip and stays in it unless he refuses to believe or act on what God has said. False faith begins only when people reject true faith. To protect their pride, people who join things that they later know or find out are wrong must try to cover over all the exposed unreality in what they are doing and saying. This leads to lies or deliberate pretenses, especially by the leaders of the group. They will keep real beliefs and practices secret from an interested new member until the novice is too deeply involved to leave without a great cost to his or her own pride and reputation. False faith always puts on a nice front, but is not what it seems to be on the outside (2 Pet. 3:15, 16; John 3:20).

It is here that so many mystery cults and secret orders fit

in. Secret doctrine or practice has no place in the life of a true disciple. God's work is "not done in a corner" (Acts 26:26). Jesus people have nothing to hide. We do not fear exposure (Matt. 24:4, 5, 11, 23, 24). Jesus says, "He that does truth comes to the light, that his deeds may be shown to be done in God" (John 3:21). Beware of any work that has concealed doctrines or teachings only for their own members.

5. Deviation from Christ

One test every disciple of Jesus should know and always use is, "Does it make me hate sin more, and love the Lord Jesus more?" No faith is true faith that does not both save from sin, and love and talk about the Jesus of the Bible. Phony religions always get away from the things God considers most important. Any religion that does not, in word and deed, center around the Lord Jesus and His kingdom is a false religion, no matter how spiritual it sounds and no matter how good it looks (John 3:24; 31-36; 10:25-28; 12:44-49; 14:6; 15:4-6, 23). This does not just mean *saying* Jesus is Lord. It means *living* like it. It means putting Him first in everything—in teaching, living and speaking (Matt. 7:21-27; 15:8-9; 1 John 3:18-19).

6. Division of the True Disciples

Any teaching or religion that splits up true disciples and tries to turn them against each other does not come from heaven, but from hell. True faith is marked by the love described in the Bible, not by envy, strife or contention. It is true that disciples must stand up for the right and constantly be on guard against wrong. And we do not unite by just overlooking anything that is against God and His Word. However, all true Jesus people love each other, despite differences of opinion. The group that goes on an exclusive trip, the group with the "we are the people and wisdom will die with us" attitude is not a group with the mark of true faith (Rom. 16:17, 18; 1 Cor. 11:18-19; 12:20-26; James 3:14-16; John 15:12-14, 17; 17:20-26).

Each of the following Scripture references refers to one specific sign of a false religion. Look up each verse in your Bible and try to match it with the appropriate sign, without checking back in the material which you have just read. Then check your answers by reviewing this section on how to tell false faiths. When you are convinced that your answers match up properly, spend some time memorizing each of these six ways of identifying false religions.

1. Romans 12:5—desire for money or merchandise

2. 1 Peter 1:23-25; Proverbs 30:5, 6—drive for power
3. 1 Timothy 6:9, 10—denial of absolutes
4. Luke 4:5-8—deception of onlookers
5. Matthew 23:27, 28—deviation from Christ
6. John 14:6—division of the true disciples

Whenever you are faced with a decision regarding some new religious group, draw on this storehouse of knowledge and take the time to evaluate that new religion in terms of these standards. Then you will decrease your chances of getting sucked into a false religious cult, and you may be able to help a brother or sister facing a similar situation.

8

Counterfeit Conversion

"Not every one that says to me, Lord, Lord, shall enter the kingdom of heaven; but he that does the will of my Father who is in heaven" (Matt. 7:21).

Not all people who use the name of Jesus are true disciples of Jesus. Some said they were when being disciples became popular, because they did not want to feel left out. Today some come from homes where Jesus is known in some way by others of the family. Because their parents say they know Jesus, the children assume they know Him too. How can you tell the counterfeit?

People can be led only in two ways: by force or by trust. We can live by rules based on fear, or we can live by love based on trust for the One who leads us. Someone who is not a true disciple is still selfish at heart and is motivated only by bribes or punishment. But true disciples know what it means to be free from the rule of threats and bargains. They are free to love Jesus. They are confident that the Holy Spirit can direct them by God's Word, and they obey the Father because they really trust Him.

Think of two children in a home. One obeys his dad because he trusts him. He has a faith in his father which works by love. The other wants all he can get from his father. He obeys only under force because he does not really love or trust him.

So are the lives of the true and false disciples of Jesus. God's true child has a confidence and trust in Jesus that leads him to wholly give himself to God and His will. The phony, like the devil, submits only partially and still has a selfish heart. He "believes, and trembles" (James 2:19). This person may believe Christ came to save sinners, may want to be saved (for his own safety), but yet never gives in *at heart* to be led and ruled by Christ. His "faith" is based on the selfish condition that God will make him happy. It never results in unreserved trust and love that leads God's true child to say, "No matter how tough it gets, your will be done."

False faith is a religion of law, not love. It is totally selfish and totally unlike Jesus. It is outward only, and plastic. True faith is a faith of the heart, and this is the only faith God honors.

You can recognize the person who has not yet discovered the faith that works by love. Here are some of the signs:

1. He Serves God Like Taking Medicine

The phony obeys only to get something good for himself. The true child of God delights in doing God's will because he loves God. If you love Christ for His own sake, you will not find it a weary struggle to do what He says. His commandments are not hard (1 John 5:3; Matt. 11:30).

The man or woman in the religion of fear does Christian things because he knows he should. It would not do for him to say he is a disciple of Jesus and not act like a Christian, even though he doesn't enjoy being one! This person's only real happiness is the hope that life will be better for him in the next world. He never enjoys serving God in *this* one. But if you are a true disciple, you already enjoy peace in Christ, and heaven for you has already begun. You know you *have* eternal life, not just hope for it some day. You are sure of God's love, and because you can relax in that love you do not have to drive yourself to do His will.

2. His Heart Is Ruled by Fear, Not Love

A phony lives by conviction and condemnation, not by affection. He is driven by warnings, not drawn by God's love. He is filled with a spirit of fear. He is always afraid that he will make the wrong move or do the wrong thing. He has never known God as a loving, compassionate Father. His picture of God is always that of a ruler and judge because he has never found mercy himself. He may be very active and strict, and he may know a lot about what God asks. But the more he learns, the more it hurts if there is no love. Here is a key difference. The true disciple prefers to obey; the phony person purposes or intends to, but usually fails because his heart is not really in it.

3. He Is More Afraid of Punishment Than Sin

The man in the religion of fear keeps on sinning because he is not saved from sin. He doesn't really hate sin—only the punishment for it. As long as he is not found out, or as long as he gets away with it, he will go on sinning. He loves the things that hurt the God he says he serves. He talks himself into committing the same sins again and again by telling himself that God will overlook it and that he can always repent afterwards.

The person who doesn't really hate sin may even argue about how secure his salvation is, because he does not have relaxed assurance in his heart. Listen to a phony, and you will soon discover his whole life revolves around his own salvation. He still worries about it because he doesn't really have it! The true disciple *enjoys* his salvation, and he doesn't need to talk about what he knows by experience is his. His own salvation is not his main concern at all. Instead his thoughts are taken up with worshipping Christ and working to see others saved (1 Cor. 10:23-33; Rom. 14:5-8; Matt. 25:31-46).

4. He Is Ruled by a Spirit of *Get,* Not *Give*

True disciples of Jesus enjoy giving and helping others because they really love. Their truest, deepest, sheerest joy is to be able to do good for others. But counterfeits are always looking for ways to get from others what they can. This may be anything from money or possessions to new members in the particular religious group they have joined. This is especially true in business. If selfishness rules there, as sure as God lives they are still in the religion of fear. Men in this religion find it hard to *give* anything to God. They give only if they can get something in return (Luke 6:30-35; 16:11-16; Matt. 25:41-45).

The true disciple of Jesus denys himself many things in order to give to the work of God and to help others. The phony never enjoys self-denial unless he feels it will earn him a reward from God. The true disciple sets his heart on God's kingdom, and enjoys saving everything he can to give to it. The more he saves from other things to give to it, the more he is excited and pleased. Can you see why the phony finds it hard to give to the work of Christ? His heart is not in it at all. He can't understand the joy a Jesus person experiences in giving, because giving drains money and time from his *own* little world where *he* still rules as king (Deut. 15:7-21).

5. His Concern for Others Comes from Being Paranoid Over His Own Life

A counterfeit is desperately afraid of hell or punishment and of being wrong. His witnessing may even be a reflection of this fear. He drives to win others only to convince himself that he is right. The phony has only two ways to spread his faith. One is scaring others into his religion. He is more likely to do this when he is talking to strangers and he doesn't have too much to lose if they don't listen. The other method he uses is to promise rewards. He is more likely to use this method on friends or relatives. In either case, however, his words will be full of tension and judgment.

Many counterfeits feel sorry for lost sinners, but not for the right reason and *not* God's way. He feels more concern for the sinner than for the God whose heart the rebellious sinner has broken. He can never understand how God could allow a loved one to go to hell, so he will try to explain it away if he can. Christ's words asking supreme love from His followers over all earthly loves mean nothing to the counterfeit. He does not really love God at all; he loves himself and everything connected with his own happiness.

It is sad to say it, but many people do not meet these Bible tests of true faith. The religion of fear is radically wrong. It is bad, right at its heart. It differs from true faith just as much as the Pharisees differed from Jesus; as much as the gospel differs from legalism; as much as hell differs from heaven. We must ask ourselves and our friends, "Is Christ the center of our lives, or are we still trying to fit Him in for our own happiness? Is our faith the faith that works by love, or are we still trying to live in the religion of fear?"

TRUE DISCIPLE OF JESUS

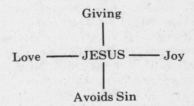

Giving

Love ——— JESUS ——— Joy

Avoids Sin

COUNTERFEIT DISCIPLE OF JESUS

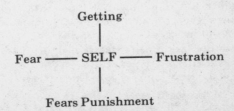

Getting

Fear ——— SELF ——— Frustration

Fears Punishment

9

How to Stay Close to Jesus

"Abide in me, and I in you. As the branch cannot bear fruit of itself, unless it abides in the vine, so neither can you unless you abide in me. I am the vine, you are the branches; he who abides in me and I in him bears much fruit; for apart from me you can do nothing" (John 15:4, 5).

Christianity is not a set of rules but a daily friendship with a living, loving Lord. It is "Christ in you, the hope of glory" (Col. 1:27). In this life of grace and faith we will be marked by the sign that "sin shall not have dominion" or rule over us (Rom. 6:14). Christianity *is* Christ who, alive and real, brings peace and power to the heart (2 Cor. 3:18).

Since staying close to Jesus is the secret of being His disciple, three things will help us to live in the glow of His love:

1. *Be clean.* Always turn away from every harmful and sinful practice. Learn to repent, confess and be forgiven of *every* sin. Sin as a way of life is always spoken of in the Bible as in the *past* of the true disciples of Jesus (1 Cor. 6:11; Tit. 3:3). The true disciple must be able to say, like Paul, "I am dying daily" (1 Cor. 15:31), and know what it means to take up his cross daily to follow Jesus (Luke 9:23). This means simply that we are to renew our attitude every sunrise for the new day (Rom. 6:11).

Remember, too, that *sin can fool us.* Satan knows how to paint pretty pictures, even from an ugly past. You can fall back into following old mind habits of the past unless you take great care. Some of you know, for example, what it is like to fall again into the slavery of selfishness. If you have given in, you know what it means to lose the smile and sense of God's friendship.

God tells us to "*cleanse ourselves* from all filthiness of the flesh and spirit, perfecting holiness in the fear of God" (2 Cor. 7:1). We have His promise: "If any man sin, we have an advocate with the Father, Jesus Christ the righteous" (1 John 2:1), and "If we confess our sins, he is faithful and just to forgive us our sins, and to cleanse us from all unrighteousness" (1 John 1:9). So, never let the sun go down on unrighted wrong. Learn to keep short accounts with God. Pay your dues quickly. The only real way to stay close to Jesus is to stay far from sin.

2. *Be unchoked.* No disciple of Jesus can afford to waste time. The sin of wasting God's time has led more disciples back into their old ways than any other. Satan knows that no sold-out young man or woman of God would ever deliberately do some gross sin.

Knowing this, he works to divert their attention to *good* things that are not the *best* things; to get them into things they could do that Jesus has not led them to do; to turn their concern into some sidetrack that leads away from what God has for them. It is, for instance, important to relax. We must take breaks from the pressure and tension of working as a Christian in a rotten world. But our free time must *build us up* in Christ, not take our minds far from Him. We cannot keep a vision for God's work with a diet of too much television; the music of heaven can be drowned right out by rock from the radio or records; souls go to hell as Christians read comics; many young men and women have gone down the moral drain with too much time on their hands.

Every disciple of Jesus must dare to completely give up all acts that they know Jesus would not smile on. Avoid things that have no value for His kingdom. The Bible tells us that whether we eat or drink, or whatever we do, we are to "do *all* for the glory of God" (1 Cor. 10:31).

Plan your relaxing times so that you will become a better man or woman for God because of them. If you really enjoy serving God, a break time should be either some form of rest or some exercise before the Lord that is not like your normal tasks. When you relax, do the things you enjoy as an offering of worship, joy or thanks to God. God says, "No man that is in a war entangles himself with the affairs of this life, that he may please him who has chosen him to be a soldier" (2 Tim. 2:4). Many things do not seem sinful in themselves, but we must watch so that we don't get so involved in them that Christ is crowded out of our heart's first place. This is what Jesus meant in the parable of the soils when He said, "The *cares* of this world, and the deceitfulness of riches, and the lusts of other things entering in, *choke* the word, and it becomes unfruitful" (Mark 4:19).

The little poem by Robert Frost is good to remember:

The woods are lovely, dark and deep,
But I have promises to keep,
And miles to go before I sleep,
And miles to go before I sleep.

3. *Be Christ-dependent.* Jesus is your power, your strength, your wisdom! He said, "Without me you can do *nothing.*" In the book of Hebrews God tells us the secret of spiritual victory. "Let us lay aside every weight (be *unchoked*), and the sin which does so easily beset us (be *clean,* especially from that form of sin you find your strongest temptation towards), and let us run with patience the race that is set before us, looking to Jesus, the author and finisher of our faith" (Heb. 12:1, 2a).

The Lord Jesus himself is the secret of power over sin. No disciple can beat sin in his own strength. The more you fight sin, the greater it grows in power. But look in faith to Jesus and you will experience instant deliverance.

Hebrews 12 gives us an awesome picture of a giant athletics track or stadium. In it are the disciples of our generation. Watching on the stands are those that have loved and served the Lord Jesus in the past. Hebrews 11 tells us some of their names. There are Noah, Moses and David. There is Enoch who loved God so much that God took him home before he had a chance to die. There are the prophets like Elijah and Samuel. Up there also is Samson, whose last repentant act was to pull down a temple on those who laughed at his God's power. They are all watching us. They are onlookers to see how well we run the race. In the stands are all those we love who have died in Jesus.

And if through some form of one-way television screen they can see us run, what do they say and how do they feel? Do they cheer or cry? If you knew that someone you really loved could see you, how would you live? How would you act if you knew the one whom you admired was watching from heaven? That is how you can have courage. That is how to draw strength from heaven. Remember, *Jesus* is watching. He has trusted the work done in your heart. You must not fail Him.

Look over the three steps for keeping close to Jesus. Which of these do you feel most lacking in?

If you were to measure your life by His standards, would you say that you have been giving Christ the proper place that He deserves in your affections?

Admittedly, you can't really measure a relationship. But you can tell something of the quality of any relationship by looking at the amount of time that two people spend with each other.

How are you using the time God has given you? How are you using your time with Jesus?

Your day's schedule is the best place to look for ways of getting yourself "unhooked," as the second step suggests. Look at how you spend your time, and, more important, *why* you do what you do. Is the Lord speaking to you about putting some things right that have been put off too long? Here are some questions to help you in your evaluation:

Is there a goal to each day and a purpose to everything you do? Are there any activities which you would be afraid to share with Jesus? What "cares of this world" do you need to "lay aside" for Jesus' sake right now?

You know what you have to do. Now do it. Isn't it time you had that talk with God?

Enough said. Now it's up to you. Why don't you write down what you would like to say to Jesus right now? Then pray the prayer you have written.

Section III
The Disciple's
SPIRITUAL LIFE

10

How to Read the Bible

"Now faith comes by hearing and hearing by the word of God" (Rom. 10:17).

1. What Is the Bible?

Your Bible is the most important book in the world. There are keys in it for finding the solution to every basic problem you will ever face. It is a manual of miracles. It is a book from God about God, written by His men about how to be His men and women. It is the story of His love for people.

The Bible's central figure is the Lord Jesus Christ—God who became a man. It is the record of His origin, birth, life, death and resurrection. Its message is stranger than science fiction: that God who spun the worlds into space has visited our earth to show us the way to heaven, and that we may join His love kingdom and be in His very own family forever.

The Bible is no ordinary book. It is strangely different because it was written by men who listened to the voice of God. The words they wrote were more than human. They are like fire to each new generation. In the power of the Holy Spirit they are as fresh as wind and rain on a mountain.

The Bible is not just a book of *history*, although the truth of its records has been clearly upheld by modern archeology. It is not a book of *poetry*, although it has inspired the writing of countless songs and poems through past centuries. It is not an *adventure* story, though few novels have matched the sheer drama of its pages. It is not a book of *ethics* or *morals*, although civilization's finest and fairest laws have been forged from it. It is not a *textbook*, but it still astounds scientists and scholars from fields as different as sociology, medicine and nuclear physics. The Bible is the unique record of man's problems and God's answers; the good news of the love revolution begun by the Father, given by the Son and operated by the Holy Spirit.

Disciples of Jesus are people who read, use and live according to this book. There is no way to follow Jesus without also knowing and loving the book He gave us (John 14:21-23). It is no accident that Jesus and the Bible are both called the Word of God (John 1:1; Rev. 19:13). Both are divine. Both speak with power and authority. Both are fully true and can be trusted. The Lord Jesus is the living Word; the Bible is the written Word. The world needs someone to see, and something to study. God gave us a book and His Son. We must obey both. We do not love Jesus more than we love His Word. We do not obey Jesus more than we obey His Word. We do not want to know God any more than we want to know His Word.

2. How Much Should I Read?

Stop a minute and think about the last seven days. How much time did you spend per day reading or studying in the Bible? How much time over the entire seven days? How much time would you have to spend each day reading the Bible in order to read the whole Bible in one year? Take a guess.

If you read the Bible only about five minutes a day, you could finish it easily in less than a year. You would read the whole Bible through in seventy hours and forty minutes. The Old Testament would take about fifty-two hours, twenty minutes; the New Testament, about eighteen hours, twenty minutes. On some holiday period, if you were willing to spend eight hours a day reading your Bible you could finish it in just nine days.

If you read by chapters, you could finish the whole Bible in eighteen weeks by reading just ten chapters a day. That is only four chapters in the morning, two at lunchtime and four at night. The Old Testament would take only fourteen weeks; the New Testament, twenty-six days. If you wanted to read through the four Gospels (Matthew, Mark, Luke and John) and Acts, you could read them in twelve days; all the rest of the books of the New Testament would take another fifteen days.

How much of God's book have you read? Remember, you will never know any more of Jesus than you know of His book. Jesus did say, "You shall know the truth, and the truth shall set you free." But the context of that statement should not be ignored. What He *really* said is, "If you *continue in my word,* then are you my disciples indeed, and you shall know the truth, and the truth shall set you free" (John 8:31, 32).

Why not start now to read the Bible regularly? Read the section again. Ask God how much time He would have you spend reading the Bible each day. Then commit yourself to reading a certain number of minutes every day, or a certain number of chapters every day. Then ask God to help you to be faithful to this commitment—to read more, maybe, but never less. If you miss a day or more, confess your negligence, ask God for forgiveness and help, then start again. God will forgive you and help you. But *start again!* Remember, Satan will be trying to get you to stop reading the Bible any way he can.

3. How Can I Better Understand What I Read?

Ask the Holy Spirit to help you understand what you read. Take colored pencils (ballpoints will go right through the pages of most Bibles and ruin them) and mark the verses that God uses to speak to you.

There are a few simple things to remember when you read the Bible. Keep them in mind, and you will not get funny ideas from the devil or from people who don't know either the Scriptures or the power of God:

1. *Read everything in the light of where you find it.* Don't pull bits out here and there and try to make them say something they don't say when read where they usually belong. (If people would read "Little Red Riding Hood" or "The Three Bears" like they often read the Bible, they wouldn't understand those either!) Compare verses with other verses. Be sure you have read all that you can find in the Bible on a subject before you teach about it. God says that those who teach from the Bible have a solemn charge before Him to be right. So don't teach others on subjects you are only guessing about.

2. *Remember, God's Book means exactly what it says.* Once you know what He is saying, take it exactly as it is. The only time you should think a verse is symbolic is when the verses all around clearly show that God wants it to be understood that way. Use the big passages to help you understand the little ones. Carefully study verses that are details about things to help you understand other sections that are more general; and study also the ones where the writer is explaining carefully and factually what to believe, to help you grasp other ones where the writer is just talking about what he feels or is enjoying in God.

3. *If some verses do not seem to fit, don't try to force them.* You just don't see the whole picture yet. Later on, as you read more of the Bible, the Holy Spirit will help you to understand. Have you ever done a jigsaw puzzle? The completed picture was at first impossible to see. Later, as you found bits that fit together, the whole picture became clearer. It is the same with the Bible.

Don't try to understand it all at once. Just read and believe in faith that God will show you what He means as you learn more. If you can't understand something at first, try reading it in another translation or two. Read it again a couple of times. If it still doesn't make sense, leave it, and go on to something else. But mark the verse so you will remember it is something you want to find an answer to.

11

Four Exciting Ways to Study the Bible

"All scripture is given by inspiration of God, and is profitable for doctrine, for correction, for instruction in righteousness, that the man of God may be perfect, thoroughly furnished to all good works" (2 Tim. 3:16, 17).

It will help you greatly if you *study* the Bible as well as just *read* it. You spend time with other things you want to be good at. Perhaps you even spend hours at a sport or hobby or talent that you want to be "excellent" in. If you want to be of great use to the kingdom of God, then you must *study* to show yourself unashamed before God (2 Tim. 2:15).

Here are four ways to study the Bible. These are the ways the world's greatest Bible scholars have used to study their Bibles. Try them out for yourself.

1. The Wide Look (Analytical Method)

This kind of Bible study will help you see what a whole book or chapter is talking about. Start with a short chapter. Then try a longer one. Begin with an easy part of the Bible to get the hang of it. Try the harder ones later. If you like, start with a simple modern version. This will be easier to read than the one you will probably use for study like the King James Version or the New American Standard Bible.

Start by reading the portion right through three or four times. (You can see why it is best to begin with a short chapter.) Try to find the parts that break into separate thought patterns. The King James and most other versions will help you by either putting a paragraph symbol in front of each new set of thoughts, or by breaking up the chapter into paragraphs. Take a sheet of paper. Write on it in your own words what you think each smaller part talks about. Don't worry about details. Find the general idea of each bit. In your Bible study notebook draw up a chart with divisions marked at each break. Study the diagram shown below:

JAMES 1

Verse	Main Idea	Minor Ideas
1	James says "hello"	Calls himself a servant To the twelve tribes
2- 8	Testing develops patience God will give wisdom	Be happy under testing We must ask for wisdom We must ask in faith We must ask without being double-minded
9-11	Be happy with what you have	The Christian poor are valuable in Jesus The rich will one day lose their valuables
12-16	Testing brings blessing *If* we don't give in	No one must think God tempts them Temptation comes from strong desires Temptation becomes sin when you give in
17-21	God's *gifts* are all good; So should be all His *children*	God's goodness never varies We are the best of His creation Christians shouldn't get angry easily
22-25	Faith isn't listening but obeying	We can fool ourselves just *listening* to the Bible Obedience to Scripture frees us as Bible faith
26-27	Faith isn't words but deeds	False religion has an uncontrolled tongue True religion cares, and keeps away from wrong

Underneath these, try to group your small parts into even larger ones. This will help you see an even wider view of the chapter or book's message. When you have done this, write out one sentence of a few words that sums up the whole thing, and write it in as the theme of the book. You can find the author, date of writing and where it was written from other Bible study helps.

2. The Deep Look (Inductive Method)

Take another small chapter, or even one of your parts of a

chapter from the last kind of study. This time you are looking
for detail. Again, write down the basic idea or thought of that part.
What you are looking for this time is the main words of each
verse or section. Now rule up a page in your study book into four
columns:

Put questions beside each part of the verse. Ask why? what?
who? where? when? how? Try to find answers to these questions.
Put the answers in your third column. Look up the meanings of
all important words in the verse you are studying. Put these under
the words in the fourth column. Leave plenty of space in case you
want to add something more later. Work neatly. You may come
back to your study again and again to add more as you find it.

A page of your *deep look* study might look something like this
when you are finished:

JAMES 1

Verse	Questions	Answers	Definitions
But	*What* does the "but" refer back to?	The perfect result of patience; thus wisdom is also needed to live a godly life under trial	
if any man	*Who* can claim this promise?	All people; God is "no respecter of persons"	
lack wisdom	*Why* wisdom? Why is *this* so important? *What* Bible word is this?	Wisdom is the other factor of Bible godliness: God is love—virtue; God is light—wisdom	*Sophia* Skill, wisdom used 51 times
let him ask	*How* do we claim it?	The simplicity of a child's request: not beg, hint, strive or study for it	See Eph. 1:16-18 John 14:16, 26; Luke 21:14-15; 2 Pet. 3:15
of God	Of *whom* are we asking wisdom?	God is the source of infinite wisdom	
who gives to all men	What is the significance of this?	"In him [Christ] are hid all the treasures of wisdom and knowledge" (Col. 2:3)	James 3:17
generously	*How* does God give? Amplify the Bible word	Surprise! Original word means something different than "a lot of"	*Haplos* Simply, in simplicity
and		—no "hassles" from Him	

Verse	Questions	Answers	Definitions
without reproach	What does this phrase mean?	God will never get angry or frustrated with us when we have to keep coming back to Him again and again for more	Oneidizo To reproach, revile

3. The Broad Look (Topical Method)

With this you actually mark your Bible, or you could just write out in full quite a lot of scriptures. What you try to find in the broad look is how often a word is used right through the Bible, or just in the Old or New Testaments, or in one book or chapter. If you are marking a Bible, you can use different colors for each key word. If you run out of colors, you can change the way you mark words by using an asterisk, an underline, a wavy underline, a bracket, a circle, etc.

> 17 But the wisdom that is from above is first pure,* then peaceable, [gentle,] *and* easy to be intreated, full of mercy and good fruits, without partiality, and without hypocrisy.

Another way to do it is to look up a word in a concordance, and write out in full all the verses that help you to know what that word means as it is used in the Bible. You can file these Bible studies in your notebook, too. Use a concordance to find the meanings of the word if you have one with a lexicon at the back.

Wisdom—Sophia—skill, wisdom

"And the child grew, and waxed strong in spirit, filled with *wisdom*" (Luke 2:40) (Jesus as a teenager)
"Jesus increased in *wisdom* and stature, and in favor with God and man" (Luke 2:52) (Jesus as a teenager)
"They were not able to resist the *wisdom* ... by which he spoke" (Acts 6:10) (Stephen the martyr)
"And delivered him ... and gave him favour and *wisdom*" (Acts 7:10) (Joseph in Egypt)

This is the method of highlighting the key word in a notebook topical study. This is where you use a concordance to research all the times a word is used, and pick out significant passages to illustrate.

The alternative is to mark the word in the Bible itself, using different colors.

Another method is to connect identical words with "railways," or broken lines, using a pen with a ruler.

> 13 Who *is* a wise man and endued with knowledge among you? let him shew out of a good conversation his works with meekness of wisdom.
> 14 But if ye have bitter envying and strife in your hearts, glory not, and lie not against the truth.
> 15 This wisdom descendeth not from above, but *is* earthly, sensual, devilish.
> 16 For where envying and strife *is*, there *is* confusion and every evil work.
> 17 But the wisdom that is from above is first pure, then peaceable, gentle, *and* easy to be intreated, full of mercy and good fruits, without partiality, and without hypocrisy.
> 18 And the fruit of righteousness is sown in peace of them that make peace.

Two other methods of marking can be used in topical study: The color-coded letter in the margin, representing a whole principle of Scripture (like the marked Reference Bible); and the column marking of a Bible with rub-on lettering like *Letraset* or *Instantype*; asterisks, letters, numbers, arrows and other such symbols come in different sizes and in different colors. This lettering is available in commercial art stores. This method has a more expensive initial investment, but is good for marking a valuable Bible in a clean, trouble-free way. A couple of sheets will last a whole Bible.

When you mark your Bible, always be neat. Don't just scribble in it, or you might not be able to read it later. Your Bible will become like a precious friend to you. Take good care of it. Some disciples of Jesus use two Bibles. They use one at home for study. This is the one they write carefully in. They carry a less expensive Bible which they use to witness with, read during the day, and give away if need be.

4. The Personal Look (Interweave Analysis)

Some parallel passages of Scripture raise puzzling questions. The accounts of some sections differ in details from other accounts describing the same incident. How can we answer these problems? This method will give you a valuable tool to find out what really happened.

The *personal look* method is a very simple one. Remember,

the Holy Spirit used each person who recorded the Bible according to his different personality. Each author was reminded of a slightly different facet of the same scene that another also wrote about. Matthew, a Jew, saw Christ as the promised Messiah, king of Israel, and his Gospel is full of Old Testament prophecies fulfilled; Mark, a young Roman, saw Him as the divine servant, and his story picks out His power, actions and deeds. Luke, a Greek doctor, saw Jesus as the Son of man; he draws on the warm, human side of the Lord. John saw Him as the divine Son of God, the Lamb taking away the sins of the world, in all His majesty, eternity and love.

Accordingly, the Gospel accounts (and some other parallel passages of the Bible) are like an intricate jigsaw puzzle. To get a whole picture of what happened, you must take each separate picture and *interweave* them. Some writers put in details that the others left out; all you have to do is to rearrange all these events in their right place and order, inserting new details from where accounts differ. Leave out all but one of the passages repeated exactly, or you will have too many words in your final account. Here is an example taken from two books, Matthew and Mark. Matthew 22:35 gives this account:

> "Then one of them, which was a lawyer, asked Him a question, tempting Him, and saying. . . ."

Mark 12:28 tells the same story, but leaves out some details and adds other details. Here is Mark's account:

> "And one of the scribes came, and having heard them reasoning together, and perceiving that He had answered them well, asked Him. . . ."

Interweave analysis gives us a smooth, rich and full description of what Jesus said to this young man who was both a scribe and a lawyer:

> "And then one of the scribes came, one of them which was a lawyer, and having heard them reasoning together, and perceiving that He had answered them well, asked Him a question, tempting Him, and saying. . . ."

The rest of each passage (Matt. 22:36-40; Mark 12:28-31) can be interwoven into one continuous account with all the details:

> "Master, which is the great commandment in the law? Which is the first commandment of all? Jesus said unto him, and answered him, The first of all the commandments is, Hear, O Israel: The Lord our God is one Lord; and thou shalt love the Lord thy God with all thy heart, and with all thy soul, and with all thy mind, and with all thy strength; this is the first and great com-

mandment. And the second is like unto it, namely this, Thou shalt love thy neighbor as thyself. There is none other commandment greater than these. On these two commandments hang all the law and the prophets."

This method of study is extremely helpful for passages with apparent contradictions, e.g., the two versions of Paul's testimony in Acts 9:1-9 and Acts 22:6-16 would be an example of this. Interweave analysis shows that the men with Saul first saw the light but heard nothing; Paul's conversion experience was not shared with the others. But when Paul said, "What shall I do, Lord?" the men accompanying him then heard the voice from heaven, for they must know where Paul should be taken because Paul had been struck blind.

12

Using Bible Study Helps

"Study to show yourself approved to God, a workman that doesn't need to be ashamed, rightly dividing the word of truth" (2 Tim. 2:15).

If you are going to do any serious study of the Bible, you should try to invest in some of these Bible study helps:

1. *A good concordance.* This is a sort of a Bible index. It lists all the words used in the Bible in alphabetical order, and it is used like a dictionary. Say that you are trying to discover where a verse that you can roughly remember is found. There are two ways to do this. One is to read the whole Bible through until you find it! The other way is to use a concordance. Perhaps you can remember only one word of the verse. Just look that word up in your concordance. When you find the word on the list of words, go through the list of verses until you find the verse that you are looking for. It will save you many weary searches.

Of course, you can use a concordance for many other things besides just finding lost verses. You can use it for a Bible study on what God says about one topic.

Some concordances even give the original Greek or Hebrew words, besides showing you how to say that word in English. Some have a special section in the end that gives you those Hebrew and Greek words in a list, and shows you how many times they are translated as one English word or as another. This may also tell the different meanings of the words, as a Greek or Hebrew word can have more than one English meaning. This special index is called a *lexicon.* You will find a lexicon in the back of *Strong's Exhaustive Concordance* and also *Young's Analytical Concordance.*

Which one is best for you? It all depends. Perhaps the best, all-around is Young's. Strong's is more complex, but better for the more serious study. *Cruden's Complete Concordance* is good but does not give as many word meanings as the others. Some

Bibles have small concordances in the back that you can use. Try out a couple before you buy one. Concordances are not inexpensive, but you can use them for a lifetime, so choose one carefully.

2. *A reliable dictionary.* Use a well-known type like *Oxford's* or *Webster's.* With this you can look up words you don't fully understand and get ideas that will help you get more meaning out of Bible words.

3. *Other resource aids.* You can also buy a Bible dictionary (written especially for Bible study); a Bible atlas (for finding places in the Bible in the ancient and the modern world); and a Bible encyclopedia. These are helpful tools but are not absolutely needed for discovering most of the things God wants to teach you from His Word. Be careful with commentaries on the Bible. They can help, but they may also become a crutch, giving you ready-made answers based on men's tradition rather than God's truth. Some are quite useless in some areas of study. Stay simple when you study the Bible. Make sure that most of your study is that of the *Bible,* not just books about the Bible.

4. *Other translations.* The much loved *King James Version* often uses words that have since changed their meaning. Other versions of the Bible may help you understand a hard passage. Be careful if you use Bibles that have interpretive notes with the Bible verses. Some of these are comments by fine, godly men, but many times you may rely on these to explain the meaning of the Word of God without giving the Holy Spirit a chance to speak to you directly.

There is a difference between a *translation* and a *paraphrase.* A translation tries to give you the actual words used by the original author in your own language, as closely as possible, even if the translator does not understand the full meaning of the verse. Translations of the Bible other than the King James are the *Revised Standard Version*, the *New American Standard Bible*, the *Moffatt* and *Berkeley* versions, and the *Amplified Bible.* There are also translations of the New Testament like *Good News for Modern Man.*

A *paraphrase* is not always as accurate as a translation. In a paraphrase, the writer takes a verse and tries to put into his own words what he thinks is the meaning of the original words. Sometimes he may use words that get across the sense of the passage, although some of the words he uses do not actually appear in the original at all. *Phillips*, the "Living" series (*Living Letters, Living Gospels* and the *Living Bible*) are paraphrases. They are good to read for a fresh look at the Bible, but do not rely on them always for accuracy. Remember, an author may put in what he *thinks* something means. Sometimes he will be wrong, although most paraphrases try to be both clear and careful.

5. *A notebook.* You will need a place to record your studies. Use a well bound loose-leaf notebook, or if funds permit, a loose-leaf or a wide margin Bible. Some groups, like the American Bible Society, have printed inexpensive Bibles for study with big margins for notes. They come in loose-leaf notebooks.

When you write down verses, you can use a "Bible shorthand" for noting references: The First Epistle of John, chapter one, verses nine through ten, becomes 1 John 1:9-10. The first part of verse 1 is written 1a, the second part, 1b.

13

Why Are Some Prayers Not Answered?

Have you ever wondered why God doesn't seem to answer some prayers? Check *your* prayer life for any one of these "answer-blockers":

1. *The wicked prayer.* Prayer for something God has forbidden will not be answered. To pray we must stay in God's promises and laws. If we get out of these, God will not hear our petitions. The Bible says, "You ask, and do not receive, because you ask amiss, that you may spend it on your lusts" (James 4:3).

2. *The unforgiving prayer.* If you try to pray with bitterness in your heart, God *cannot* answer until you are willing to repent. The only reason we can expect answers to prayer at all from God is that we have forgiven and been forgiven for all our wrong and for the wrong others have done to us. "And when you stand praying, forgive, if you have anything against anyone, that your Father also who is in heaven may forgive you your trespasses. But if you do not forgive, neither will your Father who is in heaven forgive your trespasses" (Mark 11:25, 26).

3. *The selfish prayer.* Sometimes we pray with our own personal interests in mind, not God's glory. We are to pray in the name of Jesus. We are to come to the Father as Jesus himself would have come. To come in the name of a *country* is to come with its best interests at heart, and with all its rights and powers represented in your request. To come to the Father and pray in *Jesus'* name is to come with the best interests of God at heart, and to come representing the Lord Jesus. And Jesus did not live for himself. He did not pray just so that He could be more happy, but that His Father and the whole of heaven could be more happy.

4. *The clueless prayer.* Sometimes we do not understand what we are praying for, and don't know enough of the Word of God to pray wisely. Paul asked God three times to take away his "thorn in the flesh," but the Lord left it there as a safeguard

to protect His apostle from getting too proud of what God had done in his life. "For this thing I besought the Lord three times, that it might depart from me. And he said to me, My grace is sufficient for you, for my strength is made perfect in weakness" (2 Cor. 12:8, 9).

5. *The self-righteous prayer*, secretly comparing ourselves with others, and thinking of ourselves as better. This kind of prayer only bounces off the ceiling. We don't come to God on the basis of how far we have advanced in the Christian life. We come only on the basis of the cross and the blood of Christ, as people whom He has brought back from sin and death by His grace. "And he spoke this parable to certain men who trusted *in themselves* that they were righteous, and despised others . . . the Pharisee stood and prayed thus *with himself.* God, I thank you that I am not as other men are, extortioners, unjust, adulterers, or even as this publican" (Luke 18:9-11).

6. *The doubting prayer.* Faithless and wordy prayers won't get answered. To pray and get answers, don't pray unless you really believe that God will answer. And strip your prayer life of all wordy, foolish talk just for the sake of hearing yourself speak, or that may be all that will happen.

Pray in Jesus' name. It is not just a charm, or a nice, Christian way to end a prayer. It is our *authority*; it gives us a right to speak with a holy God. It is a *seal* that ensures that all we pray for is in line with the will of God and is for His final glory. It has *power* over the enemy and his evil hosts. In that name we can command evil forces to release their holds!

14

How to Pray and Get Answers

God will answer our prayers when we are careful to meet His conditions. Catherine Booth of the Salvation Army gave these three basic conditions as the golden links by which prayer connects with heaven's "switchboard":

1. *Living and abiding union with Christ.* Jesus said, "If you abide in me, and my words abide in you, you shall ask what you will, and it shall be done to you" (John 15:7).

2. *Systematic obedience* to the teachings of the Word and the Spirit of God. "Beloved, if our heart does not condemn us, then we have confidence towards God. And whatsoever we ask, we receive of him, because we keep his commandments, and do those things that are pleasing in his sight" (1 John 3:21, 22).

3. *Unwavering faith* in the truthfulness and faithfulness of God. "But let him ask in faith, nothing wavering. For he that wavers is like a wave of the sea driven with the wind and tossed. For let not that man think that he shall receive anything of the Lord" (James 1:6, 7).

Mrs. Charles Cowman tells a story of a philosopher who pleased Alexander the Great. The philosopher asked Alexander for money, and was allowed to receive from the royal treasury whatever he requested. The philosopher asked in his king's name a sum of £10,000 (about $30,000). The treasurer refused to grant it until he had told the king. The king listened, then said he was delighted, and demanded that the money be instantly paid. By the greatness of his request the philosopher showed the high idea he held of Alexander's greatness, riches and generosity. And if Alexander gave like a king, shall not Jehovah give like a God?

"When we learn to live in these promises of the Bible we shall learn what it means to have our prayers answered. '*All things*, whatsoever you shall ask in prayer, *believing*, you shall receive' (Matt. 21:22). God must be true; and if your experience does not match the promises, you know that there is probably something wrong with your experience! Examine yourself. Repent from all known sin. Then prove Him in prayer, and you will know what it means to have power with God. You will know how to pray and get answers.

" 'Men ought always to pray, and not faint' (Luke 18:1). That little 'ought' is emphatic. It implies obligation as high as heaven. I confess that I do not always feel like praying when, judging by my feelings, there seems to be no one listening to my prayer. And then these words have stirred me: I 'ought always to pray.' I ought to pray, and should not grow faint in praying. The farmer often plows his field when he does not feel like it, but he expects a crop for his labours. If prayer is a form of work, and our labor is not in vain in the Lord, should we not pray regardless of our feelings?"—Samuel Logan Brengle.

As your prayer life begins to deepen, you will discover some of the key principles on which power in prayer can be built. Here are a few of these for you to deepen your prayer life and make it more effective for the Lord Jesus and His kingdom:

1. *Faith.* It's important that we really believe God for what we are asking. If we are sure it is in His will, by His Word and by His Spirit, then we should be bold in faith. God will answer no matter how difficult or even impossible it may seem to us as humans. Jesus said, "*Have faith in God.* For truly I say to you, Whosoever shall say to this mountain, Be taken up, and be cast into the sea; and shall not doubt in his heart, but shall *believe* that he says those things that shall come to pass, he shall have it whatever he says. Therefore I say to you, what things you desire, when you pray, *believe* that you *have received them,* and you shall have them" (Mark 11:22-24; see also Matt. 21:21, 22). "If you have faith . . . nothing shall be impossible to you" (Matt. 17:20). "Let him ask *in faith,* nothing doubting" (James 1:6).

2. *The Spirit.* We need to ask the help of the Holy Spirit for direction in prayer. Often we do not know *how* we should pray, or *what* we should ask for. It is His gracious ministry to lead us into what we should ask from our heavenly Father. Charles Finney says in his autobiography, "The Lord taught me, in those early days of my Christian experience, many very important truths in regard to the spirit of prayer . . . it came upon me in the sense of a burden that crushed my heart, the nature of which I could not understand at all; but with it came an intense desire to pray . . . I could not say much. I could only groan with groanings loud and deep. . . . For a long time I tried to get my prayer before the Lord; but somehow, words could not express it." "Likewise

the Spirit also helps our infirmities; for we do not know what we should pray for as we ought; but the *Spirit himself* makes intercession for us with groanings which cannot be uttered" (Rom. 8:26). "I will pray *with the spirit,* and I will pray with the understanding also" (1 Cor. 14:15).

3. *The Word.* One of the best ways of praying is to get a promise from the Bible, fulfill its conditions and then remind the Lord about it. God has promised to honor and back up His word; you can pray with confidence! "A spirit of importunity sometimes came upon me so that I would say to God that He had made a *promise* to answer prayer, and I could not, and *would* not be denied. I felt so *certain* that He would hear me, and that faithfulness to His promises and to Himself rendered it impossible that He should not hear and answer, that frequently I found myself saying to Him, 'I hope Thou dost not think that I can be denied. I come with Thy faithful promises in hand, and I *cannot* be denied.' I cannot tell how absurd unbelief looked to me and how certain it was, in my mind, that God would answer prayer—those prayers that from day to day and from hour to hour I found myself offering in such agony and faith" (Charles Finney's autobiography). "And this is the confidence that we have in him, that, if we ask anything according to his will, he hears us; and if we know that he hears us, whatever we ask, we know that we have the petitions that we desired of him" (1 John 5:14, 15).

4. *Fasting.* If you really want an answer from God, try fasting. Prayer and fasting in operation together convinces ourselves and God that we really mean business. In a fast we are giving up things we really need in order to give ourselves more to God and to prayer. Fasting intensifies our prayer lives. It enables us to concentrate wholly on the Lord Jesus. Try missing a meal or two and spending your normal eating times in prayer. Sometimes God may lead you into fasting by taking away all your appetite for food before a big test or prayer-battle for someone else. When the disciples failed to cast out a demon from a boy, Jesus said, "This kind can come forth by nothing, but by prayer and fasting" (Mark 9:29).

5. *Tears.* If all else fails, try tears! It sometimes helps to get away somewhere where you can be all *alone* with God, where there will be no one around to disturb you or where you will not disturb anyone. Go up to a forest, or on a lonely hill, or in an empty house, and lock yourself away with God. Learn to *cry* to the Lord; to pour out your soul in earnest, desperate prayer; to really cry out your needs in a holy shout to heaven. Do you really want to get through to God's throne in time of great need

and agony? Then learn to cry. "The eyes of the Lord are upon the righteous, and his ears are open to their cry . . . the righteous cry, and the Lord hears, and delivers them out of all their troubles. The Lord is nigh to them that are of a broken heart . . . " (Ps. 34:15-18). "Who [Christ] in the days of his flesh, when he had offered up prayers and supplications with strong crying and tears . . . [He] was heard in that he feared" (Heb. 5:7).

6. *Intercession.* Pray for others. Put yourself in their place. When you pray for them, feel their problems and difficulties. A rule of intercession is this: always pray when God lays that person or group on your heart. Never be disobedient to the voice of God. Carry them in prayer until God lifts the burden from you. Intercession has been called the highest and holiest ministry. It is the highest form of prayer, and must form the backbone of every real move of God in a nation. Catherine Booth said, "Prayer is agony of the soul—wrestling of the Spirit. You know how men and women deal with one another when they are in desperate earnestness for something to be done. That is prayer whether it be done to man or God; and when you get your heart influenced, and melted, and wrought up, and burdened by the Holy Ghost for souls, you will have power, and you will never pray but that somebody will be convinced—some poor soul's dark eyes will be opened and spiritual life will commence." God moves when His people are moved.

Section IV
The Disciple's STAND

15

Is the Bible Really God's Word?

The Bible does not try to prove its claim to be God's Word; it simply states it. The writers of Scripture keep saying their message was not human opinion but divine revelation. Genesis opens with the words "and God said" 9 times in the first chapter. The statement "saith the Lord" appears 23 times in Malachi, the last Old Testament book. "The Lord spoke" is used 560 times in the first five books of the Bible; Isaiah claims at least 40 times that his message was from God, and so do Ezekiel and Jeremiah 60 and 100 times, respectively. Bible writers claim that their message was God's message at least 3,800 times in the Bible.

The Lord Jesus quoted from at least 24 Old Testament books. He quoted from Daniel 22 times, Isaiah 40 times, the first five Bible books 60 times. He also quoted from the Psalms. He never implied that the Bible's stories were just fables or folklore. He talks of Bible people as real, historical people. In Luke 24:24-27, Christ said that He was the subject of prophecy throughout the Old Testament. He also said many times that the Scriptures must be fulfilled (Matt. 13:4; Luke 21:22; John 13:18; 15:25; 17:12). He told people that His own words were given from God and that the "scripture cannot be broken" (John 10:35; see also Mark 13:31; John 6:63; 8:42-47; 12:46-50). His own claims as God in human flesh and the claims of the Bible stand or fall together. We cannot say Christ was true but the Bible is not, nor that we believe the Bible but not Christ.

New Testament writers who knew Jesus likewise said that God had in a special way inspired their words. Paul preached that his message came from God in God's power (2 Cor. 2; Gal. 1:11-17), and Peter said that Paul wrote by "wisdom given to him" (2 Pet. 3:16). There are at least 600 Old Testament quotes and references in the New Testament. Both are locked together as a whole.

The Bible says about itself, "All scripture is given by inspiration of God [God-breathed]" (2 Tim. 3:16); "No prophecy of the scripture is of any private interpretation; for the prophecy came not in old time by the will of man [not just human ideas], but holy men of God spoke as they were moved [carried along by] the Holy Spirit" (2 Pet. 1:20-21).

Survival

Why has the Bible survived century after century of determined persecution? No other ancient book has such a vast number of surviving copies. There are thousands of Old and New Testament manuscripts. Variations between these are minor and insignificant and great care must have been taken in copying them. It is said that Jewish scribes would use a new pen each time they came to the word *Lord* and at that point carefully compare everything they had written so far with the original copy. Men have been killed for owning copies in every century. Each era brings a renewed attempt to stamp out the Bible, but history shows that it has been impossible to destroy the Scriptures.

Voltaire said, "In one hundred years, this book will be forgotten." *Voltaire* is forgotten. Exactly one hundred years after his boast, his house was being used as the headquarters for the Geneva Bible Society.

Jesus said, "Heaven and earth shall pass away, but *my words* shall not pass away" (Matt. 24:35). God's Word is "quick" or living (Heb. 4:12). It has stood the test of scholarship and the trials of all its enemies for centuries.

Social Influence

A book's true nature is revealed by the effect it has on society. The Bible gives laws for human relationships that have never been excelled or equalled. Whenever the Scriptures have been taught and lived, they have transformed nations. The Bible has brought consideration for others, tenderness and compassion for the elderly, sick and needy. It has dignified womanhood and guided childhood.

Whenever the Scriptures have been freely circulated in the language of a people, it has released astonishing power for good, elevating society, overthrowing superstition and opening the door to progress in the sciences, arts and humanities. The Bible message has delivered thousands from the chains of fear, sickness and sin. It is the most powerful book in the world for the renewal of man.

Practically applied it teaches and inspires industry, fairness and justice; it stands for the welfare of the individual, the family, the community and the state. It has created more benevolent enterprises than any other book in history. Study for yourself the record of history. Watch what has happened to the nation that has honored the Bible and its Author; see what has happened to progress in countries that have tried to supress, reject or misinterpret its message.

Wherever the Bible is loved and applied, the nation is exalted. Whenever men become forgetful of its Author and ignorant of its truths, fear, war, disease and hatred will stalk their streets. The Bible injunction is clear, "Happy is the nation whose God is the Lord."

Its Span of Time in Prophecy

If there is one thing the Bible dares to do that no other book in the world does, it is to accurately predict the future. God arranges the situations of history to bring about His glory in the lives of those who respond to His call. Working with the moral choices of men, He directs circumstances together into a pre-planned series of patterns laid down before the foundation of the world. The outline of many of these patterns is revealed in the Bible.

There are about 3,856 verses directly or indirectly concerned with prophecy in Scripture—about one verse in six tells of future events. God's challenge to the world is that we might prove Him. "I am the LORD: I will speak, and the word that I shall speak shall come to pass" (Ezek. 12:25; see also Jer. 28:9; Ezek. 24:14; Luke 21:22). Buddhists, Confucianists and the followers of Mohammed have their sacred writings, but in them the element of prophecy is conspicuous by its absence. The destruction of Tyre, the invasion of Jerusalem, the fall of Babylon and Rome—each was accurately predicted and fulfilled to the smallest of details.

In the life of the Lord Jesus himself there are over 300 fulfilled prophecies. It is ridiculous to imagine that these prophecies would all be fulfilled *by accident* by one person. Only *one* chance in a number followed by 181 zeroes! To give you some idea of the size of this immense figure, think of a ball that is packed solidly with electrons (two and a half million billion make a line about one inch long). Now in your mind imagine this ball expanded to the size of the universe—some four billion light-years in diameter (a light-year being the distance that light travels in a year at the speed of over 186,000 miles a second). Multiply this by 500 quadrillion. Out of this vast container of electrons, remove just *one* electron, and "color" it red and return it to the container, and stir it with the other electrons for a hundred years. Then blindfold a man and send him in to pick it out the first time. Impossible? With the same chance, Christ lived and died according to the Scriptures by "accident!"

16

Why Is Jesus the Only Way to God?

A lot of people get defensive when a disciple of Jesus says, "Jesus is the only way to God." The usual thing they answer is that words like these show nothing but prejudice and a narrow mind. The next thing they say is, "What about all the other great religions or teachers?" We will talk about this next. But first of all, we must see that to stick up for something based on true facts is not prejudice. Do we call a man narrow-minded if he sticks up for the fact that a man who steps off a ten-story building without aid will fall down? It is up to us to find out whether what we believe is based on opinion or truth and to change our views as we learn more.

When disciples of Jesus say "one way" it is not because they are prejudiced. Of all the people in the world, the true disciple must be the one most open to truth, and change his views because of truth when necessary. We say "one way" because the Lord Jesus said it. If there is a real truth at all, there is also untruth. If there are real rights, then there are real wrongs. And if there really is only one true God, then it is wrong to serve any other. When Jesus came, He did not speak like any other man. He did not say, "Follow me, and I will lead you in the way." He did not say, "I will teach you the truth." He was not like any teacher who says, "I will show you life." He said, "Follow me. I *am* the way. I *am* the truth. I *am* the life." And no other important religious teacher has ever said that before and proved it. Jesus said things like this, making Him unlike any other spiritual leader in history. If someone does not agree with this, his contention is not with us. We did not say it. Jesus himself said it.

It is one thing to say things like that. Anyone can say, "I am the way." But when someone as important as Jesus Christ said it, there are only four things that can be true about Him. You see, Jesus made the biggest mark in history. There is more space given to Him in the *Encyclopaedia Britannica* than that given to any other religious leader of all time. He never wrote a book. He never marched an army. He was born poor. He only lived about thirty-three years. But He made the biggest impact on our world that any man has ever made. And someone this important cannot be ignored if He says the kind of things that Jesus said. C. S. Lewis said that Jesus can only be one of four things:

(1) *He was a legend.* He did not really exist. But that is silly. We have records in history besides the Bible that Jesus really did live here on earth. And if you read on a calendar "1977" it tells you that about one thousand, nine hundred and seventy-seven years ago, someone came who split history in half. Our time is broken into two big pieces—B.C. and A.D.—before Christ and after His birth. No one else has ever been thought so important as this. No, Jesus was not just a dream or myth.

(2) *He was a liar.* Some kids say, "Oh, I believe Jesus was real, but He was only a great moral teacher." If Jesus was *not* what He said He was, then He was no great moral teacher. He was the biggest liar in history, because He made the greatest claims in history. But the life and words of Jesus are without fault. Not even His enemies could show that He had ever lied or been untrue to His word. He could say, "Which of you can convict me of sin?" (John 8:46), and no one could. He was no liar.

(3) *He was a lunatic.* About the only other thing you can say (apart from trying to prove that He did not actually say what He said in the Bible) is that perhaps Jesus really did think He was what He said, but He was mad. However, we know a lot about madness today, and Jesus showed none of the signs of madness, even when He was in great stress or pressure. No, He was not mad.

(4) *He was who He said He was*—the Lord of glory. Hundreds of thousands of people of all ages, races and cultures have come to Him and found Him to be all that He claimed to be.

17
What About People Who Never Hear of Jesus?

"When they do what the Law tells them to do, even if they do not have the Law (written down) it shows they know what they should do. They show that what the Law tells them to do is written in their hearts. Their own hearts tell them if they are guilty" (Rom. 2:14-15).

How can God judge people who have never heard about Jesus? First of all, know this—God is very, very fair. He is the Judge of all the earth, and will do right. He is kind and loving. He will always show mercy and pardon whenever He possibly can, as long as it is wise for Him to do so. The Bible says, "God will give His greatness and honour and peace to all who obey the truth. Both Jews and those who are not Jews will receive this. God does not show favor to one man more than the other" (Rom. 2:10, 11). Every man, no matter what his culture or religion is, is going to be judged fairly and justly by God. He will never overlook anything or make a mistake.

The trouble with our world is that people do not want to honor God. They all know some things about truth and right, but do not obey even this. No one is lost from God just by ignorance. People who have never heard about Jesus are not judged for rejecting the name or person of Jesus. They will be judged for rejecting what they knew about the Truth, which one day every man will see *is* Jesus. The man who has *not* heard of God's law is judged on what he really did know about right and wrong from his own life and the world around him. The man who *did* hear God's law has twice as big a responsibility. The more we know, the more will be held against us if we do wrong. You can see it is no help to know more about Jesus than someone else if we still do not obey Him. It is worse for us to know more and then not do it. The more we know, the more we are held responsible before God.

God is not lost. He is always here. All men can know something about Him. "This True Light, coming into the world, gives light to every man" (John 1:9). If any man will only obey the light God has already given him, God will find a way to bring that man more, enough to bring him to Jesus. The man who is willing to do what he knows is best and to try to honor all that he knows about the true God, will be shown more about Him. God will find a way to speak to him about Jesus and His sacrifice for sin. Cornelius (Acts 10) and the Ethiopian (Acts 8) are examples of this. There are a number of people in history who have been found by Jesus in this way, like Sundar Singh of India, and Sammy Morris of Africa. If any man really wants to know about the real God, God will speak to him, even if He has to do it directly as He did to the Apostle Paul. That proud Pharisee fought the Lord Jesus out of his zeal for what he thought was the One True God. "The Lord's hand is not short that it cannot save, nor his ear heavy that it cannot hear; but your iniquities have separated between you and your God, and your sins have hid his face from you, so that he will not hear you" (Isa. 59:1, 2). All that God asks of any man is true honesty towards Him. He says, "Then you shall find me, when you seek for Me and search for Me with all your heart." God cuts himself off from us only because of our selfishness and dishonesty. *He* is not lost. *Man* is! And when He is drawing us and calling us to come back to reality in His love and light, the next move is not up to Him. It is up to us.

God does not judge us for things we don't know about. He does not get angry because people don't understand. These are not the reasons why God is going to judge the world. God only judges men for what they do know about right and wrong, and have not been willing to obey. And what do people know of right and wrong who have never even heard of Jesus? Think about a man who knows nothing about the Bible. He may belong to some religion; he may not be religious at all. His parents may believe in God; he may not even know who his parents were. He has never met a Christian. He has never read a gospel tract. He may not even be able to read. He says he does not know anything at all about the laws of God. Is this true? How much can he know about what God expects of his life? Is it true that you can only know about real rights and wrongs by being taught about it from parents who learned it from the Bible?

The Bible tells us that such a man knows quite enough about true rights and wrongs without any of the advantages that a child from a Christian home may have. Many people today do not realize just how much a man or woman can know about right without ever being taught by someone else. And remember, to grow up in a Christian home, to go to church and to listen to the Bible being preached is no advantage if all this moral light is not obeyed. It is a terribly scary thing to learn a whole lot about God and the Bible and not do anything about it. It is better that you had never heard at all, than for you to have heard and then rejected, because your judgment will be far worse. In the next chapter we shall see how God judges a man who says he didn't know right.

18

If Hell Is Real, Is It Fair?

"As the weeds are gathered together and burned in the fire, so will it be in the end of the world. The Son of man will send His angels; they will gather out ... all things that cause people to sin and those who do sin. They will put them into a stove of fire" (Matt. 13:40-42).

Perhaps one of the main reasons why people do not think hell is real or fair is because they do not believe people are bad enough to be given any kind of punishment. Today most people in the world live their lives as if man himself was god. Human life has become the ultimate value. And human life *is* very important. Life, freedom and happiness must be guarded for all moral beings. That is why God has given us His laws. They protect everyone's happiness, including God's. And we have already seen that the law of love is the most important law in the universe. It is even more important than the life of the individual who violates it because it cannot be safely broken without beginning a chain of sin that would finally end in the ruin of the whole universe.

Human life is very, very important. But if a man does something that is worthy of death, his life must be forfeited as a punishment. And sin is the ultimate wrong. Sin, if left unchecked, would murder the universe, and would, if it could, tear God off His throne. The Bible fixes the most serious penalty for this most serious crime. It tells us that "the wages of sin is death" (Rom. 3:23).

But what about the man who does not know right and wrong? If there were such a man, you can be sure that God would not punish him. If he really did not know what right and wrong was, no one could accuse him of the crime of selfishness. First, think about the idea of "right." We all know that some things seem more important than others. When we have to choose, we ought to act on what we really see to be the best choice.

The value of something tells us how important it is. This is a simple, first truth idea of our minds and hearts. We all know we must pick the most important of two things when we have to decide. It is the *real value* of an object, its own true importance that tells us what to do. This is true for little things (like picking between two pairs of jeans in a store with similar prices), and for big, important things like fair play between nations. It is also true in peoples' responsibilities to one another and to God. The most important things must be put first. All things known to be of lesser value are to be put second. Anything known to be actually harmful or wrong to us, others or God is to be refused.

With this goes the idea of fair play too. We all know we ought to be fair with others. No culture or land has ever admired people for being selfish. Every person in the world knows he ought not to be selfish, even if he *is* selfish. No one likes to be badly or unfairly treated by others. This is true all over the world. It is true with people in lands that are cultured or primitive, religious or agnostic, advanced or backwards. People dislike and despise selfishness. So does God. He calls it "sin."

These two things are the basis on which God judges people. It all depends on what they really know of right. God has a way to find out how much a man really knows about right. It is very fair. He will put every man to the test to see if they have done what is right in all that they knew about right. He will judge them for nothing else. And when someone does wrong, he must be punished for it. This does not help him, but it does help other people to see that what is right must be honored. God's love-law does not work by force. He only shows us what is best, and we must do this for happiness.

No one ought to be selfish. Selfishness costs too much and hurts too much. It can only hurt ourselves, others and God. And no man or woman who insists on being selfish can be trusted in the universe. They would turn it into a hell. Something must be done to stop people from hurting each other and God. And God has done something. He has given us limits to stay within. If we break these rules, we ought to be punished. A penalty must be as big as the law it is designed to protect. The bigger the crime, the bigger the penalty must be to be fair. And sin is the worst crime in the universe. God must judge sin. He would not be wise if He did not. Whoever is in charge of the universe must see that everyone is fair.

God has put a very serious penalty on sin. It is the worst one He could think of. It is endless death—being cut off finally and forever from the good things that come from serving God and living right. Hell is simply the place a man sends himself without God. And what is hell like? Think about a man who has lived all his life to please himself. He has not honored God. He has pushed from his heart all that God did to try to bring him to reality. He has said in his heart, "No God for me!" He rejects everything that God's love can use to bring him to surrender up his sin. Now if a man cannot be changed by God's love, nothing, not even a million years in hell, will change his mind. Punishments do not encourage happy trust. And hell is the kindest place God can think of for the man who dies still selfish. All his life he has refused to honor God or other's happiness, except where it served his selfish ends better. He has always wanted to live for himself, and not have to think about God or others being happy. And at death, God in infinite sadness gives him his last request. He goes to a place where there is no one else he can hurt or injure. He can be with himself, and live for himself forever. And *that* is hell. Heaven would be worse than hell for the sinner. Hell comes out of the love of God. It is the kindest place God can put a man who refuses to live under God's loving rule. No sinner would be happy in the holy light of God and with the saints of God. He gets very uncomfortable just going *near* a church or listening to someone praise the Lord!

19

What If Your Friend Says He Is an Atheist?

An atheist is someone who says there is no God or who does not believe in God. A better way of thinking about the atheist is to think of him as a man who lives as if God did not exist. A lot of church people live like that anyway. The man who says he is an atheist is perhaps a little more honest than others like him about his life.

Why do people say they are atheists? Is it because they have sat down and with honest and true study looked at all the facts and were not *able* to believe? Is it too hard for a man or woman who really thinks to believe in the Bible God? Do people call themselves atheists because they are so smart and brilliant that it is impossible to have any faith at all? No, that is not true.

The Bible tells us many times why people will not trust God or have faith in Him. It has nothing much to do with how smart a man is. There have been many smart men who did not believe in God. There have been many more who did, although not all of them would serve Him. There have always been a number of really wise men who not only believed in God but also loved Him. Being an atheist has nothing to do with being a thinker or not. Many people who are atheists are not very smart at all. No, people call themselves atheists for a different reason.

People call themselves atheists for four main reasons. All of these reasons are not based on reason. Usually what happens is that they begin to live in a certain way that hurts God. Deep inside they know this is not right. God bothers them. He begins to show them their sin. Now if this happens, what can he do?

Think of a man who walks into a dark room with a flashlight. The room is full of people doing evil things. He turns on his light and shines it on someone. What do you think that person will do? He can do one of three things: (1) He can let himself be *shown up* by the light. He can be honest and admit he is doing wrong and stop his sin. When Jesus does that with a man, he becomes a child of God. (2) He can *run away* from the light to another dark place so he can go on sinning. (3) He can try to *put out* the light so it will not show him up. Which one of these do you think the atheist you know is trying to do?

The atheist's problem is not mental but *moral*. His real problem is not that he does not have enough facts to trust in God. His problem is that he is bothered already over the facts he does know about truth and God. His problem is not with his *head*, but with his *heart*. Do not forget this. He is not an atheist because he lacks facts, but because he does not *want* facts to think about God. The Bible says, "They did not like to retain God in their knowledge" (Rom. 1:28). Jesus said, "Men loved darkness rather than light, because their deeds were evil. For every one that does evil hates the light" (John 3:19, 20).

The four kinds of atheists all have this same problem. People choose to reject talking or thinking about God because of these four kinds of sin:

1. *Pride.* The man who is on his own ego trip is trying to live like he is God. He really does believe in a God, but his god is himself. He worships himself, and finds it rotten to have to care about the real God.

2. *Bitterness.* Some kids get hurt at home, school or in the system. They blame God for what happens, like Judas Iscariot on the "Superstar" album. Little do they know how much *more* God has been hurt by the things that have happened to hurt Him.

3. *Sex sin.* Many times a man's chase after pleasure trips gets blocked by one of God's limits, like his conscience, or the Bible or a Christian's witness. This man finds it easier to pretend he doesn't believe in God than defend his sin. A lot of people who like to argue about God or the Bible fit in here. Check out their lives and you will see.

4. *People-pleasing.* What if you grew up in a home where Daddy was a Red Guard or president of the local Rationalist Society? What if your crowd were all into the three kinds of sin above, and called themselves atheists? Well, if you wanted to stay "in," you would call yourself an atheist too. And you may not even bother to find enough arguments to defend your sin before a disciple of Jesus who gets on your case. That would be a shame because, even at best, an atheist's "faith" is very shaky. It takes a lot more blind faith to not believe than it ever takes to know and serve God.

She made a little shadow-hidden grave
The day Faith died;
Therein she laid it, heard the clods sick fall,
And smiled aside.
"If less I ask," tear-blind she mocked,
"I may be less denied."

She set a rose to blossom in her hair
The day Faith died;
"Now glad," she said, "and free at last I go—
And life is wide."
But through long nights she stared into the dark
And knew she lied.

—Fannie Heaslip Lee

Section V
The Disciple's
SHARING

20

Everyone Must Know the Good News

"The Son of man has come to seek and to save that which was lost" (Luke 19:10).

The Lord Jesus knew one soul was worth more than all the world. Most of His time was spent in just talking to people about how they stood with God. He did not write any books, although He could have. He didn't give out one tract. He never had a course on soul-winning. He never learned one plan on how to win souls. The one thing He did every day was "to seek and to save that which was lost."

The true disciple of Jesus follows Jesus in witness. He does not just *do* witnessing; he *is* a witness. The task of reaching a world is not just for preachers or ministers. Jesus has given it to each one of us as our lifework. Whatever our job of living is—whether we preach, pray, write, design, build, trade or travel, labor with our hands, or keep house or state—everything we do must tell of and for the Lord Jesus and His kingdom.

You must consecrate all you have and are to this task, and ask God for the promised power to carry out the work. Jesus said, "You shall receive power after the Holy Spirit has come upon you; and you shall be witnesses of me both in Jerusalem [at home], and in all Judea [our immediate neighborhoods], and in Samaria [the outcasts of society], and to the uttermost part of the earth [every nation and tongue God calls you to reach] " (Acts 1:8). Every disciple of Jesus is a missionary; everyone else is a mission field. Your friend may cross the world; you may just cross the street; but all of us have a call to be missionaries for the Lord Jesus to help Him reach the world.

You do not have to learn to be a witness. You already *are* a witness. Each day the world sees by your words and by your deeds who really means most to you in life. You always get across to people what you really get most interested in. Your actions tell the world what you love most. Anyone who follows you around can tell who is "number one" in your life.

Every day you are a witness. Who are you a witness to? Your god is the person or thing you show the most interest in. It is the person or thing your thoughts turn back to when you have nothing else to do, what you most like to talk about, what you like most to read, what your life revolves around. *Your God is the person or thing you most love and live for.* If it is anything or anyone but Jesus, your close friends already know what it is.

If you call yourself a disciple of Jesus, you have already been witnessing, for or against Him. If you have claimed to belong to Him, but your life does not back up your words, people may have been turned off to the good news because of you. The Lord Jesus said, "He that is not with me is against me; and he that gathers not with me, is scattering abroad." If you are going to show Him, you must really know Him.

What does it mean to witness? Jesus put the life and love of His Father on show to the world. To be a witness is for someone to share their life with another; to stand in their place as best as you know how; to be for others what that person is really like. This is true witness. When the world is lost and running from God, He must go looking for men. He has chosen to do this through men and women who love Him. Through their lives, He will speak in person to lost hearts; through their hands, He will reach out to His lost world.

To be a witness means to be real—absolutely real. God hates phonies. If you have any reason in wanting to witness apart from a real concern and love for both God and for people, forget it. You will do more harm than good. Only love will win hardened street people. It must come from the heart of God to your heart. It means concern for the God whose heart has been broken over the sinner and his sin. It means living a life of true giving, a giving of strength and time and care. And this love is not just something you feel. It is something you do, measured directly by sacrifice.

To be a witness means to live like Jesus did. Our world is filled with selfish people who think only of themselves, care only for themselves and live only for themselves. Jesus' friends must be different. It will do no good to go on the streets to say, "Don't look at me for an example. I'm filled with greed and lust and bitterness and hate. My life is an awful mess. I want you to look at Jesus." That sounds spiritual but it is not. The sinner cannot see Jesus. He can see only you. And he has a perfect right to say, "But I can't see Jesus. I can only see you. And if He can't help you, what makes you think He can help me?"

To be a witness for Jesus we must live so far above the world's standards and values that unbelievers will take notice and ask us what is the secret of our lives. We must live so that with Paul we can say, "Those things which you have both learned and received and seen in me, do; and the God of peace shall be with you." Men must be able to be followers of us and of the Lord at the same time.

Everyone must know the good news. They will only know it if we live such a life of joy, faith and love that we can say, in the energy of God, "Be followers of me, even as I am of Christ" (1 Cor. 11:1).

We are the only Bible
The careless world will read;
We are the sinner's gospel,
We are the scoffer's creed.
We are the Lord's last message,
Given in deed and word;
What if the type is crooked?
What if the print is blurred?

—Author unknown

21

How to Begin Sharing Jesus

"Go into all the world, and preach the gospel to every creature" (Mark 16:15).

It is not hard to talk about someone you love, neither is it hard to speak about something you are excited about and have been thinking a lot about. It is like this in sharing Jesus. If you live in His love, it will come out in witness. I have never known a man or woman who once walked the streets in sin and who was delivered by the power of the living God, who needed to be told they must witness. They *want* to. And why not? If Jesus is the only way; if the one way is only *His* way, then we have something that burns in our hearts that we must share with a lost world.

If you do not feel like sharing Jesus, there is something wrong. Go to God. Get your heart broken and clean before Him. Find out how He feels about people. Learn to rest in His love until you grow strong in His strength. When the fire burns inside so strongly that you must speak, you are ready to begin sharing Jesus.

There are many witnessing plans around today. Some have been used of God to bring many people to the Lord. Thank God for the plans and outlines that Christian people have learned and were able to use in witnessing. But plans have limits. Many young people are on the streets in revolt against things like plans and programs. The whole hip culture began to reject a machine way of living and thinking. Some plans just plainly don't work on the streets. Some kids turn off fast when you share a plan. And they have a right to. We are not called to give out plans. We are called to simply share Jesus out of our hearts and out of the Word of God.

Marvelous things are done in people's hearts when we learn to get our "lines" from the Holy Spirit on the spot for each meeting with a man or woman without God. Share a plan with street people and they may think your *plan* is after them. Share the Lord Jesus with them, and you *know* what the street people will think! Another thing to think about is this: if too many people try to use the same plan on one man, his conviction may turn into anger. He may think he is being used by some group on a trip. And that is not the way to meet needs in Christ.

Spend more time on getting yourself ready than in learning plans. God doesn't care about the plan half as much as He cares about the man. *Men* are God's methods; *men* are God's plans. E. M. Bounds, a famous man of prayer, said, "The church is looking for better methods; God is looking for better men."

Let us suppose that you see a man in a park. You look and see that he is fishing. When you get up close you see he is fishing in a bucket. There are no fish in it. You ask him kindly, "Have you caught anything?"

"No," he says, "but I think I know what is the matter."

(You think to yourself, "I know what is the matter, too!")

"The reason why I haven't caught anything yet," he says, "is that I'm using the wrong hook and wrong bait. When I change my bait and hook, I'll probably have more success."

As you walk away, you know two things about this man. One is that there is something wrong with him. The other is that he is fishing in the wrong place.

These are the problems with most people who do not know how to fish for souls. There is either something wrong with them, or they are fishing in the wrong place. Get cleaned up! Then you will have something to say and the courage to say it. Then go out where the people are. Don't expect sinners to come to you. If you read your Bible, you will know that men and women are running from God, not looking for Him. Expect them to avoid you. But love them like God loves them. And go where they are. If you live by a beach and that is where they are, go there. If your mission field is on the streets, go to the streets.

But use your head. Don't go up to a person who is busy doing something else and try to start talking to him about Jesus. Ask God to lead you to kids who are doing nothing. Try to find the lonely ones, the ones that have time on their hands, the ones that you can make friends with and tell them what has happened to you. Go where people can listen.

Try railway stations, or bus stations. Try airline terminals. A lot of people have time on their hands, and you may get a chance to share with them there. If you have reading material about Jesus, they might be more ready to read it there than if you tried to give it to them on a street or in a supermarket or store.

Try parks and park benches. A lot of times people just sit around waiting there for something to happen. *You* be the happening! Get there with a smile and the love of God.

School is a huge mission field. If you are still in school, you have one of the biggest lot of kids to speak to that you will ever be with over a long time.

You can go house-to-house. You can go to big sports meetings where a lot of people will be sitting, waiting for the game or race to start. Any place where there are a lot of people is a good place to go. Ask God to help you to be wise. God will show you the ones that are hungry for something real. Ask Him to direct you by His Spirit. You will feel drawn to different people as the Holy Spirit gives you a nudge in their direction. Learn to hear His voice. And swallow your fear! All of us get scared at times about what people will think of us or say to us when we speak to them about Jesus. It is natural to be afraid; it is supernatural to go ahead anyway, and speak whatever God lays on your heart because you care for the one you are speaking to.

Prisons and hospitals may give you permission to visit and share. Universities and schools empty out hundreds of young people that you can talk with and give tracts to. Take along Jesus literature everywhere. Send it through the mail. Decorate your envelopes with messages for the postman. The best way to learn to share Jesus is just to begin.

> Suddenly, before my inward, opened vision,
> Millions of faces crowd upwards to view—
> Sad eyes that said, "For us there is no provision;
> Give *us* your Saviour too;
> Give *us* your cup of consolation;
> See—to our outstretched hands this never passed,
> Yet ours is the desire of every nation and—
> Oh, God—*we die so fast."*

22

Do It God's Way

"And as Moses lifted up the serpent in the wilderness, even so must the Son of man be lifted up, that whoever believes in him should not perish, but have eternal life" (John 3:14, 15).

You don't need to know a lot to witness God's way. You will see in the next chapter how witnessing is very simple. One basic step will bring a person to Jesus. If they will take it, they will be saved. But you, as a disciple of Jesus, ought to know more when you share salvation's good news. The greater wisdom you have in God's Word and ways, the more effective your outreach will be. Some things usually happen in every true conversion. A person realizes his guilt before God, and is willing to see, hate and forsake his sin. He gives his wholehearted trust to the Lord Jesus. Keep in mind these things when you talk to a man or woman who is careless towards God.

All happiness depends on our living unselfishly. Selfishness is the root of every problem we face today. It is wrong because it always hurts someone, somewhere. Without selfishness we would be free to build a beautiful world.

We were made to be led by trusting a wise and loving leader, not to be ruled by force. For this reason, people need a governor who can both show us what is most wise and tell us what to do. That leader must be wise and trustworthy, always fair and perfectly loving. The one who has a supreme right to lead the world is the one who is the strongest, the wisest and the best.

The God of the Bible is the only person with an absolute right to guide and direct our lives and that of everyone else in the universe.

He does not have this right just because He created our race, or because He is the strongest person in the universe, or even from the fact that He loves us the most. He has the right to be our leader because we need a person like Him to be happy and live together in harmony, and He is the only One qualified for this job.

Why should He be our leader? He is in all places at once, so He knows what is happening everywhere always. He knows everything that can be known, fully and perfectly, so He has perfect wisdom. No problem is too hard for Him; nothing is a secret to Him. He has endless energies and power to help us and to back up what is right. He is the only example of perfect justice and total unselfishness in our universe. He is the only One who has never been at a loss to know what to do.

God's qualifications both oblige us to follow Him and oblige Him to lead us. Selfish refusal of this kind king is something so stupid, so dangerous to everyone and so hurtful to others' happiness as to deserve punishment. Sin or selfishness is the heart of wrong doing. It consists of our refusal to honor God as God. Left unchecked, it would rise up and murder the universe.

Because sin is such a terrible evil, God guards against it by an equally terrible penalty. This penalty is called endless death. It is like a death sentence in human government, but on an eternal scale. The man who refuses to live in wisdom and love, who sets himself up against this highest happiness, must be cut off from the universe of which he has refused to be a happy part. This penalty grieves God, but He may not wisely suspend it without putting in its place something that will do the same job. To throw it out to show mercy would degrade the standard of right. A penalty protects a law. Any law without penalty is only advice, and God's love-law is much more than advice. It is the basic rule of the universe. Everything hangs on it. We *must* do that which is right, or terrible, universal destruction will result. This is only fair for everyone. It is the only just way of making sure that no one selfishly uses others; no one will buy power or pleasure with others' lives and happiness.

Live in these truths until they burn in your soul. Read your Bible until you start to see as God sees. Study how it speaks of God's great and wise kingdom. Find for yourself how good He is, why serving Him is the most valuable act in the universe. To say it in a sentence: *God deserves to be first, because He is the greatest!*

Remember the story of the man who found treasure hid in the field? Once he saw the jewels, he sold all he had to buy the field. Why? Because he knew its value. We are made to choose what we really see is the most valuable. It is God's loveliness, who the Lord Jesus is, the Holy Spirit's beauty and power that can make a man see truth, then surrender to it. Do you see why

Jesus said, "If I be lifted up from the earth, I will draw all men to me" (John 12:32)? He is the Friend of sinners. He is the supremely lovely One. And one look of faith to His love will save.

Don't be surprised if the one you are talking to doesn't care about God. It is no surprise to Jesus, who knew what it was like to have His own "receive him not." To be convicted, people must really see their selfishness. They must realize what sin has done to them, to others, to God.

Give them a glimpse of Christ in your life. Light shows up deeds done in darkness. Let them see Jesus' love for them in you. (A rose will do more than a packet of seed to make a man want to grow flowers.) If they don't care, show them that *you* care, because *God* cares. This is what Jesus did. This is what you must do to do it God's way. God has supreme right to everyone's life. He *deserves* to be first and *must* be. And every man who will not let Him be his God is both foolish and dangerous to the world.

Sometimes you will meet people who have already been spoken to by the Lord. It will amaze you to find out how many people have the Spirit of God deal with their hearts long before you came along. Ask them, "Has God ever dealt with you before?" You may find them not careless, but convicted. Many people really know their lives are wrong. They know they owe God a debt they can never pay. That is why they are afraid to talk about Him. Deep in their hearts they know they are wrong, but they don't know there is a way out. For some, suicide seems the only answer to their guilt and grief.

God, in His loving wisdom, has found a way to restore people caught in the web of selfishness. He has given us an offer of mercy in two wonderful ways:

1. *Indirectly*—by telling us He wants to pardon us through men and women who knew and loved Him. The Bible is this story collected. It tells us why He made us, what He wants for us, and what has happened because of our sin. The most astonishing part of this story is that, despite our wrong, despite our refusal to seek Him, He still loves us! He is not bitter towards His wayward creation. God is only grieved, terribly grieved, and longs to restore us.

2. *Directly*—by meeting men in person. The most amazing of all these contacts happened about 2,000 years ago. It split history in half; God himself became man, and lived among us for about thirty-three years to show His care and concern for our race. God came to us in human flesh as Jesus Christ. He was born uniquely, lived incomparably, died prophetically, and rose again from the dead triumphantly.

His earthly mission was threefold: (1) to show us what our Maker was really like; (2) to show us how we were supposed to live; (3) to die an agonizing death out of love for us as a substitute for the penalty of our sin.

Now He can forgive, pardon and restore us to His family on two conditions: *repentance*—that we are willing to forsake our previous selfish way of life, whatever it costs our plans, our pride or our public image; *faith*—that we will trust Jesus Christ as our own personal stand-in for the penalty of sin, and that we will love and obey Him as our Lord and God.

This surrender is one of the heart (our ultimate choice). It centers around one particular point of obedience. This is usually the one thing we are most unwilling to do for God. When this is yielded, a transforming climax from selfishness to love occurs which the Bible calls being "born again."

Obedience to God over this one critical point will set us free, for Christ himself will enter our lives. If you do something just because God asks you to, your life will change. You can tell a man or woman who doesn't know Jesus anything that leads them to give up their selfishness and surrender to God's love in Christ. Listen carefully, and the sinner will tell you his "god." If he says, "Do I have to give up—?" don't say, "Oh, don't worry about that." It is the *very thing* the Holy Spirit is dealing with him on. Say instead, "Yes, you will; and that's probably the *only* thing you will have to give up, because that is your God, that is the very thing you are a slave to."

Witnessing God's way, then, is so very simple! Our task is to help a sinner see himself as he is before God, then just point him to Jesus. If our lives are a picture of God's friendship, love and concern, he can see the gospel on display. If he will then give God His rightful place, he will never be the same again. All that it takes is two steps: give *up*, and give *in*. But don't cover up the cost when you speak to the convicted sinner. Don't make it easier than Jesus did. There is only one way, and it is His way. We can't break His pattern without something going wrong.

23
What to Tell New Christians

What instructions do you give to the person that you want to lead to Christ? If you are sure he understands what it means to give everything to God, and you believe he is ready to know Jesus, first help him to pray. You can suggest what he ought to tell Jesus. Go over this a couple of times to make sure he understands. Give him instructions that are *complete*.

Include the instruction that he must turn totally from all known sin and make a wholehearted surrender to Christ as his Lord. Ask him, "Are you ready to give your whole life to God? Do you understand what this will cost? Are you willing to do anything He wants you to do? Are you ready to give up anything or anyone that stands in the way?" If he hesitates, you still have some work to do. Find that hidden god of his heart. He must pray in total honesty and from the heart or God will not answer.

If he says he is ready and willing to do whatever God requires, ask him, "Do you want to talk to God and tell Him that you need Him?" If you think he doesn't know what to say, ask instead, "Do you want to pray with me now?" If he does, put your hand on his shoulder and bow your head with him. Sometimes it helps if you both go down on your knees before God. Listen to the Holy Spirit, and let Him tell you what to do here. Then, you yourself should pray first. Talk to God on behalf of your friend. Say something like this: "Father, here is —— who has come tonight to give his heart to you. I have told him what it will cost to serve you. He is willing to pay that price. Now he wants to talk to you himself and tell you with his own words that he is finished with his selfish past and that he wants you to change his life. Father, this may be the first time in his life that he has ever been real with you. Show yourself to him as he is honest from his heart. Here he is now to speak with you."

Wait for the other person to pray. If it seems hard for him, tell him again quietly, with your eyes still closed, what God is waiting to hear. Say, "Go ahead. You tell Him now that you are finished with your sin and you want to serve Him." If he can't remember what to say (many people feel shy when they first talk to God) or if he doesn't seem to get very far in his prayer, just step in and lead him to pray after you. Say to him, "Just pray after me, 'Dear Lord Jesus, please forgive me for my selfish way of living. I admit to you as honestly as I know how that I have hurt you. I have hurt others. I have hurt myself. I have really wronged you most of all. I am sorry for my rotten way of living. I turn from it. I hate it. I forsake it. Cleanse me by your blood. I give you my heart. I give you my life. Change me now. Give me a new start in life. Come into my heart. Make me your child. Save me from my sin. Right now, Lord. Right now. In Jesus' name. Amen.' "

When he finishes, test his honesty. Begin the moment after he has prayed. Ask him quietly, "Did you really mean what you just asked?" Don't threaten or sound suspicious. Just look him right in the eye and ask. If he is still not sure that the work is done, go back and see what has been held back. Something has not been yielded. Don't be afraid to dig deeply when you sense doubt or uncertainty.

The Spirit of God knows when a real change has taken place, and can let you know. If you get a firm, clear "Yes," then say, "Would you like to thank the Lord Jesus for what He has just done for you?" Then let him pray out loud on his own. It may be a good idea to leave him alone with his new Lord for a little, while he learns how to thank God. You could get some follow-up material for him. Ask him to come back and see you when he is finished talking with God.

There are a few *don'ts* for you. Don't tell him, "It's hard to be a Christian." The Bible says, "The way of the *transgressor* is hard." Jesus said, "My yoke is easy, and my burden is light." You can tell him that he will have trials, but the love of God can keep him in victory.

Don't tell him, "Now you are saved!" It is better that you leave it between him and God. His life will prove whether his experience was real or not. You don't keep the Book of Life; your job is to make plain the way. Don't "play God" by trying to give him assurance of being saved. If you tell him he *is* saved, and he is *not,* it will be your word that he will rely on rather than that of Jesus. Then if he doesn't come through properly, *you* will have to keep him straight, not Jesus.

Don't ask him, "How do you *feel*?" The Christian life does

not depend on how we feel. If he really gets saved he will feel something all right! But let *him* tell you, and don't draw undue attention to it.

Don't say too much. Save some instruction for the next time you see him. And don't prepare him to backslide by giving him scriptures on what to do "when he falls into sin!" (If you do, don't be shocked if *he* does.)

Before he leaves, be sure you get his name and address. Give him a piece of follow-up literature that has your name and address on it. Then ask him to write or to contact you again within a week. Encourage him to get in with real disciples of Jesus who love God with all their hearts. Take him yourself, if at all possible. Don't let him go off and end up with a bunch of back-slidden hypocrites who will kill his new joy in Jesus. Teach him to enjoy God's love and favor. Explain that his heart should always have inner peace and should enjoy the smile of God. Tell him that the only real proof of his salvation is that he really does love and obey God from the heart. Everything he is and has now belongs to Jesus. And don't let him leave until you pray for him one last, short time. Pray that God will bless and use him and make him a real man of God.

It is a powerful thing to get a new Christian involved in some form of work or witness for God as soon as possible. It is the one who confesses with his mouth the Lord Jesus that is saved. Use the principles of confession and restitution, forgiveness and the yielding of his rights to do this. Ask him to go home, make a list of all the things he has done to hurt God, then burn it as a symbol of his burning the bridges back to his past life. Ask him to pray that the Lord will put in his mind one person that He wants him to get things right with. Then show him how to write a letter or ask forgiveness. Fix a time when he will do it, and pray for him during that time. All the work he begins to do for God will not only involve him right away in God's service but will also be a mighty proof of his changed life to his world.

Section VI
The Disciple's
FAITH

24

Making Friends with Christ's Friends

One of the things that the Pharisees didn't like about Jesus was that He had too many friends. No one ever came to the Lord with a need and was not made to feel welcome. He never shut people out of His life. Every disciple of Jesus must be a friend to all. If we really love God, we love the One who so loved the world—and that means everyone. Perhaps you have had trouble making friends before. You may be shy or not feel that people will like you. And it is true that some people in the world will never like you. If you live for Jesus, there will be selfish people, runaways from God's love that will not want to know you too well, in case you get through to them about their souls. You will meet bitter people who have been hurt and do not trust anyone. Disciples of Jesus don't expect to be popular with everyone. But the Lord Jesus had many friends. He was a supremely friendly, understanding person. You could come to Him and always be sure of a welcome.

The world always has a funny idea of disciples of Jesus. They think of us in terms of being too far out in religion, not tolerant of others' faiths, not able to enjoy a little fun in life. The world always has a miserable picture of Christians. But remember, that is not why the Pharisees criticized Jesus. They said He was the friend of publicans and sinners. Sinners liked Him too much for their liking. Jesus had the knack of mixing with people and building them up even while He was putting down their wrong. He made friends because He loved people.

How can you be more friendly? If you have been shy and have found it hard to make friends, it is time that you take stock of yourself. Here are things to help you:

1. *Get properly clean before God.* If you are holding onto fear, guilt, anger or worry, you will give off bad vibes wherever you go. If you have been hurt, forgive. If you have some things

to get right, *do it*. You must be clean or you will always be afraid of meeting people in case they spot your secret sins. Remember, the disciple of Jesus is to be totally clear. He is to be as transparent as a mountain stream. God has given you the promises and power to be free. Go to Him first and get your heart clean. This is the first step in making friends. Do it now.

2. *Learn to forget yourself*. Shyness is only a form of pride. One of the big reasons why people don't make friends is that they try too hard. They do crazy things and say too much to be real. People get scared off when you try too hard to be friendly. You can never be friendly when you are thinking all the time, "I wonder what she thinks of what I just said? I wonder if he thinks I am friendly?" Relax. Be natural. Be yourself under God. You don't have to try to be anyone else than who you are. But be a loving "who-you-are."

You can do two things to conquer shyness and make friends. First, think of some time when you really felt at home, relaxed and at ease with someone. Carry it in your heart. Remember how you felt. Think about how easy it was to talk, to say things that people listened to and liked. And when you have to meet someone new, bring back to your mind that time of relaxed happiness. Practice living in the feelings and thoughts you had that day, and you will find your tenseness draining away; you will be more relaxed and loosen up better with new people.

Another way to stop thinking of yourself when you are trying to make new friends is to change your way of thinking about people. Instead of thinking what you can *get* from the friendship of this person, think of how you can *give* to them. Think instead of what *God* is doing in their life; how you can be of help to them; what you can do to serve them in Jesus. God has been dealing in some way with this person you are meeting; you are there to help Him in His work. Don't worry about what they might be thinking of you; concentrate on their needs. This is the way to project a real spirit of friendship.

Another way to make friends, especially with those who are hard to like, is to make a list of the good things you can find out about them. Try to write down the things you would find attractive or pleasing or praiseworthy in them if you were their friend, even if they have all kinds of problems and faults. Then pray for them. Bring these difficult people to God in prayer. Ask God to bless them, to help them. Thank Him for the things you find are nice about them. You will be surprised at how much you can find if you open your heart. Then ask Jesus to help them in His love to solve their problems. Tell Him that you are ready to be of service to that person.

Some more important things to help you make friends. Say hello *first*, even if they don't say it to you first. Go out of your way to do it. Learn their names and remember them. To help you do this, say it back to them when you first meet them and they tell you. Use it right away (a couple of times at least) when you first talk to them. Repeating it helps you to remember it. People like it when you use their first names. Write it down somewhere, after you have met them, to remember it even better. People almost always like you if you remember their names. When God calls someone, He always calls him by his name. If you want to be God's friend as well as people's friend, do the same thing.

Do what the book of Proverbs counsels in showing yourself friendly (Prov. 18:24). Every disciple of Jesus must go out of his way to help others in studies, introductions, jobs needing doing. You can *choose* to be a friend. Think these thoughts: "If Jesus loves this man, I can love and care about him too. If I can help him, I will offer to. God has left me here to serve, and this is someone I can show His love to" (see Prov. 17:17).

3. *Look out for the lonely and neglected.* The world is filled with people that others brush by without even looking at them. Make it your ministry to say a kind word to at least one new person each day. All around you are people who have no friends, with no one to care or even notice them. Some have been hurt, and they have in return hurt others so much that they have become sour and bitter, driving away all their friends.

You be a light to their darkness. You speak kindly to them despite their rude ways. Some you brush past today may go down the road to suicide, death and hell by tonight. Will they say, "No man cared for my soul" (Ps. 142:4)? Be one of the first to meet newcomers to church, school or work. Don't just hang around in little cliques that you feel safe in. If you care for others, speak to them.

When you do talk to others, don't talk about yourself. Talk about them. Be really interested in them, but not nosy; give them the feeling that you enjoy being with them. Look them in the eyes and smile. Ask them about their problems, their needs, their work. Learn to be a good listener; learn to make people feel important when they are with you. Learn to build them up and make them feel worthwhile. Of all people, the disciple of Jesus knows that man is important. We know that people are not nothings. We know they are important and valuable because they are made in God's image. We can love them because God made us all, and we are related by His creation. This lonely man is made in our Father's image. This lonely girl is made to be a tiny, finite copy of our great Creator's love and wisdom and value. I can love them and make them feel important because they are important to God, and therefore they are important to me.

Of course, your closest friends will be Christ's friends. Although we are free to find out what most people love and want to do, what are the problems they have and what God is doing in their lives, our closest friends will be only a small circle of people. They will be ones we really enjoy sharing with, those we spend a great deal of time with. Close friends are people we can share our deepest feelings and hopes with, people with which we can really have fellowship. We feel more free to help them grow spiritually by throwing in our efforts with them in some common task for God. We can expect them to lovingly show us if we are doing something wrong, and they expect us to do the same. We cannot have too many close friends; there is not enough time to share everything with many in one lifetime. But this inner circle will be close to our hearts, and we must make sure they are Christ's friends.

The Lord Jesus gave us an interesting principle. He said, "If two of you shall agree on earth about anything that they may ask, it shall be done for them by my Father who is in heaven" (Matt. 18:19). That phrase "two or three" that follows in Matthew 18:20 is important. Unity in prayer comes only by a close, common bond of understanding, affection and friendship. Jesus put His team of disciples together on that basis. Your closest friends should be people of similar likings and interests, people who think like you do in most situations. They should also be ones with a similar level of spiritual growth in Jesus. They should be ones with whom you can share new discoveries of the work and Word of God in your lives.

Sam Shoemaker has pointed out that true unity is not just two people who agree in the same things, but more like a pyramid where two people form one line; God forms the third corner of the base, and the common task or ministry they have together forms the peak. When we walk together with God, under His control, doing a common task He has given to us, we will really begin to know the joys of divine friendship. With friends that are Christ's friends, we can know God's love among us every day.

Because you prayed for me
I found the strength I needed for thy task,
The courage I lacked before, the faith to see
Beyond my narrow world; new joy for pain
I found, and zeal
To press forward, strong of heart again—
Because you prayed.

Because you prayed today
I found it was not hard to face the dawn,
Take up again the work I laid away
But yesterday, and shoulder it and dare
To smile a bit,
And find a blessing I'd not dreamed was there—
Because you prayed.

Because you prayed for me
Tonight, I seemed to reach and find your hand
Close by, as I had known that it would be,
And somehow toil and turmoil must needs cease;
It was as though
God to our heart had whispered softly, "Peace"—
Because you prayed.

—Ruth Margaret Gibbs

25

Steps to Bring You Closer to God

"Draw near to God, and he will draw near to you" (James 4:8).

Every Jesus person sooner or later feels what Paul the Apostle felt when he said, "That I may know him, and the power of his resurrection" (Phil. 3:10). Disciples of Jesus of all ages have searched for ways that would help them learn more about the Lord Jesus and His love. Here are some of these ideas for you to use. Anything that brings before us spiritual light, anything that helps cast us on Him can be used as fuel to feed the flame of our love for Him.

1. *Read the biographies of God's great men.* Try to read at least one book a week, other than your Bible. John Wesley said to his early Methodists, "If you don't read, you'll never preach." There are so many exciting things that early men and women of God learned. You will find them in old books about their lives. Think over the lessons they learned. Time has had a chance to prove their work. What were their secrets? What mistakes did they make, and how did God help them? What things could you copy from their devotion? What problems can you avoid by learning from their failures? When did God first start to use them? What prices did they pay for their ministries? How did they affect their world for Jesus?

Try especially to find books on the giants of evangelism and revival. To help you choose, ask yourself, "Were they wise to win souls?" Christians who were had the wisdom of heaven. Learn from the words of such men because they learned from God. These men were successful in drawing people to Jesus. They were good at winning others to God's way. We could call this their vision, and the crowds they drew heavenwards tell us something about the time they personally spent with God. And the people who came to Jesus under their ministries remained true to God. They went on with Him. They were fruit that remained (see John 15:16). They don't give up easily if their faith is real and solid. This is the mark of a man's ministry done in God's knowledge. The closer he gets to God by experience, the more he can draw people to Christ; the more he knows and teaches the truth of God's Word, the better his results will last.

Subscribe to all the good Christian magazines you can afford. Pick those with real outreach and love in their writings. Grab every bit of free Christian material you can lay your hands on. Be open to new ideas, but let your reading be careful and thoughtful. Let it jog your thoughts into new lines for Christ. Every disciple of Jesus should read as much as possible besides his Bible to stay ahead of what is happening in our world, so he will know where a happening needs God to deal with it.

2. *Take notes on messages from real servants of the Lord.* Every sermon or message you hear, every rap time when disciples share something "heavy" should be written down. Always make it a habit to carry paper, or a little notebook, and pen into a meeting for Jesus. Learn to listen and write at the same time. Take careful, full notes. Get down the words and thoughts that help you most and lift you closest to the Lord. File these away carefully and neatly. Use them to help stir your heart.

The Holy Spirit may recall to your heart as you read the same ways you felt when you first heard that message. This will carry your heart quickly into God's love in times when you feel dry.

The best way to keep notes is to invest in a little loose-leaf notebook. You can add or replace its pages as your knowledge of God's Word and ways grows. You can also type up your notes and make the folder very neat and compact. As your notes grow, you can split them up into other folders.

One other thing you may like to do is to keep a daily devotional diary. It is simply a little book in which you write the things you learned from life with God each day. Put down in it each experience that taught you something about Jesus, or verse that spoke to your heart in need, or times of trial and blessing. Saints did this long ago, and copies of their diaries still bless us today. Read those of George Mueller, John Wesley, David Brainerd and Jim Elliot.

3. *Spend as much time as possible with men and women who are used of God.* Don't be a pest, but if they will let you just listen or be with them you will learn much. Jesus first called His disciples to "be with him" (Mark 3:14). They may help you a lot in the practice of Christian living. Don't bring all your problems to them when you can get answers from God or from the Bible. But they may have learned things about walking with God that have never

been written or preached about. Ask God to help you meet those people. Ask Him to open doors to meet the men and women He is using, so you can learn from them.

4. *Guard your tongue.* The mark of the man or woman of God is the control they put on their tongue. Don't talk too much. Talking without thinking, the loose use of words, and lightness of speech all signal the sin of foolishness. The Lord Jesus never wasted a word. We are told we will be weighed for every idle word we say. Only God can tame the tongue. They are the expressions of what we are. If you want to be a man or woman of God who is known for your walk with Jesus, don't waste words (see Eccles. 5:1-7; Prov. 13:3; James 1:26; Matt. 5:37; 12:36-37).

5. *Spend much time alone with God.* Go to a "desert" Bible school—simply a place of silence and solitude. Moses, Elijah and Paul all learned great lessons there. Jesus spent much time alone with His Father in the desert. Too many words, too much mixing purposelessly with people can take the edge off your spiritual axe. There is nothing more beautiful to the soul than to go off quietly somewhere late in the afternoon, evening or early morning to spend an hour or two with God. Disciples of Jesus must not be so busy *doing* things that they don't have time just to *be.* Love is sweetened by stillness. If you don't have time to spend alone with God, make time.

26

How to Deal with Trial, Trouble and Temptation

"You have never been tempted to sin in any different way than other people. God is faithful. He will not allow you to be tempted more than you can take. But when you are tempted, He will make a way for you to keep from falling into sin" (1 Cor. 10:13).

Why are Christians tempted? As long as we are able to do *right*, we are also able to do *wrong*. No one can be good unless he is also able to do wrong if he wants to. Think of a talking doll. Pull the string in her back and she says, "Hello." Pull it again and she says, "My name is Kathy." Pull it again and she says, "I love you." Now God could have made us like chatty Kathy dolls. He could have made us so that when He would pull a string we would say to Him, "I love you." But would it really be love?

To make us able to freely *obey* Him, we have to be free also to *disobey* Him. God is looking for people He can trust. We talk about trusting *Him*, but can He trust *us*? God cannot have people in His new world who want to give into sin. This life is our testing time. If we really love Him, we will not give in to sin. If tests come, we must learn to lean on God and be strong in Him. Tests prove what is in our hearts. Tests show us how much we love God. "A man who does not give up when tests come is happy. After the test is over, he will receive the prize of life. God has promised this to those who love Him."

Temptation is not sin. To be tempted is to have an idea or feeling put into your mind that you know you must not give in to. You can have very strong temptation, refuse it and stay as holy as Jesus was. "When you are tempted to do wrong, do not say, 'God is tempting me.' God cannot be tempted. He will never tempt anyone. A man is tempted to do wrong when he lets himself be led by what his bad thoughts tell him to do. When he does what his bad thoughts tell him to do, he sins" (James 1:13, 14).

Temptation comes from three main sources:

1. *Temptation can come from worldly people around us.* Old friends can come to try to pull us back to our old way of life. The Bible calls this the "world." Satan said to Jesus, "I will give you all this power and greatness. It has been given to me. If you worship me it will be yours" (Luke 4:6, 7).

2. *Temptation can also come from our old memories,* of habits we once had when we lived in sin. God cannot just wipe out our memories, because they are the only record we have of who we are. He has a better way to deal with our past. When old thoughts or feelings come back, we are to use these as a signal to turn again to Jesus. We can find in Him all we need. If we are lonely, we can ask Him to show us himself as the great friend who sticks closer than a brother. If we have done wrong, we must know Him as our great high priest. When we are confused, we can see Him as our leader and guide. When we feel tired and dry, He can show us himself as the living water. In this way, He can give us beautiful times with himself in our pain and trial. These times with Him will make a curtain of new and happy thoughts over our old ones. They will make it hard for us to dig back into the old clay of our bad past.

Becoming a child of God is like learning to drive on the other side of the road. When you come to Jesus, you really do "change sides." No real Jesus person stays on the same side of the road he used to live on. He now lives for Jesus. A change has happened. But for a while he must be careful. He has brought to his new life some memories of the way he used to live. He cannot afford to do things by habit. He must be careful until he has learned the new ways to live.

3. Finally, *temptation can come from the devil.* He waits until we are either up or down before he drops a thought into our mind.

When you are tempted, do not think about what you used to do. If you dig back into your mind and think too long on what you did wrong before, you may do it again. This will only make bad habits stronger. This is not the way to deal with temptation. The way to beat sin is to say a firm "no" and turn your mind right then to Jesus. Sin can be beaten only by faith in Jesus. We can win in the world only by faith in Jesus.

Section VII
The Disciple's
FRIENDS

27

First Make Friends with Yourself

"No man ever hates his own flesh; but nourishes and cherishes
it, just as the Lord does the church" (Eph. 5:29).

When I was small, my mother used to leave my little sister
to watch the shop for her while she had a cup of tea. My little
sister ruined a lot of my mother's business because whenever
some stout matron with a lot of money would come in, my sister
would call out in a voice you could hear for a block, "Mother,
there's a big fat old lady in here to see you!"

That's the trouble with little kids: they say what they think
and feel. They have not learned to pretend as well as grown-ups
have. They are real and they are honest. It is not until they get
older and more sophisticated that they learn how to play "let's
pretend" *all* the time, even when it is serious and not playtime
anymore. Perhaps that is one reason why the Lord Jesus said,
"Except you . . . become as *little children,* you shall not enter
into the kingdom of heaven" (Matt. 18:3). One of the most beautiful
things about the gospel is that it has power to make us see like
little children again.

One trouble with grown-ups today is that they have lost the
eyes of a child. People have forgotten what it means to wonder.
That is sad, because when you lose your wonder you also lose
your ability to dream. I saw a painting once in San Francisco.
It had two little children, a boy and a girl, standing in a field.
Everything in the picture was browns and greys; the grass, the
sky, the earth itself seemed dead. Even the sun was a dull white
disc in the sky. There were no clouds, no trees, no birds or animals.
The only blue in the whole picture was the blue in the children's
eyes. Their eyes were big, like those sad pictures of street waifs
that make you want to cry. But the frightening thing about the
picture was this: the children had their eyes open wide; they
saw everything around them, but their eyes were like two chips
of blue glass. There was nothing inside them. They were just
two dead dolls in a dead world. And when the children lose their

dreams, it is the end of the world.

Have you ever wished you could be a child again, a child that could dream and wonder? It is time you made friends with yourself. If the Lord Jesus has truly changed your life, you know what it means to be "born again." That means you can start all over again with a brand-new life from God. All the rotten past is over. All that belonged to your former life is dead and buried. And one thing God can do in your new life is to give you back your sense of awe and wonder. No disciple of Jesus can spend an hour in the presence of the living God and not begin to feel like a small child. Becoming a true disciple can strip you of all the old sophistication and phoniness. He can make you honest, open, frank and clear as a snow stream. This is the first step in making friends with yourself: bring your old life to God with all its rottenness and smallness. Let Him finish it for good. Learn what it means to be "born again"—and to become as a little child.

Becoming like a child means going back to the time before you learned to pretend. And that is what it means to be humble before God—being willing to be known and accepted for what you really are. Anything else will take you into a world of unreality and phony living. And if you are knowingly living a lie, you cannot be friends with yourself. If you are not friends with yourself, you will also find it hard to make friends with others. If you have not been honest with God about who you really are in His sight, you will find yourself guilty of these things:

1. *Crowd fear.* "No one loves me; no one likes me; I'm always left out." Are you shy? Do you find it hard to make friends? This points out one thing: you think too much about yourself. You have not been to Jesus to get yourself clean enough and honest enough to enjoy living with yourself. And if you don't like yourself, you surely won't like showing that self to others.

2. *Concern for looks.* Do you catch yourself saying all the time, "I just look rotten all the time; I never have the right clothes; my hair always looks a mess; my face looks terrible"? Too much concern for looks is another sign of a self-centered heart. Your problem is not outside but inside. When you learn to be clean before God, your face will begin to change to match your heart. And you will start to forget what people might be thinking of you because you will be thinking about their needs instead.

3. *"Creepy" Christianity.* "No one really understands my walk with God; God has called me to do a work that no other Christian will recognize; I have a special ministry that no one else has ever had or will have." Words like this reveal a spiritual trip

that is not founded on a relaxed, happy fellowship with God. There are some people who seem to try too hard to be disciples of Jesus. No one could ever say they are not keen; they go to every meeting around. They may shout louder than anyone else, jump higher and pray longer in public than anybody else. They try to be spiritual superstars. You can spot them quickly; they always point out what is wrong with everything and everyone else around. God has apparently called them to a ministry of condemnation.

But there is something wrong somewhere, and all free disciples of Jesus will sense it. Their zeal doesn't quite ring true. The fruit of the Spirit does not show at all in their lives. They give off bad vibes when they are around. They seem to live on the edge of spiritual breakdown. And the cause of much "creepy" Christianity is the same as the others: a failure to love and accept ourselves and ministries *as they are* before the Lord, with their weaknesses and failures.

"Creepy" Christians have not accepted their own personal limits, the things they plainly can't do or be. They have not learned to be satisfied in Jesus' love alone. Their trip is just another form of pride, and it will not get any better until they are really humbled before the Lord and honestly own up to the fact that God was not in 99.9% of all the things they said He told them to do.

4. *A critical spirit.* Do you always seem to be saying, "Nothing I do turns out right! How come she always does things so well, but mine turn out so lousy? What right does he have to get all the lucky breaks?" Are you always getting into arguments with others? Are people around you openly or secretly getting criticized? Do you feel like your own life is just one big war?

These things are all signs of the person who has not made friends with himself. Now, I don't know why you are this way. Maybe it is because you always wanted to be like someone else you liked a lot but you never could be. Perhaps you had some scar or deformity either by an accident or from birth that has made you look, in your eyes, far worse and uglier than others around you. Maybe deep in your heart of hearts you are mad at God because you think He is to blame for the way you are. Any one of these things could give you a reason to hate yourself. But none of them are good reasons. All of them are simply forms of pride. And this breaks every basic command of the Bible.

When you are proud like this, it doesn't mean you think you are *better* than others; it can mean you treat yourself as *inferior* to others. Pride is not just thinking too *much* of yourself; it means also thinking too *little* of yourself, despising your own special life as one of God's creations. Pride means thinking too much about

yourself and not enough about others. That breaks the first of
the Ten Commandments; you make yourself a god by always worrying and thinking about yourself and letting your whole life re-
volve around yourself. You are not content with what you have
and are; you break God's law that says, "You shall not *covet*."
You put up a false front to others, pretending you are a different
person than what you really are. God's law says, "You shall not
bear false witness." Your funny dress or actions take peoples'
eyes off God and put them on you. That broke the law that says,
"You shall not *steal*" because you stole the center of attention
that ought to belong to the Lord Jesus. And holding hate in your
heart about someone else, including yourself, is like *murder* in
the Bible. What a terrible thing to be proud! A man who has
refused to accept himself for the way he is before God breaks
every basic law of the Bible.

Have you accepted yourself for the way you are under God?
Will you give up your ambition to be loved, accepted, wanted
or even liked by anyone in the world except by the Lord Jesus?
Give *Him* this right, no matter how much *you* want it. You can
be sure of His love. You don't have to prove anything to Him.
And He is hurt when you keep pretending that you are someone
else that you know you will never be.

If you are like this, it is time you learned to make friends
with yourself. It is a Bible command: "You shall love . . . your
neighbor *as you love yourself*." Now, have you obeyed this command? If you really love Jesus, learn to love your own special
life, and treasure it as a gift from God despite its limitations.
Stop running from reality. Face yourself. You are what you are.
What is sinful can be repented of, cleansed and forgiven. What
is just you can be accepted and lived with happily. You don't
have to be anyone else. You only have to be yourself; Jesus loves
you the way you are.

28
Stay Out of the "In" Crowd

"And these are they likewise which are sown on stony ground; who, when they have heard the word, immediately receive it with gladness; and have no root in themselves, and so endure but for a time; afterward, when affliction or persecution arises for the word's sake, immediately they are offended" (Mark 4:16, 17).

Some people today say they belong to Jesus as long as it is popular to belong to Jesus. But take a close look at their lives and you will see they are still living for themselves. Their one rule of life is the current crazes of the "in" crowd. If some kind of religious trip is in, they want to be in it too. If religion is not in, however, you will soon see them change their faith. How can you recognize a man in the "in" crowd? If he says he loves God but really only loves his own reputation with religious people, how can you tell? Try these tests:

1. *They measure themselves among themselves* (2 Cor. 10:12). The man in the "in" crowd sets his standards by the pulse of the world around him. His "good" is the good opinion of others. He asks himself, "Am I doing what others expect me to do? Am I doing enough to get by without anyone telling me off?" *Church* "in" crowd people aim to keep up a respectable religious front. Instead of seriously asking themselves what the Lord and His Word requires, they simply try to copy the current Christian crowd. If one-way signs are in, they learn to give one-way signs; if buttons, bumper stickers or bagpipes are in for a church crowd, they will use them too! They aim to do that which is *respectable*, not that which is *right*.

2. *They never bother to raise the standards of right.* "In" crowd people always dislike someone who tries to stir up the church to higher levels of consecration to God. They have set their spiritual levels by the crowd's *minimum* standard, and anyone who aims to bring it higher is in for criticism and trouble. People pleasers stand against a man or woman who is not popular with the crowd,

even if he or she is right; then they turn about face if the same crowd begins to honor them. There is only one exception to this: when they have said so much against him that they cannot change without disgrace. And then they will be silent, until they get another chance to criticize.

3. *They divide God's laws up into the ones they want to do and the ones they won't.* Any sin that people are against *as a crowd* they also are "against." If hard drugs are out, they give up theirs too. But if no one is saying anything about pot or cigarettes or petting, they go ahead with it. When someone by habit disobeys any known law of God, the obedience he seems to have to His other laws is not from a true love of God; its stems from selfish motives.

This means that the "in" crowd man is apt to sin away from home. Many a professing Christian who is outwardly very religious and respectable with his own church crowd drops his mask at a distance and begins to live the way he really wants to live. If he is fairly sure no one will recognize him elsewhere, he will sin. If he is a religious man at church, away from church he is ready to "let his horns grow." If you are a true disciple of Jesus you will not lead a double life. The things that make you happy in church are the same things that make you happy a thousand miles from it. The man in the "in" crowd often lives in secret sin. Here is a test by which you can know your own stand. If you allow any sin in secret when you know how to get out of it, you have sold out to the "in" crowd.

4. *They try to make friends on both sides of the line.* It has always been so for centuries that people could make a good show of religion without ever being labelled holy. The standards are still so low that in many places people can get by having a religious stand without being written off as reprobates or laughed at as Christian fanatics. They are *fashionable* Christians. Their life-style is fashionable and popular, and they do what the world says in their dress and ways of living. No matter what God says, they are careful not to offend any of His enemies. If they are ever faced with a choice of offending a crowd or Christ, they will offend Jesus.

5. *They care more about what people think than what God thinks.* Their one "unforgivable" sin is to fail in the eyes of man, or to be rejected by the crowd. They have never been with Jesus to Calvary. They are ashamed to stick up for God because they do not love Him. How could they? If a man really loved a girl, would he be ashamed to defend her if she were put down? If a woman's children were being abused, would she let it go

unchecked? Not if she loved them. The people pleaser does not really love God; he loves *himself*. When among Jesus people he may be very bold for the truth and may make a good show of his faith. But put him among Christ's enemies where it would be a reproach to be called a Christian, put him to trial, and he will sell Christ out like Judas, or deny Him before His enemies.

But for their love of reputation, how many people would break into open rejection of God? All that holds them back from sinning is public opinion, fear of disgrace, and wanting to get credit for being thought good. If you are good because you love God and honor His authority and value whether the crowd frowns or smiles on it, you have true faith. If you do it for other reasons, you have your reward. You do it to gain credit in the eyes of men, and you will gain it. But if you expect honor from God, you will surely be disappointed.

Will you agree to take the Bible as your rule and the Lord Jesus as your pattern, doing what is right in all cases whatever men may say or think? If you are not willing to take this kind of stand, you are a stranger to the grace of God. A people pleaser is by no means His child. If you will not purpose to do what is right whatever the crowd says, you love the praise of men more than the praise of God.

Friend, I have been honest with you. If I did not really love you or care, I would not have said these things. I have told it like it is. If you mean to be a Christian you must give yourself wholly up to Christ. You cannot float along to heaven on the waves of public sentiment. I will not pretend you can when God says you cannot. "Wherefore come out from among them, and be separate . . . and I will receive you, and will be a Father to you, and you shall be my sons and daughters, says the Lord Almighty" (2 Cor. 6:17, 18).

Will you do it? Who is on the Lord's side? Who is willing to say, "We will not follow a multitude to do evil, but are determined to do the will of God in all things, no matter what the world says or thinks about us" (see John 12:24-26)? "Search the scriptures; for in them you think you have eternal life; and these are they that testify of me. . . . I receive not honor from men. . . . How *can* you believe, who receive the honor one of another, and seek not the honor that comes from God only?" (John 5:39, 41, 44).

So he *died* for his faith. That's fine—
More than most of us do.
But say, can you add to that line
That he *lived* for it too?
In his death he bore witness at last

As a martyr to the truth.
Did his *life* do the same in the past
From the days of his youth?

It is easy to die. Men have died
For a wish or a whim,
From bravado or passion or pride.
Was it harder for him?
But to *live*—every day to live out
All the truth that he dreamt,
While his friends met his conduct with doubt,
And the rest of the world with contempt—
Was it thus that he plodded ahead,
Never turning aside?
Then—we'll talk of the *life* that he led—
Never mind how he died.

—Earnest H. Crosby

29
What to Do About Bad Friends

"Love not the world, neither the things that are in the world.
If any man loves the world, the love of the Father is not in him"
(1 John 2:15).

Perhaps for a long time you have run with a crowd of bad
friends. If you have been in a gang, you know how dangerous
it is to try to walk out. Here is a way to cut free from your
old crowd. It is a costly and dangerous way, but it is the best
way I know to leave without making them suspicious and angry
at you.

1. *Give all of your friends to Christ in prayer.* Take them
one by one, beginning at the one you like most, and give up your
rights to have them like you anymore. You must make such
a total surrender of your rights to their friendship that you will
be able to go on with Jesus alone if necessary. Tell the Lord,
"If You want me to lose every friend I now have, I will be content
to know that You are my friend. I am willing to stand alone for
You. Give me the courage to do what is right, no matter how
much it will cost."

You have made full surrender of all your friendships when
you are willing to go on *alone* with Jesus, even if no one you
now know and love ever serves Him, and all of the ones you
now call your Christian friends turn their backs on you and Him
together. And that will hurt, but it must be done. Are you willing
to stand alone? Jesus did—for you. Even all His friends, the disciples, "forsook him and fled" at the hour of His greatest need.
Will you follow in His steps? It will not be easy to do this. Some
of the people you know now have been very close to you. But
it must be done. Jesus said, "Whoever does not forsake *all* that
he has, *cannot* be my disciple" (Luke 14:33).

2. *Go to your friends and apologize to them.* Go to one at
a time if possible. Tell them you are sorry for not being a real

friend to them. If you have been religious but not really Christian, you will also have to apologize for being a religious hypocrite. Genuinely love your lost friends. God will give you a real love for them that transcends anything that you had with them before. Show them by your attitude that you are not against them and that you are not putting them down personally. Then give a straight-from-the-shoulder testimony about what has happened between you and God. Be direct and honest. Pray a lot before you go, and wait for the right time to see them so you won't blow it. Ask God to give you favor in their eyes. Your aim is to win their respect for what God has done in your life, and to convince them that what has happened is real and will make you a different person.

3. *If there is something you can give them, like a book or tract that has helped you, give it to them.* If there is a meeting where you know the gospel will be preached, invite them to it. Ask them if they want to go with you sometime to learn what happened to you. One of two things will happen: either they will want to come along, or they will say, "No, you go, but leave me out." It is important that you don't sound like you are putting them down in any way if they refuse. Just make the way clear for them to come, and then go. Tell them, "I've never been so happy in my life. I want to learn more about Jesus for you, so if you get interested, just let me know. I'd be happy to take you along with me." Then leave.

4. If some of your friends do want to go with you, explain all that you can about what it means to be a child of God. Give them time to ask questions, to try to understand. Take them someplace where the gospel will be preached in their language on God's terms. Give them a chance to think it over and to give their lives to God.

If there is a clear rejection of Christ's claims, and they show no further interest, you will have to take a stand on Christ's side. Say something like this: "I can understand how you feel, but you can see what Jesus has done in my life. He means more to me than anything else in the world. I can't hurt Him now by going back to my old ways. If you want to change your mind about Him, remember that I'll always be here to help you know Him."

5. *Pray for and write to your friends.* They may not answer at all, but keep it up. Don't preach in your letters; just share as a small part of your letter what Jesus is presently doing in your life. Be positive; don't condemn. Lift them up often before God in prayer, that He will sow the seeds of hunger for change

in their lives. Be ready to help whenever you can, because when they really get into trouble, God may use you to meet their needs and lead them to Him.

6. If a non-Christian friend asks you to go out with him to some place that you know would not be right, thank him, but tell him you really wouldn't like to go there. Then suggest an alternative place or activity that you would be able to attend, where you can spend some more time with him, and wait for God to give another chance to talk to him about Christ.

Don't be afraid to be natural with your old friends; just love them with God's love, but don't compromise to keep their friendship.

If a non-Christian guy asks a Christian girl out, she can thank him, tell him she appreciates his invitation, but that she is not able to accept it. If he asks her why not, she can tell him that she has given her life to Jesus and has decided that she will only go out with guys who love Jesus. She can say, "Since I've given my heart to Jesus, I'm going out only with guys who love Jesus. I don't know you well enough to know if that's true or not." If he says, "How will you know if I do or not unless you go out with me?" she can say, "I'd be happy to have you come to a Christian meeting with me and have you meet some of my friends." Then at the meeting the Christian guys can take the non-Christian guy under their wing and maybe bring him to the Lord.

If you have been living sexually with someone, you must break off with that person immediately, preferably by letter. Use the words, "I want you to please forgive me for not setting you a decent standard." Say good-bye for keeps. Make sure the person understands by repeating it a couple of times. To make it final, tell the person not to contact you again, not ever, especially if you are a girl. The break must be total, or you will fall back into sin.

Here is part of one girl's letter: "I've known for some time that I should end our relationship, but my selfishness has caused me to hold on to you, and both of us have suffered. Please forgive me for any unhappiness I have caused you, and please understand that I must ask you never to see me again. You have your work and your own life to straighten out and I have been interfering with both. Please forgive me; don't even try to call me again. It is better that things are ended now before more pain and suffering is caused. This is best for both of us, and again, I beg you, don't try to contact me in any way, not ever. . . ."

If you have been going with a rotten boyfriend and have just become a Christian, you have a simple way to break off with him. Tell him, "I'm sorry, but I can't go with you anymore; I've just met someone who has totally changed my life, and I got *married* to Him!" (Since every disciple of Jesus is now in the "Bride of Christ," and since the Lord Jesus is called the "Bridegroom" of the church, you have a Bible right to say that!) Then if he asks who it is, give him a testimony and say good-bye. Whatever you do, make sure you really break off completely. It is hard sometimes for you as a girl, but you must do it, or you will only go deeper into sin and wind up even more hurt.

30

Date Differently: Do It God's Way

Thousands upon thousands of couples are divorced every year. Over the last few years over three million people in the United States alone called it quits and broke up forever. In some places there are more divorces each week than marriages. Homes are falling apart. Mothers are giving up; husbands are walking out.

For every home that is split by divorce and separation, there are children who will learn what it means to be hurt and to hate. Each one of these kids will want to hit back some way at his world. Maybe that's why, during the time it takes you to read this section, hundreds of people will have been robbed, raped, bashed, beaten and murdered by children from homes like these. Maybe you can see why God is so concerned about marriage.

Some brilliant people have come up with an equally brilliant solution: If marriages are so messy, why not "can" the whole thing? Why not just throw them out? Why not just live together on a trial basis, and if it doesn't work out, split, with no ties—no responsibilities?

That makes about as much sense as putting a screen door on a submarine. There are other ideas about as smart as this, like outlawing jails because a lot of people like a life of crime, or banning bridges because people jump off them sometimes, or stop eating because some people are gluttons.

There's nothing wrong with marriage. But marriage, like a game, or like life, has rules. When rules are broken it is not really fun. It is the end of the game. For some it has also meant the end of *life*.

We have more books on sex than ever before. We have more information on how to make out, more data on how to be a sexy swinger. But we have left out God's laws, and are paying a tragic price for it! To hear some people talk, you would think God is against sex. But it was *His* idea; He invented it, and He knows how it ought to be run.

It is precious, and like all precious things it must not be used too often but treasured for special times. You must learn to use its power within God's controls and to preserve its beauty or you will again join the ranks of the lonely and the bitter and reap the harvest of a broken marriage, a broken home, a broken life and a broken heart.

God made us different. He took Eve from Adam's side, and she has been near him ever since—never far from his heart or side. The marvelous relationships possible between a man and his woman are tiny reflections of the happiness God planned for us. Human friendships are but a shadow of the friendship we can have with God. You should know the differences God has put in our personalities so that you can understand how to court in God's way.

Physical. Apart from fairly obvious sexual differences, God has made most men physically stronger than women. I know there are exceptions; I know all about the woman who weighs four hundred pounds, has a black belt in karate and can kill a moose with her breath! But usually God has made man stronger physically so that he can protect his girl and take care of her.

It's true, of course, that for a time girls grow up faster than boys. Girls physically turn into women sooner than boys physically turn into men. When most boys are still playing marbles, running in gangs or flying kites, girls are falling desperately in love with their English teachers. This means a girl can have a woman's body but a little girl's mind. It can lead you girls to dating older guys. It can also lead to trouble unless you know what's happening and get ready for it. That's why some fathers freak out when they discover their little girl is going out with an older guy. Dads have been around. They know what's happening. Listen to them sometimes. They may ground you because they care about you, or because they remember something of their own past with a great deal of fear and regret.

Mental. There are usually mental differences between men and women. It has nothing to do with intelligence. It does have to do with the *ways* God designed us to use our intelligence.

Now this is important. These two basically different ways of looking at things make each sex superior to the other *in the role God has given them.* The girl is superior to the guy in her way of thinking when problems of life require an inspirational, unprogrammed, unstructured approach. She gives color, surprise, wonder, adventure. The guy is superior to the girl when a problem needs logic, fact, analysis, detail to solve it. He gives form, stability, structure to life.

If each one stays in his/her role, God will be able to bring the maximum blessing to their partnership. Right through the Bible, beginning at creation, God has set up a role for each sex: The man must *lead*; the girl must *inspire*. This is God's pattern. When we do what we were designed for, we will find maximum happiness in our friendships with each other, in our courtship, and in marriage.

Because the men are supposed to lead, here are some rules for growing hair on your chest:

1. *Get smart.* The Bible says, "In understanding be men" (1 Cor. 14:20). If you are to be the IBM computer, "study to show yourself approved before God." A girl likes to have the man she depends on to be informed and to know how things work.

2. *Get a sport.* Develop your physical body so that you will be strong enough to take care of her and protect her. Pick something you enjoy, then really work at it. "Bodily exercise profits a little" (1 Tim. 4:8). Even if you look like the "before" picture on a Charles Atlas advertisement, do the best with what you have.

3. *Be a gentleman.* The Bible tell us to be courteous to one another, kindly affectionate; in love to serve one another (see Rom. 12:10). Watch your manners. Give her the respect due to a woman of God. Most girls do not mind being treated like a princess. If we are sons and daughters of the King of kings, you treat your girl like the princess she is.

4. *Don't tell lies.* "Speak the truth in love" (Eph. 4:15). Never lead a girl on to think you care for her more than all others if it is not true. Don't you dare indulge in some mild power trip just to feel that some girl is under your spell even though she means nothing much to you. Girls get hurt easily. Don't forget it. No guy has the right to tell a girl, "I love you," unless he is ready to say in the next breath, "Will you marry me?" If you can't say the second sentence, don't say the first. Don't tell lies.

5. *Be a man of God.* If you have one epitaph on your tombstone, strive to make it this: "Here lies a man of God." Unless you know how to love God and serve Him wholly, you will never learn the tenderness, care and concern that makes a guy a worthwhile leader, a sweetheart and, one day, a husband. If you are going to lead, be a leader where it counts—*spiritually.* Brother, hear me now. Nothing counts more than your walk—your personal,

daily walk with Jesus. It will save you, and every girl you befriend, heartbreak, trouble and wasted, irrepairable years.

Now you girls have been saying too many "amens." Here
is your list for loving living:

1. If you are smart, *don't show it off.* No brother wants to
feel like Charlie Brown. God doesn't want you to put on some
dumb blonde, brunette or redhead acts; but, remember, he is
supposed to be the leader, and your job is to inspire him (see
Prov. 31:26).

2. *Don't gab.* Sister, here is a secret. If you want things to
talk about, ask him what he thinks. Learn what it means to build
a man with admiration. You can do it by just asking a few questions and doing a lot of listening. Don't just listen to the words;
listen to the man who is saying them. Smile a lot, admire greatly
and say little. He will love you for it. Be simple and honest like
a child. If you are serious about marriage, talk about your walk
with God, ministries, children, a home, finances and parents. But
don't gab (see Prov. 11:22).

3. *Be fragile.* Let *him* be the strong man. *Him* Tarzan! *You*
Jane! Have you ever seen a weedy little man call his two hundred
pound wife "my little baby"? She learned the secret of being
fragile to him. It is not just how you look; it is an attitude. Don't
go around killing your own spiders. Let him do the strong man
stunts. Things like this make a man feel like a man. Generate
a dependence, a little-girl look. That's the kind of girl a man loves
to be leader for (see 1 Pet. 3:3).

4. *Dress and look like a woman.* And that woman must be
all girl and all lady. Stay away from the tough-as-nails look. God
has given you one marvelous attraction. You are a woman and
you are God's girl. Use those facts to the full. Don't dress cheaply
or lewdly so that you look no better than a hooker. God is your
Father, the Lord Jesus is your Brother. Dress like it. Be clean,
be simple and be sensible.

5. *Be a woman of God.* There is nothing more beautiful and
mind blowing to a man than a girl who is really in love with
Jesus. There is no better source of beauty than living in the joy
of perfect obedience to His will. Learn to be someone Jesus can
be proud of. You will understand what God means when He says,
"Delight yourself also in the Lord, and he will give you the desires
of your heart" (Ps. 37:4).

Men, in any outings with a sister, take the lead. Decide before the Lord where to go. Commit such times to God in prayer.

Live so that you will lead the girl you meet closer to Jesus.

Girls, you are to live so close to God that by your very life you will draw your boyfriend closer to Christ. Inspire him there. That is the Christian way to live in love.

Not merely in the words you say,
Not only in the deeds confessed,
But in the most unconscious way
Is Christ through you expressed.
Is it just a beautiful smile?
A heavenly light upon your brow?
Oh, no. I felt His presence
When you laughed, just now.

For me 'twas not the truth you taught—
To you so dear, to me so dim;
But when you came to me
You brought a sense of Him.
And from your eyes He beckons me,
And from your heart His love is shed,
'Till I lose sight of you
And see the Christ instead.

—Author unknown

31

The Tests of True Love

"For God so loved the world, that he gave his only begotten Son, that whosoever believeth in him should not perish, but have everlasting life" (John 3:16).

Do you really love your boyfriend or girl friend? Test out your personal friendships and love life against this "John 3:16 exam."

"For God. . . ." All true loving must be done for God. We don't know what it means to love until we can unselfishly put the Lord Jesus first, and because of our love for Him care for all we meet. Christian love must happen within real Christian fellowship and witness. Our love is to be holy, set apart as sacred under God. The man who has never given up his selfish way of life has never really learned to love at all. Everything he does can only be to make himself more happy. Then if others fit in to his own pleasure and interests, he will make them happy too. If not, he won't. And this is in no way real love.

You do not know the real meaning of *any* kind of love until you have first experienced the love of God. This love will be the control, the guide, the underlying care behind all our actions and words. Without it, there will be nothing but surface friendships based on our own interests or sexual attraction that is based wholly on physical lust. Honestly now, are you loving your friend for God's glory? Did you start this friendship to please and honor God, or is it just a sidetrack of the devil and his crowd? Love doesn't seek her own.

"So loved. . . ." Real love, God's love, is special. It can feel more deeply than any other kind of love, but it is not just a feeling. It is tremblingly alive to all the joy and pain of the world around it, but it is not just a sensitive compassion. Love is far more than a feeling; it is also intelligent. No one who loves with God's love ever "falls in love"; that is romance. Though romantic feelings are beautiful and exciting, they are not enough to hold a marriage together.

The love of God is first of all a wise choice for the highest happiness of the one loved. Love is an act of the will; love is something you do; it is sure and careful. If you are a girl, you must promise the Lord that you will bring your boyfriend to Him for His approval, and not just rely on your feelings to tell you whether he is all right to go with. It is too easy for you just to let your feelings run your heart, but you cannot do it if you want to be a woman of God.

If you are a man, is your first motive in going out with this girl to bring her closer to Jesus? You may feel strongly about her, but remember that feelings can come from anyone who is interesting and attractive, who shows some interest or attention in you. And you can't marry or live with everyone who does this. Enjoy your feelings, but do not let your affection run ahead of your mind and will. Love takes time; it thinks before it commits itself. If you trust your feelings, you may be hurt very deeply. Trust God. Learn what it is to "so love." Don't blow your purity and your future over a supercharged gland. If you love God, don't cheaply sell the body and affections He has given you.

"The world. . . ." Love wants everyone in on its happiness; love has a great heart. If you love your friend with God's love, you will want the world to know about it. Do you love like this? You can always tell shallow, counterfeit affection. It is selfish; it wants to keep to itself and for itself.

If you love with true love you won't try to control your friend's life exclusively; you won't be envious or worried if he spends time with others because you will trust him. You leave the one you love free to make his own choices before God. True love cares for all creatures and doesn't willingly inflict pain. It is not partial to a select few; it is color-blind. Do you mind sharing your love with others? Do you want to tell the world about the one you love? If you are envious, you do not love with God's love. If you cannot witness or pray with your date, you don't love him. Now, do you trust your loved one enough to share him with others? Do you admire him so much that you can be sure he will not let you down in any situation or with anyone else at any time?

"That he gave. . . ." True love always wants to give gifts. Love works out ways to make others happy all the time. It would help everyone the same way if it could; but it does whatever it can. Love from its very nature will deny itself to promote a greater good whenever it is wise to do this. You can give without loving, but you cannot love without giving! Love is concerned with God's happiness, and others' needs; it only thinks of its own in

the context of these. Love never uses the other person as a tool for personal pleasure or popularity. Now, do you want to share with your love? Do you want to give gifts, even if it costs a lot to do it? When you see her, do you think in terms of what she would like? When he calls, do you just naturally have something for him? Is he worth your giving him the full devotion of your heart? Do you think she deserves the loving labor of your hands?

"His only begotten Son...." There is always a cost to true love. Love cost God His Son; love cost the Lord Jesus His life. Love means you are willing to give up everything for the one you love. When love rules, you choose things for their true value, and not just for personal gain. Love counts the cost, but doesn't keep on counting it. Now, how much do you love God? Do you love Him enough to even say good-bye to one who grows in your affection if you learn this will interfere with God's will for you? Do you have that unreserved trust in God that leads His true child to say, even if it hurts for a while, "Your will be done, Father"?

This is a costly test, but you must be prepared to take it. Do you love God enough to give up earthly love if He asks? When you pass this test, you will know the joy of listening to God for a happy love life.

"That whosoever believeth in him...." Love involves absolute trust. To fully love, you must first trust yourself and the other person wholly. Love has faith in the other person's character and integrity. Love hardly even notices when others do wrong; love is able to live with another person's failures and weaknesses, because love knows the other person for what he is and is willing to be known for its own true character. Love does not seek to impress or pretend. Ask yourself, does it encourage you on to greater things to think that she would like what you are doing? When questions come up, do you quite naturally think about what she would say? Do you think a good deal about him? Whatever you are doing, is she never far from your thoughts? Do you trust the one you love anywhere, with anyone? This is one of the reasons why God puts limits on premarital sex. To hold back from sex before marriage with the one you love is a proof of your trust of each other.

"Should not perish, but have everlasting life...." "When you love someone you will be loyal to him no matter what the cost. You will always believe in him, always expect the best of him and always stand your ground in defending him." Love is an eternal thing. True love will last, regardless of the trials it will face.

Do not rush into deciding whom you will marry. Love always has time, and it is never in a hurry. It will be hard, if you are a girl, to wait on God and trust that He will arrange for you the one that will bring you the greatest happiness and usefulness. Here is the final test: are you willing to wait? You can test that out very easily in your dating. If you cannot discipline your life to wait for God's time, you have not learned what it means to love with God's love.

If you are getting serious, give your relationship the test of time. "Love is patient, and is kind." Get to know the other person really well—not sexually, but personally. Do you have a good time together, no matter what you are doing? Do you think alike in many of the things you do together? Do you have the same basic, heart-feelings about Christ and the work He has called either of you to do? Do you quite naturally think of the future with him? Do you see her standing with you as you stand up for God?

If you think it is serious enough for you to get engaged, but you are not sure, give yourself a separation test. Now it is not good to have long engagements as it is too much of a strain on you both. Once you are sure, you should marry soon. But first spend a period of time really apart from each other—some six months. In the Bible days, if a man wanted to marry a girl, he announced his intention to do so, then left for a year to raise money for his future home. At the end of the year, if he still felt the same way about her, he would come back, and they would invite over all their friends and relatives and make a formal commitment to each other. Then after a big party, they simply would live together as man and wife.

If you are going to spend the rest of your life with this person, you can afford to give it these two tests—time and separation. The time-test will show you if your love is genuine and deep, or if it is only a feeling of attraction that may pass when you see someone that looks prettier or nicer. The separation test will help you know the difference between excited, romantic feelings and serious, loving commitment. You will want to write a lot during the separation-test; it will give you a chance to learn to know the one you love without their physical attractiveness getting in the way. Bring all the trials and tears you have at this time—all the tests to God. If it is of Him, it will last; what God joins together, no man can break apart. "Love endures all things." What is of God will last forever, and you can trust Him to guide you in this, your happiest and most important human decision.

No voice is heard, no sign is made,
No step is on the conscious floor;
Yet love will dream, and faith will trust,
Since He Who knows our need is just,
That somehow, somewhere, meet we must.
Alas for him who never sees
The stars shine through his cypress trees,
Who hath not learned, in hours of faith,
The truth to flesh and sense unknown,
That Christ is ever Lord of Life,
And Love can never lose its own.

—Author unknown

Section VIII
The Disciple's FAMILY

32
What God Says About Your Home

"Honor your father and your mother, that your days may be long... and that it may go well with you in the land which the Lord your God gives you" (Ex. 20:12; Deut. 5:16).

There is an old song that says, "Be it ever so humble, there's no place like home." It doesn't mean what it used to mean to a lot of kids today. There *is* no place they can really call home. They feel the loneliness of Neil Diamond's song, "I Am, I Said," when he sings, "L.A.'s fine, but it ain't home; New York's home, but it ain't mine." Home for thousands of young people is living hell where they stay until they get old enough or mad enough to leave.

No one really knows what goes on in your home as well as God. His eye is in every place. He sees all that happens. Every wall is transparent to Him. Whatever is carefully hidden from the eyes of the crowd is not hidden from Him. He sees the lies, the bitterness, the greed that goes on under a cover of virtue. He sees the kid who steals from his parents, the one who is shooting up in his bedroom, the ones who use their house for a place to have "free" sex. He knows all about the fights, the quarrels, the drugs and the drinks. He sees your family members as they really are. But still God cares about your home, even if it is as bad or worse than I have described. He really understands when you feel afraid or sad or alone, instead of having peace and happiness. And He wants to change all that is rotten and wrong in your family and make it right and clean.

If Satan can wreck your home, he knows he can turn you on a path that leads straight to hell. Under a hundred covers, in a thousand subtle ways, he can tear up your family. The Bible says that when a man and woman marry, they "cleave" to one another. The word means "to stick" as with paste or glue or cement. When that joint is ripped open, it tears and hurts. Satan pulls at this love-tie. He works on your parents when they are tired or ill or bound by habits, hoping to slash apart their love and split your family in two. He tries to turn brother against brother, sister against sister, parent against child, father against mother, with stupid little differences or big, horrible past memories that keep growing into explosions of hate and bitterness. And too often he has done it. And it is our sin that has given him the open door to move in and make home into hell.

Your nation is only as strong as its homes. When the family is ruined, the nation is on the way to the end. It is the foundation of order. When homes begin to fall apart, riot, rebellion and anarchy will stalk the streets. Civilization is murdered when the home is put to death. Kids have walked out from their homes; dads have left by the hundreds of thousands, never to come back; mothers have dumped their kids on the doors of adoption agencies and just split. If something is going to be done for the world, it must begin at home. And that means your home!

How do you think God feels when He sees your family? He first planned the home for happiness. He began the first marriage, blessed the first family. From the start, He chose to use the home as a picture of how to love and obey Him. He gave laws for the home, laws that have been broken by our generation to give terrible results. Every family that breaks apart hurts more people than we can realize. If each family should have only four children and the kids should make the same foolish mistakes their parents did, within a hundred years (four generations of twenty-five years) over six hundred and eighty people would be messed up. And every hurt that happens in each heart is felt in all its pain by God. Here are His laws to keep our homes happy. Here is what He planned as a Father for those families of His children:

1. Parents should love Him with their lives as well as their lips. Too many religious parents are just phony church people without a real experience of the Lord Jesus. They totally turn off kids from real faith. Too many radical young people today come from church homes—even preachers' homes. Not always is this their parents' fault. But often parents have not done what God said. Do you parents spend real time with you? Have they taught you to work and play and love and laugh? God wants them to be a source of strength and guidance. Your home was meant to be a place of peace, love and security. And God longs for it to be like that even more than you do. He wants your parents right with Him. And now, here is a question for you: Are you helping Him to affect their lives by doing your part?

There is a set of directions in the Old Testament that almost every disciple of Jesus has heard about and read. It is called—no, not the Ten Suggestions—the Ten Commandments. And only one of them has a built-in beautiful promise with it. It is the one special command for kids. God knows how hard it is to obey and honor some parents. He put a special promise with His command. The law is, "Honor your father and mother." The promise is "that your days may be long . . . and that it may go well with you" (Ex. 20:12; Deut. 5:16).

In this command God promises us two things if we obey. One is a long life. The other is a good life. If we break this command, we set in motion laws of judgment that will bring us two tragedies. The first is a rotten life. The second is a shortened one. You will not live long, and you will not live well. Fail to honor your parents and you will get bitter over their faults and sins. That bitterness will lead you to reject all authority. Loss of respect for any guidance or control other than your own will open the flood gates to all kinds of sin. That sin will bring guilt and with that guilt will come loss of respect. No self-respect means that you will no longer love yourself. And when you stop caring about yourself, the door opens to suicide.

The Bible says, "The eye that mocks at his father, and despises to obey his mother, the ravens of the valley shall pick it out . . ." (Prov. 30:17). The result of dishonor and bitterness over parents? —a short life and a rotten one. No, we cannot afford to break the laws of God. Even for your own sake, if not for God's or your parents', you must obey the law, "Honor your father and mother."

2. The Lord Jesus must be first "Boss" of your home. Dad is to be next, then Mother, in that order. The rest of the family are to be subject to them. Dad is to lead the home under God and provide for all its needs. This provision is not just "things." God expects Dad to take care of his wife and children, of course; the wife should not have to work for the bare necessities of the home. That is Dad's job. God says, "If a man provide not for his own, and especially for those of his own family, he has denied the faith and is worse than an infidel" (1 Tim. 5:8).

But provision also includes love and time with his wife and children. It also means time with God on behalf of his family. If parents fail to meet spiritual and emotional needs of their families as well as the physical needs, they may lose them. The Beatles underlined this when they sang, "She's leaving home after living alone for so many years," while her parents are saying, "We gave her most of our lives; sacrificed all of our lives." Dad must spend real time with the kids, not just give them things.

Mother is to be the inspirer of the home. She is to stand behind Dad and encourage him on in his work and leadership, and be there when she is needed for comfort and advice (see Eph. 5:22-23; Col. 3:18, 19; 1 Pet. 3:1-2; Tit. 2:4, 5). Now if this is not true of your family, do you really want it to be? Are you willing to obey God so that He can show you what you can do to begin to effect it?

. 3. You are to love, honor and obey your parents as you would obey the Lord. Now *I* did not say that. The same Holy Spirit who gave us the Bible said that in God's Book (see Eph. 6:1-3; Prov. 23:22; Luke 2:51; Col. 3:20). And He did not say, "Love your parents if they are nice to you," or "honor them if they always do the right things." He just said, "Obey your parents in the Lord . . . in all things." And this doesn't mean that if they are not Christians you can tell them to go jump in the river! It does mean that as long as you live in their home, and as long as they ask you to do anything that God doesn't forbid in His Book, you are to do it for Jesus' sake.

Did you ever think that maybe God could use your unsaved parents to speak to you? It is easy to blame them for all their wrong. But what if God is using them to point out to you your own lack of love for people who are rotten? If love involves meeting others' needs, and not just expecting them to meet yours, do you really love your parents? It is easy to love people that are lovely. Anyone can do that. But it takes a person really changed by Jesus to love people who are not. Do you believe that God could speak to you through your unsaved parents? Do you see that every rotten thing they do could be just another chance to show them the love of God? The question is not what have they done to make you feel ashamed of them, or be hurt over them; the real question for you is, "Have I obeyed God by doing what they asked me to, even when it didn't fit into my own plans?"

Loving your parents doesn't mean feeling good about them, especially when they do wrong or cruel things. Remember, love is a choice to do right even when you feel like acting the same as they, and returning evil for evil. No, loving them means swallowing your pride and hurt and doing what is best, even when it is hardest. Honoring them means respecting their God-given authority over your life, even when you think you know better. Obeying them means doing what they tell you, even when you would like to do something else. God has ways of dealing with problems. But as long as you take it in your own hands and don't do it His way, He then has two problems—your parents and you. He will do something in your home. But let it happen His way. Begin on His side. If anyone can win your parents to Jesus it should be you.

33
Forgiving Your Family for Wrongs Committed

Have you been hurt by your family? It is easy to see the signs. Your face gets hard; you avoid other people; you expect favors from everyone without gratitude; you spend a lot of time and attention on people who feel like you, and because of your attitude you wind up with only a few friends you are really afraid to lose. Bitterness makes you sensitive, touchy, ready to "fly off the handle."

The worst thing about not forgiving those that hurt you is that you get turned totally into yourself, and you get so hard you don't care anymore. And when you give up on others you also start to give up on yourself; you just might want to finish the whole thing by jumping off a bridge or with a deliberate O.D. Bitterness is deadly. It sends more kids to the street of death than any other sin.

Bitterness keeps getting worse and takes you deeper and deeper into trouble. You trust someone; they betray your trust. They shun, disgrace and reject you. Today that horrible happening is still painfully burned like fire on your mind. That hurt makes you want to hit back. Other bitter young people have done it before; they left behind them a trail of more wrecked lives.

A young man got hurt once; now he specializes in hurting girls who fall for him. I met a girl who got deeply hurt once too often, but now she says she is insensitive to pain. She has learned the frightening art of being tough, hard as rock, calloused to tenderness and care. Now she tells me she doesn't get hurt anymore. But the trouble with not feeling hurt is that you can't feel happiness either. When you get hard, you stop feeling anything.

Bitterness makes you blind to others' needs. It wraps you up totally in yourself. It poisons everything and makes everything you do poisonous. You lose all your friends except those who feel hurt and mad as you do. Up goes an ice wall around you that no one can break through with love. Proverbs 14:10 says, "The heart knows its own bitterness, and no stranger shares its joy" (RSV). Bitterness starts you blaming everything and everyone else for problems. You get the idea that if you point long enough at others, people won't look too hard at you.

Bitterness is the basic sin of the streets. Ask one hundred kids why they dropped out and blew their minds and lives in one trip after another, and you will almost always get the same answer: "I got hurt; this was my way of getting even." Hurt kills love dead. It wipes out your trust for any authority.

Bitterness attracts rotten "friends" like dung gathers flies. I have this funny feeling that some marches for various causes are only convenient vents for bitterness. Lives that once trusted now burn with the acid of revenge, and come out in protest against all rule or control. Yet in the face of all this, God commands us to forgive!

Now maybe you feel like joining the thousands of people who just laughed. It is a cynical laugh, compounded from a hundred thousand hurts and trusts betrayed. It came from both old and young people, flag waving sixty-year-old patriots and angry young sixteen-year-old anarchists, street kids and church kids—people with thin lips and unsmiling eyes.

I hear those voices. If they talk at all, they say, "Forgive? Are you putting me on? What for? My parents? My kids? Them? You don't know. You just don't know."

But God *does* know. That is why He commands us to forgive. We ignore this law at the cost of our lives. Forgiveness is God's way to spare your happiness. Look at your life. See what bitterness has done. Face it! Think back over all the things you have said and done because someone, sometime hurt you. Was it worth it, this getting even? Was it worth what it has done to you? Look in the mirror. See what you are becoming—a walking grudge against the world. "Forgive." If you do not do what God says, bitterness will destroy you. Yes, being hurt *is* their fault. But being bitter is always your own. And you must forgive or you will change, step by step, until you become like the ones you most despise.

If you have been hurt by your family, or by others that you know you must forgive, here is what you can and must do to be free. It will be hard, but you can do it. Choose to. God will help you and strengthen you. Take His help and do these things:

1. Make a list of all those who have hurt you. Take time. Leave plenty of space under each name. You won't have any trouble remembering them.

2. Under each name list the wrong things that person has done to hurt you. Sum up individual acts in principles. Sum the little things into basic wrongs. Get it all down. It isn't hard to remember when you are hurt. You've been thinking about some things for years. "Let it all hang out."

Funny about bitterness. It is pain, but you can actually half enjoy feeling hurt! It is like biting down hard on a sore tooth so that a smaller pain is swallowed up in a larger one. Being bitter includes the sin of intense self-pity.

You have held onto wounded feelings long enough. Write them down. Perhaps your parents failed to give you the kind of example you wanted. They told you not to do things you saw them do. The word "hypocrite" was easy to say. Maybe Dad just wasn't there when you needed him; maybe he took out his drink or his guilt on you with a belt. Your parents expected too much from you; they always told you how in their day they had to "walk five miles through the snow to get to school," and, "Why couldn't you do better when they had tried to give you the chance they never got?" Or maybe they couldn't care less what happened to you. Perhaps they kept harping on how good your brother or sister was, and "why couldn't you be like them," until you just wanted to kill that brother or sister. Write them all down. This is the poison that has eaten your life.

3. Now, take another list. On it, write down the things *you* did to hurt *them!* It is strange how your normally excellent memory can fail you about now. But ask God to run his plough through your heart. Let Him bring to light all you did to wrong them, and write them down. Maybe you just froze them out of your life the day you found out what they did wrong. Then you didn't love them enough to do what they asked, even if it was right. Or you lied to them, and made a habit of it, because they had lied to you. You smoked pot because Dad drank highballs; you dropped acid because Mom couldn't sleep without her tranquilizers. You just went out and got pregnant from the rottenest guy you could find because she was always so concerned with the family name. He hurt you; so you never said thank you, no matter how much he tried to make it up, just to show him you couldn't care less. You did things with friends you never did before because you gave up thinking real decency existed.

How many lies have you told yourself because of your hurt? How many times have you punished your own body and mind because of something someone else did to wrong you? How many others have you hurt because someone hurt you? Write it all down. Be as honest as you can. Put on your paper all you have done to hurt your family. I know you are not too proud of it. I know it is not easy to bring it all back. But you must really see what the sin of bitterness has done to you. And you will find a strange and terrible thing.

A lot of what you have on your list is exactly the same as what you have on your parents' list. You have judged and condemned them; but *you* have done the same things! In a multitude of ways, you have become like the ones you despised.

4. I think you know what the next step is. Get on your knees, and ask God to show you how much the things you have done have hurt Him. You are not finished yet; it is not over until you glimpse what has happened to His heart. Oh, what a terrible thing bitterness is! And remember—in every hurt you ever felt, in every hurt your family has felt, in everything where your bitterness slashed into someone else, *God* felt it all. He who has total experience has been put through the sum total of all that pain. Isn't it time you stopped hurting yourself? Isn't it time you quit infecting others? And isn't it high time you stopped hurting God?

No excuses. Everything you have felt in all your deepest hurts are only a tiny fraction of what God has felt for you. There is healing in His heart. Only Christ can carry this burden and live. If with all this He can forgive you, you can draw on His grace to forgive. Deeply repent of what you have done. The way of bitterness is a street that dead-ends in hell. Hurt put you on that street, but you were not made to be its slave.

You must let God set you free, but freedom is impossible if you hold onto the very thing that is changing you into the kind of person you hate. Spread out your horrible list before the Lord. Let Him break you over what you have done. Maybe it's time you cried. No one, not even you, is too hard to let Christ's love melt away the years of hurt and anger. Let His blood cleanse your stony heart of hate. Bring your list to Him, and ask His forgiveness. Get it as clean as you would want it on the Day of Judgment.

Charles Warner said:

> In the very depths of yourself, dig a grave. Let it be like some forgotten spot to which no path leads; and there, in the eternal silence, bury the wrongs that you have suffered. Your heart will feel as if a weight had fallen from it, and a Divine peace has come to abide with you.

Apologize to God for what you have done. Say, "Oh Lord, I have been hurt, and I hit back in horrible ways. I have been just like the ones that hurt me. I have become filled with bitterness and callousness and pride. Forgive me for my rotten attitude. Forgive me for my sin. I know I couldn't help being hurt. I know that you understand that. But I could help what I did to hurt back. Wash me and make me clean again. Take away my bitterness over these feelings, these grudges I have in my heart. Wash them out, oh God! Restore to me the joy of my salvation."

5. Now, the hardest part. Get off your knees. Take the list of what your parents have done. Pick it up, and rip it up. This is the last time you are going to think about it. Tell the Lord as you do this, "I forgive them, Lord, right now. I refuse to hold this hurt that has bound my life any longer. I will not be the slave of others' wrongs. I choose with my will not to hold these things in my heart or mind any longer." Then take a match and burn your torn list. As you burn it, see those old resentments going up in smoke. See the old past turning into ashes. Crush it when it is dead and cold, and blow it away in the wind. Let your grudges, your hurt, your past go with it.

6. Call, write or go to see them right away, as long as you know what to say, and if you can speak with them for a minute without interruption. (Write only if seeing them or phoning them is impossible.) Now, what do you have to do? You have to *apologize to them* for what *you* have done to hurt *them*. Take the worst thing on your list, and use that. Do it humbly, sincerely, with a broken heart. It will do you good to break before the ones that have hurt you. Do not mind their reactions. That is not your concern. They may be surprised; they may be embarrassed; they may be so convicted that they rip off at you. Leave this in God's hands. They themselves may also break, and God will be able to heal in seconds a breach that has taken years to split. But you must do this, even for your own and God's sake, if not for theirs. And you will find you can never be sure that you have forgiven them until you have first asked their forgiveness.

You could say something like this: "Dad, something has just happened to me that should have happened a long time ago. God has showed me how my ——— has really hurt you. I know I've wronged you in this and I want to ask you, 'Will you forgive me?' "

When you have done this, you will open a channel on your side for healing to begin. Your own heart will be cleared by the Lord. Many others may even be healed from hurt too. Now you must begin the process of living in love towards them. It will be a challenge. You must prove by your life that you really feel differently towards them now. This will not be easy. Bitterness causes suspicion, indifference, ingratitude. You understand all this. You have been there yourself.

You know you will have to work at it. It may take months for the breach to heal. But God will do things in your life that you never would have believed possible.

Through it all, pray for the ones who have hurt you. Don't you dare pray, "Oh Lord, I have tried. I have done my bit. Now I am right, but they are still wrong. Now get them for me, Lord! Judge my rotten father! Really smash my hypocritical mother! Deal with them for me, Lord. Wipe them out if it is your will!" Really see your parents with all their hurt, frustration, rage and sin, being loved by Jesus. See Him reach out His hand and touch their hurt hearts. The Bible says, "Bless them that curse you, do good to them that hate you, and pray for them that despitefully use you, and persecute you, that you may be the children of your Father who is in heaven, for he makes his sun to rise on the evil and on the good, and sends rain on the just and unjust" (Matt. 5:44, 45).

7. The final step for you in forgiving a family that wrongs you is to begin to list ways in which you can help the ones that hurt you. Are there things that they need that you can work to buy for them? Are there jobs around the house that no one likes doing that you can do for them? Are there things that they have asked you to do that you have not done before? Then do them in the name of Jesus. The Bible way is to will their highest good. And you will find something strange happening to your heart. As you do these things, step by step God will restore the love that you once might have had for them. It may even bring them to Jesus. After all, if you can't be an effective testimony to your family about the wonderful change the Lord Jesus can make in a life, who can?

34
What to Do If Parents Go Wrong

Maybe your story is like the fourteen-year-old girl who said, "I don't hate. I don't want to hate my dad, but he started kissing me in a funny way when I was twelve. I didn't understand it then, but it got worse. Finally my mother found out and threw *me* out of the house. I don't understand; why did my mother blame me? They said they were going to call me for Christmas, but they haven't, and if they don't call soon I'm going to wind up hating them both forever."

Or like Charlotte who went out with a bad kid at school, and found out she was pregnant at fifteen. Shocked, hurt and deeply ashamed, she went home to try to tell her parents what had happened. Her dad put his finger in her face and called her a dirty little tramp. She had never gotten over it. "I don't hate him now," she said, "but give me a year and I'll hate the ground he walks on."

Or the fifteen-year-old who bitterly admitted, "My dad's going to leave Mom. They don't know that I know, but just you wait. The day he walks out on us, I'm going to become the dirtiest little hippie the world has ever seen."

How do you live with problem parents? There are no easy answers to problems like this. Every kid who has lived in the streets knows what it's like to have problems at home. The world is filled with rotten parents. They come in all kinds. But remember, parents are just people, and people have problems. And some people have far worse problems than others. If you have given your life to Jesus, stop looking at your parents like they were a problem, and start looking at them as people you have a chance to help where no one else probably can help.

Mario Murillo tells of the time when in the middle of his big home problems he threw himself on God, and the Lord spoke to him. It seems as if the Lord looked down through time and knew that in the last days homes would fall apart. So He said, "In the last days I will pour out my spirit upon all flesh." That spirit is the spirit of adoption. God thought, "If no one will take care of the kids in the last days, then *I* will. I will be a Father to them. I will make them My children. If no one will love them, then *I* will love them."

Alcoholic parents. Perhaps one or both your parents are a slave to alcohol. You have felt the shame of having to move bottles to get into the house, the agony of having friends come around when your mother or dad was drunk, the pain of having them fight in drunken rages. Perhaps God has called you to help your parents. There are reasons why they are alcoholics. Part may be medical, but another part is spiritual.

You must take steps to really love them. First ask their forgiveness for not being the kind of kid you could have been. Tell them you love them and that you are praying for them. Gain their confidence by being trustworthy and by not showing revulsion over their problem. God loved *you* when *you* were a mess. You do the same with them. Ask God for His gift of peace in your heart so you can work from His calm strength. Ask them if you can help them in any way. Contact the A.A. or other Christian social welfare agencies that can help them with this problem. Try to bring your parents in contact with a minister or man of God who can counsel and help them spiritually. And *care* for your parents by cleaning up for them, choosing their highest good despite the pain and the grief their alcoholism will cause you. They need Jesus very, very much. And He can sometimes touch them through the fog of a ruined life and bring them to repentance and new life.

Atheistic parents. Maybe your father is president of the local rationalist society, or your mother specializes in giving lectures on atheism. But despite this, you have discovered the love of Jesus is real. Remember, most people who call themselves atheists have not calmly sat down and thought through evidence on both sides. Usually it is because they have been hurt in some way with some kind of church connection. Every rampant atheist I know has had bad contacts with some kind of religious situation.

Pray for your parents. Never allow yourself to get bitter over *their* bitterness, or you will find yourself becoming just like them. Don't argue about faith with them. If they take you to task over your faith, never raise your voice or fall into the trap of getting angry over their words. Speak quietly. Spend much time in the Bible. Don't antagonize them by deliberately trying to show them up by doing spiritual things when they can see you. Demonstrate your changed and different life practically around the home. Your aim is to show them by your life that giving your life to God has made you a better person who loves them more because of it. Love will sometimes win them when all the arguments have failed to move them one step closer to God.

A brutal dad. Some parents learn to take out their rage and hatred on kids by beating them brutally. When the Bible says, "Honour father and mother," it doesn't mean to let yourself be bashed around until you are beaten senseless. If you have done something wrong that deserves punishment, "take it like a man." But no Christian has to suffer cruel beatings silently without being able to call for any help or protection. You have the right to rebuke a parent that is cruel. When he is over his anger, tell him, "Dad, stop it! When I am wrong, I know I ought to be punished. But be fair. It's not right to take out your own problems on me. I am your son. I want to love you and respect you. But I can't do it when you are cruel." Be sure you first apologize for not being the kind of child you should have been. Then tell him that you will respect his wishes and will do whatever he asks you to do that is right; but if he will not be fair, you will leave the house until he calms down.

Try to find out why your dad is so cruel and angry. Does he trust you? Does he do this because he has made a mess of his own life, and can't find anyone else to take out his frustration on? And if you can, try to help him by bravely walking with God in the midst of his rotten life. Love him, care for him, but be firm. And stay out of his way when he gets a bad temper. Tell him that if he gets angry, you will leave until he has cooled down, to help him not hurt himself or God or you anymore.

Parents practicing black magic. Spiritism, occult activity in the family are growing problems. Many parents are involved in satanic activity expressly forbidden in the Bible. Your house may be filled with demonic powers and fear because of occult activity that your mother or dad are involved in. You must steadfastly refuse to take part in any way. The occult arts are like a deadly, contagious disease; a small contact contaminates and begins to infect others.

Resist the temptation to experiment in any way, or to take part in anything that involves occult activity. Go to a friend's house while your parents are doing things connected with the devil. Take a number of Christian friends with you to your house and pray in and over each room that you can. Have your friends make you a special subject of prayer to guard your mind and spirit from the wiles of the enemy. Get rid of any music at all that is vaguely connected with the world. Fill your room with Christian music, and stay away from all hard or acid sounds and the depressing "downer sound" of blue and minor music.

Learn to praise and pray in the Spirit, not for yourself, but for others. Demonstrate the reality of a life lived in the love and power of the Holy Spirit. Know in a real and practical way the power of the Holy Spirit. "Greater is he that is in you than he that is in the world." Refuse to read any books on spiritualism, even for fun or curiosity.

Careless parents. Sometimes you have parents who think they love you so much they don't want to set any limits on your life. That is foolishness. God loves us, and that is why He gave us limits. When we know what is right and what is wrong and how far we can go without causing trouble, we have freedom to build and create and grow. If your parents say they "care so much" or, frankly, just don't care at all what you do, *you* care. Set yourself limits. Ask God for help to learn the fruit of the Spirit that is called self-control. Set yourself a time to be home, and be home by that time. Regulate your own hours of play and work. Read Christian books and biographies that will give you a model for living that your parents have not been able to provide.

Church-going, non-Christian parents. Some parents aren't really evil people; in fact, they may go to church every week. But you know they don't really love Jesus because it is not much more than a social or reputation thing with them. Don't condemn them or try to preach to them about their hypocritical lives. They may not know anything more than what they have been in for the last fifty years. At least they are trying to set some kind of religious example, even though you may have learned more about Jesus yesterday than they ever have in their whole lives.

Live joyously around your home, be helpful, and sing Jesus songs while you wash the dishes, clean your room and make the bed. After asking permission, bring home friends who are sold-out disciples of Jesus, just to fellowship and to meet your parents (again, not to preach to them). Your job is to provide an example of genuine Christian love and reality. Let *God* give them the rest of the message.

Divorced parents. Maybe your parents have split up for good. You may be staying with your dad, or with your mother, or maybe you have moved away into a separate flat or apartment. Don't develop bitterness, and if you have, get rid of it. Ask forgiveness of both parents separately; this will help you clear your heart of hurt. Do things for both of them out of love for them. Spend an equal amount of time with them, whenever you can and whenever they will let you or want you to. Don't take sides with either of them. No matter how wrong one of them was, don't side against that one and stick up exclusively for the other. Love them both, the lovely and the unlovely, the loved and the unloved one. Maybe God will use you to speak to both of your parents about the love of Jesus. Maybe they can both make a new start one day because they both have a new heart. And if they are remarried, don't hold grudges against your stepparents. They are legally and scripturally the ones you are to listen to because the court has given them custody. Your true parents can advise you and you can go to them for counsel, but they have no power to command.

Parents of different faiths. Perhaps your parents belong to two different faiths, and that has been a source of tension to both them and you. Treat them the same way as you would divorced parents, because this situation is like a spiritual divorce. When you witness, stick to the main issues; don't get off into minor doctrinal differences. Be positive about the love and harmony you have found in Jesus. And, if possible, go to a service or two with either or both of your parents with their promise that they will come to one that you attend. Then really pray for both of them to find spiritual unity in Jesus. If one parent is a Christian and the other isn't, buy books that will help the Christian one to win the other.

A dead parent. Maybe one parent has died, and your mother or father is alone in trying to bring you up. It is sometimes harder when it is your dad who has died. Mother has a double responsibility to provide for the needs of the home and to bring you up as well, with any brothers or sisters you may have.

Carry more than your share of the load. Look for ways to get extra work, and help to support your mother. Help her carry the load by being responsible and trustworthy yourself. Give her extra love because she is alone now and it is harder for her.

If your mother is a church woman, have her take her needs to God in the weekly prayer meeting. It is the church's responsibility to help out widows and those who are in need. You make sure you belong to a body of believers who follow that Bible command. Have some Christian men in the church pray weekly for your mother, that she will have the wisdom and strength to make the right decisions in raising her family. Lighten her load as much as you can.

A doting mother. We are usually close to our mothers, but sometimes they can try to live their lives through us. It is an old trick of the devil to convince a mother that her children, especially her sons, need her more than anyone else in the world, even God. Our mothers are very important in God's pattern of training in the family; they can give us both love and inspiration in God's order. But if mothers get too possessive or too domineering, a lot of pressure is put on their children. When mothers have problems like this, boys are pressured towards homosexual or Hitler-type living.

You must take steps to rebuild your father's leadership in the home. In the presence of your mother, say things that honor and uphold your dad. If your mother asks you to do something that is a family decision, do it; but if it comes to a choice between what your mother says and what your dad says, follow your father's directions each time, unless it is a command to specifically commit sin. God has put Dad in the home to be leader. Help him do it. Resist the temptation to undercut his leadership by working on poor old Mother to give in when Dad has already said no. Go to your dad and ask him permission first when both parents are home. But don't put your mother down while you do it. Just smile, recognize her authority, and say "Right, Mother; I'll just have to check with Dad first to see if he thinks its O.K."

Overly strict parents. Have you ever wondered why some parents seem to be far too strict with you? Put yourself in their place for a little while. Why would *you* be strict on *your* kids? Maybe it is because you remember what you did when you were a kid, and you are getting uptight now because you recognize (or think you recognize) the same sort of things you used to do? Maybe some parents remember their own lives as kids with a measure of fear and regret.

In the Billy Graham film, *The Restless Ones*, April Harris, a young prostitute with an alcoholic mother, is being questioned by her mother as to how she got the money to buy an expensive dress. (The dress was bought with money she got by selling her body.) Suddenly April turns on her mother and says, "What did *you* do when *you* were young that makes you so suspicious of *me*?" Silence! Remember, sometimes parents are too strict because of either guilt or fear.

You must learn to build trust with them. Do exactly what you say. When you tell them you will be home at a certain time, be home earlier if possible. Do all jobs you are given. Earn their trust. It will take time. But if you can prove you can be trusted, you may find them relaxing their strictness a little.

Success-cult parents. Sometimes your parents seem to have their hearts set on your being a success. Now this is also natural. It is only right that parents should expect their kids to be some kind of credit to the world and to be successful. But sometimes they don't know what success is. Bible success is living in God's ways and living by His principles. Sometimes success to parents means fame, fortune and power. That may not be the way God is leading you, but you cannot go to war with your parents over this.

Tell them that you are happy that they want you to succeed. Say that you want to be useful and worthwhile to your world. But try to redefine success so they can understand that your values are not just based on how much money you will have or how well known you will be. Point out that a lot of crooks are wealthy and well known (see Matt. 6:33). Say that you are working to have a successful character and a good reputation, which is far more worthwhile to you than just to have a great deal of money that you can't take with you when you die. Give some creative alternatives to their own plans for your future. If you don't really feel too interested in the thing that they want you to do, explain that you will go along with it as long as you can until you are absolutely sure what God wants you to do. Thank God for your parents. At least they care enough about you to worry over your life. Some parents have never done that at all. Then pray for them.

The final step for you in forgiving a family that wrongs you is to begin to list ways in which you can help the ones that hurt you. Are there things that they need that you can work to buy for them? Are there jobs around the house that no one likes doing that you can step in and do for them? Are there things which they have always asked you to do that you have not done before? Then do them, in the name of Jesus! The Bible way is to will their highest good. And you will find something strange happening to your heart. As you do these things, step by step God will restore the love that you once had for them. It may even bring them to Jesus. And if *you* can't be an effective testimony to your family about the wonderful change the Lord Jesus can make in a life, who can?

35
Taking Your Home for Christ

If you want to change society, there is no better place to start than here at its heart. Unless you can live out Christ in front of your family, forget about trying to serve God in your world. The home is foundational. Here are where all the lessons of true social change are learned under God. Here is where you begin to change your world.

1. *Apologize to each person in your family.* If you are going to affect their lives, first get right with them and really face up with your wrong. You have broken God's laws and heart in being a bad example to your parents and other relatives. If you are going to be a different person, start off the right way. This way your new way of living will not be misinterpreted as you try to live better.

2. *Begin to live in love towards your parents.* They have no other example of a true Christian than yours. What is that example like? Who else do they have that can give them a real illustration of what a Christian is like in daily life? The Bible tells us to "love your neighbor." A neighbor is someone who lives next to you. Who lives more next to you than Mom and Dad? Now loving your parents does not mean that you have to feel good about them nor to be happy about the wrong things they do. It simply means to unselfishly choose their highest good in every situation, whatever they do or say. It means treating them the way you would like to be treated, even if they are unfair or misunderstand. If you love them, you won't be sarcastic, you won't lose your temper, and you won't lash back at them if they hurt you. Read 1 Corinthians 13.

3. *Stand firm for right.* Don't compromise your testimony. If you ignore your stand for Jesus when it is inconvenient to stick up for Him, you are a people-pleaser. Your family will test you to see if you really mean what you say. Don't give in to

sin. You are on trial before your family. If your parents see you are not only willing to die for your faith, but to live it out before them also, they will begin to respect your stand. Be kind in your stand, but be firm. You must obey your parents in everything except to sin.

4. *Obey your parents.* This is the Bible way to win them to the Lord. What better way can you convince them that the Christian life makes people better? Do not say that you are disobedient because you are a Christian and they are not. Jesus said that Christians keep His commandments, and one of them is to obey parents. This is not advice. Everything your parents ask you to do must be done, cheerfully, for Jesus' sake—everything except a specific command to commit sin. If you think Jesus wants you to do something but have no Bible command to do it, and if your parents don't want you to do it, you must pray, "Lord, I feel that You want me to do this, but it is only my feelings. Your Word says I am to obey them for Your sake because it is right [Eph. 6:1-3]. I am going to obey them because Your Book says to. If You really want me to do what I feel, I want You to change my parents' minds about this. Your Word says that You can do it [Prov. 21:1]. I put this into your wonderful hands, and just look to You for the solution."

5. *Do all the dirty work in your home.* Take on all the ugly jobs. Go the second mile (Matt. 5:41-48). Wash the dishes for Jesus. Clean your room for Jesus. Mow the lawn for Him. Empty the garbage for Christ. Do everything "for His sake." When the opportunity comes to witness for Him, then you will be ready. They will want to *listen* to the gospel that they have *seen* in your life every day.

Section IX
The Disciple's
FUTURE

36

What Will Happen to Our World?

It had lasted many years, but finally the war was over. People said, "It must not happen again. We must build a better world. We must build a brave new age, worthy of the sacrifices of those that died hoping for it." Hope was born for a Golden Era. Poets wrote about it, actors dramatized the dream, singers did songs about it. Man had finally learned his lesson. Now he would build *Utopia*, the perfect planet!

The years passed. The dream sickened and died. It did not happen; they knew it never would. The world was still torn between extremes of poverty and hedonism. Government was still corrupt. Civilization began to fall apart again as moral rot ate at the spiritual seams of the nation. Religion had failed. Though most people put in a token showing at a place of worship, most were virtual atheists. In place of religion, thousands turned to magic. Horoscopes, astrology and soothsaying became commonplace. Others, scorning witchcraft, turned to philosophy and science for answers, but the schools of thought were barren and science had no hope. Man began to settle into the darkness of black despair.

Yet it was a world with unique advancements in science. There was one world government, a world communications system, universal transport and basic world language. But in spite of all this progress, fear hung like a cloud over men. People were afraid of exposure, afraid of life, and, above all, afraid of death. The grave was a subject nobody cared to talk about and rarely tried to think about.

The TIME?—Twenty-five A.D. Or perhaps the year *two thousand* A.D.!

What will happen to our world? Will it go out in one huge chain of mushroom clouds or only with a whimper? Will pollution get so bad that man will finally choke to death on his own waste? Does the disciple of Jesus have to live with an uncertain future and a blind hope that something might turn up? Thank God, no! The Bible is different from any other major religious book, and one key difference is its window on the future. One Bible verse in seven tells us something about what will happen in history, a demonstration of God's amazing wisdom and ability to foresee the future. We don't need to lay Tarot cards, check horoscopes or study the stars. God has already told us what will happen to our world. Knowing this, we can live in the awe and wonder of realizing what will happen to history—*before* it happens.

The Bible gives us *no* hopeful future for the polluted world system that selfish men have created. The "brave new world" dream will keep on turning back into the same frightening old nightmare. The disciples asked Jesus what would happen at the end of the world. He told them what would come. Wars would increase. Famines would take place as exploding world population stretched earth's resources to the limit. Strange new diseases would mutate. Earthquakes would rock the world in faraway places (Matt. 24:6-7).

But man will not bring on the end of the world. Destiny is not in the hands of some mad military leader with fingers on the buttons of nuclear I.C.B.M.'s. *God* is in charge of history. Nothing will happen without His permission. Nations will change to suit His purposes. He retains control over the affairs of His creation. And although His heart has been angered and hurt by the selfishness of His rebel race, He will not allow it to fold up on its own. When it has to fold, He will do the final wrapping. And only He has the final say when the curtains must come down.

The Bible tells us to beware of some things in the last days. It seems from culture studies that our world is dividing into two camps of people. Some are thinkers. They are entranced with the promises of science. They stake their lives and future on the hope that technology will bring some kind of answer to man. Their solutions are food farms, treated water to tranquilize populations, genetic engineering to breed out the weak and "clone off" the strong. Science has become such a sacred cow to people that when a scientist speaks as a man they hear him as a god. Some other thinkers are more violent. They think man's problems come from the society he has built; so they want to burn it down in the hope that somehow a new world will rise out of the old ashes.

But different thinkers cannot agree as to *how* the world should be changed. They need a leader, someone who can be a master of technology and force, a military genius and super-politician with the art of controlling people. If such a man showed up, he would have world allegiance of the thinkers.

Another camp of people have gone to the mystic worlds to find meaning. They care about earth, but care more for the individuals that make up our planet. Their crusades center on the search for love, beauty, truth, values and meaning. They have a deep hunger to discover the secrets of human harmony and spiritual reality. Their drive is towards universal religion, the unity and brotherhood of all humanity. They honor occult powers and supernatural forces.

But they, too, are leaderless. They want a superman too. If he comes, he will find a world of waiting worshippers. But he will have to be a man with greater mystical, supernatural powers than all other human leaders before him. He will have to be one who can unite all warring factions of sects; to combine all churches and faiths; to introduce a single, systematized experience and understanding that will put all the mystics of this world in the same basic camp. He would have to have supernatural powers beyond all those that can be duplicated by earth science. He would have to be a man that all faiths (outside of those who belong to the real Bible Jesus) could accept.

The strange thing about these two camps of people is this: both need each other, although they are at present divided. The thinkers are looking for answers to their history and society, but are losing their answers for man. The feelers are looking for answers to the individual search for meaning, but have no answers for society as a whole. What the world wants is two leaders who can unite these separate camps and then form an allegiance to unify the world.

And this is the scary thing: Jesus said such men would come. What the world is waiting for is another "Christ." There will come a man to unite nations militarily and economically. There will be another man who has supernatural powers, a "king of the witches" who can work wonders so great that all the religious world will worship him.

Both will form an alliance and they will unite the world. But it will be a world without the true God and a world that is united in its defiance of Bible truth. It will be a world that has rejected the real Christ, and enthroned instead a satanic counterfeit. And only real disciples of Jesus will be able to tell the difference. That time is almost here. What we can see in our world now is a literal fulfillment of the words of the Bible. Our generation may have the last great opportunity to see God sweep the nations with real revival before the real Jesus returns.

And He will come. That is the great hope of the church; that is the great prayer of every disciple of Jesus. Jesus will come! He sill set up His new world, a world without war, where nations learn peace and beat their swords into ploughs. His signs are in the sky. Time's last great drama is about to take place. You and I have been called on stage at the most awesome time in the history of man. You who read these words are part of the last great conflict between the powers of heaven and the powers of hell. When the real Jesus comes, all the world will know.

The Lord Jesus warned us with these words: "Then many shall be offended, and shall betray one another, and shall hate one another. And many false prophets shall arise and deceive many. And because iniquity shall abound, the love of many shall grow cold. But he that shall endure to the end shall be saved. And this gospel of the kingdom shall be preached in all the world for a witness to all the nations; and then shall the end come" (Matt. 24:10-14).

The Bible predicts a great spiritual awakening to combat the increase in occult powers. The Spirit of God is going to be poured out on the young, on the servants and the old men who shall dream dreams. We are in that awakening now. The Jesus movement is only a small demonstration of what God is going to do. The awakenings that are going on around the world—in Indonesia, Africa, Asia, South America, behind the iron and bamboo curtains— are only fuses of the mightiest spiritual explosion of all time. And we can be excited with the honor of being in on it.

37

How to Know God's Will for Your Life

From the beginning of creation, when He flung the stars into the trackless hollow of space, *God has had a purpose for you* as a tiny part of His vast purpose for mankind. To know and follow God's purpose for our lives brings the joy and radiance of a Christ-guided life. Here's how—if you are willing!

1. *Be sure you are filled with the Spirit of God.* Honestly, without this, you will never make it. To know the power of the Holy Spirit and to be sensitive to His voice is the difference between defeat and victory, failure and success, direction and aimlessness. There is a price—God wants you empty of self and sin. He is always ready to fill your heart—but you are not (Luke 11:13)! Be honest with yourself and with Him. Be earnest. Confess your sin, ask His forgiveness. Then, just as you asked Christ to come into your heart, ask the Holy Spirit to flood your soul with divine power. It is impossible to be in the center of God's will continually without knowing the guidance of the Holy Spirit. He is the Master Guide and the "dynamite" of God's power.

2. *Be sure you have fully yielded yourself to the will of God.* It's not what *you* want, it's what *He* wants! God can't direct a life that doesn't *want* to be directed. You must ask Him to direct your will totally. Now, is this unreasonable? He knows what the future holds—you don't. And who is best equipped to run your life—you or God? He has all wisdom and power, and the ability to be with you wherever you go. Nothing is too hard for Him. He has never made a mistake, never had to say, "I don't know." And He has never made a selfish decision. You don't have to be afraid of surrender to Him. He is a loving, kind, and compassionate Father who longs for your highest happiness and holiness. Make it a matter of sincere and heartfelt prayer and self-searching. Then tell Him you are willing to go wherever He wants you to go, and do whatever He wants you to do, no matter what

the cost. If you don't mean it, don't pray. God will take you up on any promise you make to Him.

3. *Count the cost.* A halfhearted Christianity is powerless and joyless. All—or nothing—is God's standard of committal. God never uses people whom He can get rid of easily. He never does business with people who don't mean business with Him. Now, are you willing? Think specifically. Are you ready to leave home? Give up your rights to a home? Friends? Family? Marriage? A specially lucrative or important career you have followed since you were little? Remember the story of Abraham. God may not ask you to give up or sacrifice your rights to any of these—but unless you are willing—honestly willing to do so, forget about Him ever using you. This is going to be hard—really hard. But if you really mean business with God—and you do—you won't want it any other way. The best things cost the most.

4. *Be willing to be called a fool.* Doing God's will often goes against the ideas of a selfish world. Usually His will fits perfectly with our minds and thoughts. Some Christians do not do anything because they say they don't know God's will. But we need not always expect a voice from the sky when the path of service is clear. God gave us common sense and He expects us to use it. God's will is usually an area of general direction in which He leaves us quite free to work for Him.

However, sometimes His words cut across all human thinking and even go right against it! This is guidance from intuition as our spirits connect to the Holy Spirit, who has promised to guide into all truth if we obey the Bible.

It is sensing in spirit what is on God's heart. People who know God's voice may be called fools for obeying Him but they will be *God's* fools and they will see His power.

5. *Be sure you have a clean conscience from the past.* God's voice will be blocked if there are still sinful things in your life that He has urged you to get right. How can He show you more if you have not obeyed in the little things?

Every time you kneel to pray, the finger of His Spirit will point back to your clear duty to get that thing cleaned up and put right. A clear conscience is a must to tell between God's voice and the voice of the enemy. Many do not know God's will because of unconfessed sin. It is the "pure in heart" who see Him.

6. *Spend time daily in prayer and the Word of God.* The Word of God is the whole basis of guidance. It contains principles and guidelines for almost every walk of life. God's will is clearly shown in His *Word.* Bible study shows us what God expects in daily living, and most Bible principles can be directly applied

to life. No guidance will ever break the fence of Bible laws. Freedom in following the Lord Jesus always stays on the tracks of right. Prayer teaches us to learn what God is like and how His voice sounds. Many do not recognize the call of God simply because they have never taken the time to really talk with Him long enough to know what He is like. It is not enough to know *about* Him; you must know *Him*.

7. *Ask Him to show you His will.* Don't expect that God will always detail everything for you, or tell you in advance all that He has in store for you. As men's choices change, so God changes the ways that *He* works. Don't get mad at God because He doesn't show you a diary of the next five years of your life. Such a diary is impossible because you are a moral creature.

Every choice you make brings into being new creations in God's universe. God will use these to fulfill His own purposes. But because they don't exist until you actually *make* them, it is impossible to give you a detailed diary of your life in the future. You will not find the word *plan* or *blueprint* in the Scriptures. You have been made free to choose, and for this reason, it is important that you learn to know God's voice on a day-to-day basis. You can expect guidance for what you have to do right away, but He may not always show you what you are supposed to do next year! And don't be hung up on words or definitions of your ministry for Him. God may call you to do something, then change it later as He feels you are better equipped to handle another task. The only thing you can be sure of is that He will use you wherever He wants you and that you can expect Him to show you what to do in each circumstance.

8. *Don't be too impatient.* A walk with God is one step at a time. He will never forget you. He will never be late in His promises. Failure can only come from your side. But there never need be disappointment, or the sense of having missed His will if you *want* to know Him—if you *want* to know your task for the present with all your heart.

38

The Ways God Speaks to Us

"My sheep hear my voice, and I know them, and they follow me" (John 10:27).

Study the men and women by whom God changed history. They were not special. Not many were wise after the ways of the world. You will not find many naturally gifted among their ranks. But all had one thing in common: they knew and did the will of God in their generation.

Those that God used in the past were ordinary people with an extraordinary Lord. They were not all champions of great faith, but little people who had put their little faith in a great God. The driving force in their lives was the sure conviction that God had called them to His work, and that as long as they were faithful to that call He would work with them and through them against impossible odds to victory.

Scripture is the story of common men and women who found the will of God. Wiley Jacob met the Angel of the Lord. Show-off Joseph in his multicolored coat had a dream. Failure Moses saw a bush that didn't burn. Disobedient Baalam heard an ass speak. Paul saw a blinding light. Little Samuel heard a voice. Old John saw a vision. God speaks in many different ways. He has not changed; what He has done before He can do again. He can speak to you and you can learn to recognize His voice.

First, have you faithfully met the basic conditions for guidance? Do this first, God cannot speak to you if there is still sin in your heart, or unyielded rights, or something yet undone that He has already told you to do. Be clean before Him first.

Now it would take too long to go into all the different ways that God has guided people before. It would take even longer to show you how to be sure it was God in each case. But if you have spent time in God's Word and your heart is truly honest before Him, you can be sure He will guide you. Leave the way up to Him. Here are a few simple things to remember about true guidance from the Holy Spirit of God:

1. *God is never spooky.* No echo-chamber type voices, weird apparitions or other fear producing, scary sights or sounds come from Him! The Father always guides His children gently, lovingly, matter-of-factly. Whatever God does, He never "shows off." He is kind, gentle, loving. The voice of God is the voice of the Good Shepherd who gives His life for the sheep. Watch out for any guidance that is tense, harsh or strange. God is very normal and spiritually natural in His ways (see 1 Sam. 3:4-5; John 10:14, 16, 27-28). Little Samuel thought that God was Eli, his spiritual father.

2. *Never decide in a rush.* If you *have* to know *now* and you have no time to think it through or pray about it, refuse it. You cannot afford to act on anything you are pushed into by pressure. The Bible says, "He that believes shall not make haste" (Isa. 28:16). We are not to be hasty in words, heart or spirit (Prov. 14:29; 29:20; Eccl. 5:2; 7:9). The Bible also says, "Whatever is not of faith is sin" (Rom. 14:23). Never decide until you are sure, or have a reasonably firm conviction that God is in it. Watch all voices that demand or are bossy or that ask unthinking obedience. No voice that keeps harping on your mind like a continuous commentary comes from God. Don't act until your heart has full peace and is at rest over your decision. The Bible says, "God has not given us the spirit of fear, but of power, and of love, and of a sound mind" (2 Tim. 1:7; 1 John 4:18). This means that even when we have to act in faith we should never have to act in unrest, turmoil or fear. Don't make rush decisions.

3. *God will never "waffle around."* He doesn't keep on changing His directions. If it is *His* voice, you can expect a clear direction, and then you can expect the silence that signals He is waiting for you to obey. God is never confused. He is always frank, direct and right to the point. If you are confused in guidance, it is probably because you already know what He wants you to do and you are looking for an easier way out or an excuse to not do it!

4. *The Holy Spirit will never depress, deaden or arouse you sensually.* He will never guide you when your head isn't straight. Never seek guidance through any means that requires you to "turn off your mind"! God speaks to our heads and hearts together. We must be alert and active. He has asked us to check what we feel by facts—facts from His Word and from what we know is right and true. Beware of any suggestions to your mind that push you to do kooky things about your food, dress, sex or manner of acting.

Sometimes the enemy will try to fool a young Christian and

wear him out by throwing in false compulsions that look at first glance to be real guidance from God. Beware of thoughts injected into your mind. If something comes to you like a bolt from the blue, with no reference at all to anything you have been thinking about or doing, and if it is to do something strange or unusual, think it through very carefully. It could very well be from the devil's side. Look out for anything that tends to either put you down or puff you up. Both are forms of pride and are first steps towards inviting satanic attack disguised as divine guidance.

5. *Most important of all: God's guidance will never break His own laws or go against what He has said in His Word.* "To the law and to the testimony: if they speak not according to this word, it is because there is no light in them" (Isa. 8:20). Every major problem you have in guidance can be solved in the pages of God's Word. His *will* is revealed in His *Word.* When you don't have enough light on something, walk within the broad principles of obedience to the Scriptures and God will always get through to you exactly what He means. You will never need guidance, for instance, as to whether you ought to lie or steal or be sexually immoral. You already know what His Book says. And that is the only guidance you need on that subject.

When you need anything else that is not specifically covered in God's Word, He will show you in whatever way He wants to. If you are fully yielded to Him, you can expect His directions just as surely as you can expect the sun to rise.

6. *Get your guidance from Him, not from a Christian friend or someone else.* No one else can guide you as a disciple of Jesus; all spiritual friends can do is to advise you and instruct you from the Scriptures for help. The Bible gives serious warnings about listening to men without first seeking God's face about a matter. God may guide in your daily Bible reading. He may bring to mind a verse of scripture you once learned to help you decide in a situation. But don't be afraid to act when something needs to be done because you are afraid you "might get out of God's will." There is an unhealthy extreme either side of happy guidance—either rushing ahead foolishly without taking time to wait on God, or worrying over every motive and decision, fearing to act when the Bible principles are plain and clear. You may at all times do anything that the Bible directs you to. This never takes special guidance, just ordinary obedience.

When you need to know the Lord's voice in a special decision and you want to be sure it is *His* voice, rather than the enemy's voice, use this method to help you hear Him speak to your heart and mind:

1. *Die to your own desires.* Take some concrete object—a Bible, a book, or a piece of paper. Use this as a symbol of your own feelings and ideas on the matter. Place it to one side, up on a shelf or in another corner of the room, and as you do it tell the Lord, "Lord Jesus, this represents all that I have on my mind and heart right now. I put these over here for You to deal with. I desire to die to these ideas and feelings of mind, whether they are right or wrong. I choose to give them up to You. Put them to death for me. I surrender them to You. By faith I ask You to crucify them for me."

Choose to die to them; then reach out in faith and *believe* God to really put them to death for you. See yourself as dead, totally dead to all your own ideas and feelings on this matter.

2. *Yield yourself to God.* Pray, "Lord, I submit myself to You. I give You my mind and heart for Your complete direction and guidance. I confess to You now that I am Your child and You are my heavenly Father. I just put myself wholly in Your hands right now. Cleanse me from all sin. I yield all my rights to You now. I want to do whatever You want me to do." Submit yourself wholly to God.

3. *Resist the Devil in faith.* Take your stand in the name of the Lord Jesus. Each child of God has a place of power with Christ the head of the church in heavenly places (Eph. 1:17-23; 2:1-7). Stand in that authority. Use a scripture verse to resist the devil to drive him away from your consciousness. Say, "Satan, the Bible says, 'Submit yourself to God.' I have done that. Then it says, 'Resist the devil, and he will flee from you.' I did not say that. Jesus said it. His Word says it. He made that promise, and *you* must obey. In Jesus' name and on His authority, I resist you and command you to take all your thoughts and suggestions out of my mind. It is written, 'Greater is he that is within me than he that is in the world' " (James 4:7; 1 John 3:8; 4:4; 1 Pet. 5:6-9).

Do this simply, clearly and without asking. Make it a command in the power of God. Jesus will back up His promises. You will feel a peace and clearing of tension when there has been a release from satanic pressures and suggestions.

4. *There is now no voice left but the voice of God to your mind.* By faith take the mind of Christ (1 Cor. 2:16). Ask God, "Father, I have done what You asked. I am Your child, and You promised that You would speak to me and show me what to do. If You would be pleased to show me now, put into my mind and heart what is on your heart for me." Take the first clear, definite direction. Do what He tells you!

39

Finding God's Man or Woman for Your Life

Do you believe that God can guide you to a wife or husband? One Bible story tells us the ways you can find the right one. There is more spiritual truth to this story than just guidelines on marriage. You can think about the story as a beautiful illustration with Abraham like God the Father, Isaac like Jesus the Son, the servant standing for the Holy Spirit, and Rebeccah as the Bride of Christ, the Church. But I want to use its outline to help you find God's girl or guy for your life. Open your Bible to Genesis 24.

1. "And Abraham said to his eldest servant . . . I will make you swear by the Lord, the God of heaven, and the God of the earth, that you shall not take a wife to my son of the daughters of the Canaanites, among whom I dwell" (Gen. 24:2, 3).

Here is your first rule to find God's one for you life: *Don't Date Canaanites!*

Who is a Canaanite? A Canaanite is a selfish person. A Canaanite is someone who really only cares about himself, someone who has never made a real surrender to the Lord Jesus, someone who doesn't practically put Christ first in his life. Canaanites don't really care. Notice how much that word looks like "canine." And Canaanite love is in its mildest form only "puppy" love; it is in its worst form the prelude to a dog's life! Date a Canaanite and don't be surprised if he treats you like a dog. A dog is something you pet, something you play with—certainly not someone to marry.

Selfish people don't know how to love because they have never loved God. Only true disciples of Jesus can really love because Christian love in marriage operates on three different levels at once. A Christian couple joined in marriage know much more than just sexual love and physical attraction. They also have a friendship love because they have learned to honor each other as brother and sister in God's family, and have shared common interests in His work. Then they are both ruled by the love of God that smooths over the rough places and brings them together under the rule of the Lord Jesus.

Don't even go out with Canaanites! There is no way you can keep on seeing some attractive Canaanite without mixing up any spiritual concern for them with purely physical attraction. And girls, don't fall into the trap of saying, "I'm going to win him to Jesus by going out with him." Maybe you can, but the odds are greatly against it. Some of the most beautiful disciples of Jesus I know went down the moral drain because they hung around too long with some sexually attractive Canaanite who would not give in to God.

I know it is easy to fool others when you are really getting into deep trouble. It is even easy to fool yourself that you are really spiritually in love with their souls. But remember, love is not just a feeling of affection. Anyone, even a Canaanite, can turn you on if they give you enough interest and attention. But love is not romance. (Romance begins when you sink in his arms; romance ends with your arms in the sink!)

I know Bible college girls who have gotten messed up by some of the worst pimps and addicts that ever fought with God. The girls each thought they were close to winning those guys to Christ; all along they were only being seduced by smooth talk and practiced lines. When these rotten guys were finished with them, they laughed and split just like they did with every other girl they used the same way. There is one safe rule, especially if you are a girl: stay away from all Canaanites.

2. "But you shall go to my country, and to my kindred" (Gen. 24:4). Find God's person for your life among God's people. Christian marriages must build first on a common love for Jesus. This will give you a forever bond—one that will never fade out, an eternal love for and in God. You may really grow to like them by finding they are interested in the same kind of things you are interested in. What has God done in their life, and what does He want to do? You may even find that you have the same basic goals in life. You want to do the same things under God, care about the same values and find that you work together beautifully. If the question of getting engaged comes up, you can begin to seek God and put your friendship to the test of true love.

3. The servant had a good question. How was he going to find the right girl for his master? Abraham gave him this word of advice: "The Lord God of heaven ... shall send his angel before you, and you shall take a wife for my son from there"

(Gen. 24:7). So the next rule is: *Date the angel that is sent by the angel from God.*

You will find great pleasure just being with God's people. You will make many friends of the opposite sex among disciples of Jesus. None of these may ever lead to a serious personal marriage type commitment. But you can be happy knowing that if God wants you to marry He will arrange for you to meet at the right time the one He knows you would be the happiest with. One thing is sure about this servant: he really believed that God's angel would guide him to the right girl. And if you want God's best, you must really trust God to lead you the same way.

There are plenty of people you could marry and make it for a while. But unless there is a sureness in God over the choice you make, you will always wonder whether or not you married the right one. What will you feel like in five years' time, looking back over the steps you took to decide? Will you have regrets and doubts over whom you married, should Jesus tarry? It goes without saying: don't flirt with anyone when you have no intention of being seriously interested in them. God keep you until you are sure.

Some kids are afraid to trust God for a girl or a man to marry. They will let God manage everything else, but have the funny idea that God doesn't know anything about picking life partners. They imagine He will punish their trust by giving them some vile creature-feature reject.

Can you see a guy who loves God and who believes he needs a wife come to the Lord? He says, "Oh Lord, I'll take anyone you want me to have. Anybody, Lord, anybody!" Then he stops in fright and says to himself, "Oh, no! What did I say?"

He thinks God now pounces on his words like Snoopy the vulture-dog and says, "Ah ha! *Now* you did it. *You* said it. I heard you. You said *anybody.* Good! I have this horrible old hag with a bun, hairy legs and wears tennis shoes, who has been praying for ninety-five years, 'Oh God, give me a nice young man!' She has been praying so long she finishes each prayer with 'A man!' Now, I can't let her go unrewarded. You were the first one who said anybody, so for the rest of your life you'll have a chance to regret your dedication!"

What a horrible picture of God. God knows the kind of person you would be most happy with better than you do. You, brother, have a fairly good idea of the kind of lovely girl you would like to spend the rest of your life with. You, sister, want some marvelous guy that you can willingly give the love of your whole being.

And listen, both of you. God knows the thoughts of your hearts even better than you do.

I know two things about God: first, He is really wise; second, He really *is* love. That means He never makes a mistake, and what He decides for us will always fit in beautifully with what in our heart of hearts we really want. God's angel will find for you another earthly "angel" to share your life. Trust Him! If you trusted Him for your eternal life, surely you can fully trust Him for short time happiness in this life. And whoever He picks out for you will be really right on.

4. "And the girl was very fair to look upon" (Gen. 24:16). Ready for the next rule? *She must be beautiful; he must be good looking.* That's what the Bible says! One guy sent a letter to a columnist and asked, "Why do girls always close their eyes when I kiss them?"

She answered, "Look in the mirror, and you'll find out."

A girl sent her picture to a boy pen-pal after he had written to her for a year without ever seeing her. She wrote on the back of it "This picture doesn't do me justice."

He sent back another letter. It said, "You don't need justice; you need mercy!"

But God is far kinder than we can ever imagine. No one knows the depth of the lovely thoughts He has for us. Yes, the one you marry must be beautiful or very good looking. At least, *to you.* You are going to spend the rest of your life with him. Why shouldn't he be? God designed physical attractiveness. It was His idea.

It would do no harm for you to pray what Catherine Marshall calls "the dreaming prayer." Ask God to give you the man or woman of your dreams. But first set your heart on pleasing Him, in delighting yourself only in Him. Don't be just running around in quiet desperation looking for someone to marry. Just be content that you are married to Jesus, that His love is the spring and source of your contentment. And God says that if you delight yourself in Him, He will give you the desires of your heart. Don't be afraid to set your sights high. Be a man or woman of God, in love with God, and your dreams will come true in Christ.

Perhaps you think you look ugly so your dream girl or man will not think you are the right one. Do not despair. You can become beautiful! Beauty is not something that comes in cans or by genetics. There are some people with pretty faces who have ugly hearts, and they are not beautiful. Real beauty begins within.

William Booth said to his sons, "You want more than a pretty face to live with 365 days in the year, my boys. Look for those deeper womanly gifts and graces with which your mother has so enriched my life."

The most outwardly beautiful person in all the Bible was not the Lord Jesus. That person was an angel of such glory and beauty that he was called the Prince of Morning. But his beauty made him proud. He sinned against God and was cast out of heaven. The Bible calls him Satan. No, beauty is not always an advantage. The only record we have of a description of Jesus is the one Isaiah gives us: "When we shall see him, there is no beauty that we should desire him" (Isa. 53:2).

People didn't come back from seeing the Lord on earth and say, "Wow! Didn't He look like Paulus Newmanus!" No, it was not what the Lord Jesus looked like that made Him truly beautiful. It was what He *was*. And you can be beautiful the same way. I have seen street people with the most awful looks changed by miracles into beautiful people by the power of the living God. Their beauty is Jesus. It comes from the time they spend with the supremely lovely One. You can change *your* face! Just forget about yourself. Give your love wholly to Jesus. Let that outpoured love spill out to others. Your whole life and appearance will change from the inside out. The Bible puts it in a beautiful way: "They looked unto him, and were radiant."

5. "Let it come to pass, that the girl to whom I shall say, 'Let down your pitcher, please, that I may drink'; and she shall say, 'Drink, and I will give your camels drink also'; let the same be she that you have appointed for your servant Isaac" (Gen. 24:14).

Here is a marvelous test. The servant wanted some kind of sign by which he could recognize the girl God had for his master. Here is a way by which you can recognize that girl too, if you are a man looking for God's girl: *Can she water camels*?

Of course, your land may have no camels. But the principle still holds true. Is the one you are attracted to willing to really *work* to make it? Is he willing not only to help, but ready also to go more than the second mile for you?

In picking kids for leadership, we found a simple principle. Each new volunteer would be given a tough physical job. The ones that stuck at it the best and did the cleanest work made the best leaders and the most trustworthy followers.

Here is a simple test you can try on that "angel" you have in mind. What do they work like? Are they willing to give marriage everything they have? Marriage only begins with a ring and a vow; it takes a lifetime to build. To begin with, find out how he treats his mother, his sister. How does she care for her father, her brothers? Talk with him and ask him what he thinks of your loved one.

Is he really serious about commitment? Has God delivered him from the casual liaisons of the street, and made him truly committed to Him and to others? Can you really trust him? Is he really giving of himself sacrificially to meet needs? That is what it means to water camels.

When she is not around one day, sneak a look at her room. Is it neat? Does she take good care of her clothes, of her appearance without being a slave of fashions? Is she really clean? Ask yourself: would I like my home looking like her room? Marriage will not drastically revise personal habits. What you see is about what you get!

And what about *him*, sister? Is he careful with the money God has entrusted with him? Is he generous where it is needed, and yet knows how to save when things get tight? Does he know how to be abased and how to abound? Is he kind to you now, or does he have bad habits that you just hope will change? It is God, not time, that changes habits. Don't marry anyone that hasn't got cleaned up from all known sin. Remember—no Canaanites!

To help take the edge off your romantic cloud, look at his father. Maybe he will look better when he is his dad's age. But then again, maybe not. Are you going to be happy with him after fifteen years even if he looks like that? ... the same goes for her mother. It may hurt, but it is better to think clearly now than to have to do it in repentance later. Remember, love is a wise, thinking choice. Don't marry anyone that doesn't pass this test: can they water camels?

6. "And the man ... held his peace, wondering whether the Lord had made his journey prosperous or not" (Gen. 24:21).

The servant learned what you will have to learn. He learned to *wait*, after he had set his signs and made his vows to God. And to find God's sweetheart for you, you must be willing to wait too. If God has called you to marry, He will bring your team mate on time. This means, of course, that you must first give Him the right to have you on His own, that you have given Him the right not to marry, if He thinks that is best. That is the only way true surrender to God can take place. Then, don't confuse the moving with the moment. If God shows you His one, that is the moving. Wait for the right moment.

40
Preparing for the Work God Has for You

While God makes plain His will for you, there are some things you can do in the meanwhile, in the years when you are seeking to know His purpose for your life. Don't be worried if you don't immediately know the night after you give your life to Jesus what God wants you to do! Sometimes He puts us through *training* to see if He can trust us before He will make clear what He has on His heart for us. Use the years of your early conversion to learn discipline and obedience from Him, and expect that He will open up the pathway for you. In the meantime, do these things:

1. *Follow your interests and abilities.* Find out what you can do well, and what you can't. Sometimes our backgrounds are part of God's purpose for us; the lessons we have learned from life, the responses and the choices we have made in the past, are all used by the Lord and woven into His ultimate purposes. God wants to use us as we are. You are different from anyone else in the world. Find out what makes you special. Sometimes God may use your talents; sometimes it is your very lack of talents that makes you very special to Him. Hudson Taylor said, "When God wanted to evangelize China, He looked for a man weak enough to use." Learn what you like to do well and what abilities you have.

2. *Have many interests in your teenage years.* Learn to do a lot of things, and be interested in more than just a few things you have already done. Try your hand out in different sports; they may help develop your body in different ways that will make it stronger and more serviceable for Jesus in the years ahead. Experiment with different *hobbies*; some of the things you learn in recreation times will become valuable tools in the future, especially ones like radio or electronics, photography, art or crafts. Try to develop the capabilities God has entrusted to you. Be enthusiastic about what you do! Really get into it, and get an

interest in as many things as you can. The more things you know a little about, the more people you may be able to reach for Jesus.

3. *Read about the things you'd like to do.* If you think God might be calling you to some form of missionary work, read biographies of famous missionaries. If you think God has called you to be a Christian artist, or a mechanic, or a scientist, read books about art, mechanics, and science. Read often and wisely. If you learn to like books, you'll have a wider picture of the world God wants to reach.

4. *Get some practical experience early.* Take a part-time job in the area of your interest. During holidays or vacation times, ask if you can just do some odd job around the place you would like to work in, and talk to others already on that job. On spare time, ask a lot of questions. Do they find it interesting? What does it cost in terms of time, study, and commitment? Can you advance in it? Will it take care of your financial needs? Of course, all jobs must be those that will honor God and help forward His creation; anything that is shady or morally tainted is totally off-limits to the child of God.

5. *Study God's Word.* Even secular jobs will benefit from a year or so in a good part-time Bible school or correspondence course in scripture. And *pray*; talk over new developments and disappointments with Jesus.

Section X
The Disciple &
SEX

41
The Purpose of Sex and Love

"For this cause shall a man leave his father and mother and be joined to his wife, and they two shall be one flesh" (Matt. 19:5).

God created and ordained sex. It is not evil or unholy. The Bible does not hesitate to praise the joys of a God-given, God-blessed sexual love in marriage. Sex is God's idea. He made it up! It is an earthly symbol of a great many things that are precious and sacred to Him as shown to us in the Bible. Marriage is the symbol of some of the deep and lovely truths of Scripture.

Study the relation of Christ to His Church and you will see a heavenly picture of the ideal earthly marriage. The wife gives up her own name and takes on her husband's. She merges her life with his; she recognizes him as her head and looks up to him as her support, protector and guide. She devotes her whole life to his happiness and to carry out his will in her love for him. She naturally looks to her husband to protect her from injury, insult and want. She hangs her happiness on him and expects that he will protect her, and he is bound to do it. Their reputation and interests become one; what affects her character or reputation affects his.

The faithful husband loves, cherishes and honors his wife; he gives of his time, his labor and his talents to promote the interests of his bride. And the faithful husband is jealous of his wife's good name and feels deeply when her feelings or reputation are injured. The Lord Jesus is the perfect picture of the faithful husband; His true Church, every real disciple of Jesus, is the perfect pattern of His loving wife (1 Cor. 18:20).

Likewise, a Christian family is the earthly pattern of God's longing for a heavenly family of sons and daughters to rule and reign with Him. In its God-designed place, sexual love is the most beautiful relationship on earth. It is His special gift to show us in symbol His ultimate purpose for man: to be in the Father's house and family, living in love and fellowship with Him and with each other forever (1 John 3:1-2).

Because God made sex in human beings such a special relationship, He set definite differences between animal and human sexual drives. Animal reproduction is sparked by automatic instinct laws that operate at certain times of the year. There is no love in these sexual couplings, just blind instinctual desires.

Human desire for sexual love and children is to be quite different. It is not automatic. It has been placed by the Creator under the sway of our human wills and thoughts. He designed it to awaken and work under our control. In early years this force sleeps hidden from our attention. As we grow older and grow up it becomes a strong energy in our lives that can be channeled into creative and joyous living, even if we are not yet married or do not use its potential in a sexual way.

Sex was given to us for two main physical reasons: to keep our race going on by men and women together bringing children into the world (Ps. 127:3-5), and as a source of deep spiritual and physical pleasure between a husband and wife (Matt. 19:4-6; Gen. 2:24-25; 24:67; Eccles. 9:9; 1 Cor. 7:2-5). The same Bible that gives stern warnings about the misuse of sex (Prov. 5:1-8, 20) clearly describes how sexual needs should be met to bring us great happiness in marriage (Prov. 5:15, 18-19).

The Bible does not teach us to hate sex, to consider it an unpleasant but necessary duty that is basically evil that must be done in order to keep the world going. People who ought to have read their Bibles more carefully sometimes thought that sex had something to do with the Fall. But Adam knew and loved Eve long before the Fall happened. Sex was not part of the sin of the Fall. God commanded sexual love. Sexual happiness and love were enjoyed by the first man and his wife long before sin came into the world. Men and women who should know better give the Bible a bad name by saying Christianity teaches people to think of sex as evil. The Bible never says that because it is simply not true. Sex is like any other gift that God gave men; used His way and in His time, it is beautiful, enriching and fun; outside of His laws which regulate its direction for happiness, it can be terribly painful and hurtful.

In the Bible we are warned that one sign of the last days will be men who "forbid to marry." There is nothing "more spiritual" about not marrying. A husband and wife who love each other can be as holy in their sexual relationships as a man or woman who have given their life wholly to others in ministry and foregone the right to marry in order to spend more time with people.

The Bible actually commands a husband and wife not to hold back from each other sexually unless it be by consent for a time so that they can give themselves to prayer and fasting (1 Cor. 7:5). This Bible command is a powerful force to weld marriages strongly together. There are many blessings realized when a husband will obey God to regularly meet his wife's sexual needs and the wife likewise to meet her husband's. The beautiful song of Solomon poetically and reverently describes some of the joys of this physical-spiritual blend of married love (Song of Sol. 6:1-10; 7:1-9; 2:3; 8:3). Marriage is to be held in honor, and sexual love in marriage is to be exalted as the highest physical pleasure gift God has given a young couple (Heb. 13:4).

Read the Bible and think hard on all the symbols that sexual love in marriage can tell us about spiritual truths. Only in the Bible is sex placed in its proper, lovely place. Only in the Bible is the woman's place in marriage uplifted and honored, where the husband is to be "intoxicated" by his wife's love, and where the Holy Spirit describes this union as a part of divine wisdom which God sees and approves (Prov. 5:1; 5:21). Sexual love in marriage, God's way, is tenderly beautiful.

In this love, there is a mutual giving and sharing which is unlike any other relationship on earth. Each partner invests of his life in the other, in a bond which makes them both grow more strongly in love with each other and more open and honest with each other. What happens in essence is that each one makes a little emotional home in the other's heart, a place where they can let down all their guards and barriers and be really honest and trusting with each other like little children. Sexual love builds this home. It is a place where two people in love can relax in each other's trust and love, secure in their care and giving for each other, a place where all the rough places of life they face together are smoothed and healed.

Sex is a precious gift. It is the way God has given us to show our love in the deepest possible physical way, to build a bridge of love that is not only the joining of two bodies in the most profound of pleasures, but the joining of two souls in a bond of happiness that will only be surpassed by heaven itself. Sexual love, God's way, God's time, is one of God's highest blessings.

42

Bible Words on Sex Without God

Sex is like fire. What happens when that fire burns out of control? Across your world this fire is burning the wrong way. Once let loose, it knows no boundaries, classes, ranks or positions. Hell itself feeds this flame with the fuel of unclean stories, dirty books and smutty imaginations.

Another name for this chapter could be "Dreams in Flames." That is what the sin of sexual immorality does. It can take a beautiful girl and turn her into a mottled diseased whore. It can take a man and make him worse than an animal. It can take your dreams and turn them into flames; it can take everything you hope for and leave you with nothing but smoke, ashes and a burned-out life.

Some of you know this from bitter experience. Thank God that to disciples of Jesus who have already suffered from this flame God gives the promise that He will "give to them beauty for ashes, the oil of joy for mourning, the garment of praise for the spirit of heaviness . . ." (Isa. 61:3).

Do you know why so many marriages crack up? Boil it down to the main reasons and you get two: people either get married too young, or get involved in some form of premarital sex that hurts them later. A fire is warm and wonderful on a cold night in a hearth under control; but that same fire if set loose can also burn your home down. There is no difference between the fire that comforts and the fire that kills; it is the same flame. When it helps it burns in the right place, under control and at the right time; when it hurts, it is in the wrong place at the wrong time, and out of control.

When you first discuss sex, it's a common temptation to want to test out sexual powers or prowess by experiment. Mothers don't help who push their little girls to act grown-up and who spend their waking hours making sure their daughters will be popular with the boys. It is often the same mother who is shocked and hurt when her little 14-year-old comes home pregnant and in tears because she became popular with the boys.

The "going steady" trip has laid the foundations of much divorce. It's nice to know that if you have somewhere special to go that Fitzroy or Tinsenella will always be there; but big problems begin when you spend so much time alone together that you are tempted to let down your standards and your moral codes. Parents once didn't let their kids get stuck in situations like this. They respected sexual chemistry enough to give kids tight discipline and limited time with boyfriends and girl friends.

It's the old story: familiarity breeds contempt. You can get too familiar with each other. Transfer it to your bodies, light the flame, let down your guards, lower your codes and you will fall right into trouble. And it's too easy to excuse sin when you get sexual attraction confused with love. You may find yourself saddled with responsibilities before you are ready to handle them.

Here is some advice about "going steady"—don't! Don't go steady unless you are really in love; don't go steady until you are both serious about getting married, unless you are ready to be a husband and a provider, or a wife and mother. Don't do it, because the odds are that you'll get into trouble. Going steady is one big reason why too many kids marry too young. They light a fire they can't honorably put out and are pushed by their own guilt into marriages that are finished before they begin. Marry too young, out of pressure from an early sex experience, and you'll have every chance of breaking up your marriage, your home and your happiness. Sex and love is not a game for children. Spend time just being friends with a lot of brothers and sisters in Jesus. Keep clear of unhealthy, exclusive attachments.

A safe rule is don't get "physically involved" with anyone until your wedding date is set. Now what does that mean? How far is too far? The Bible uses words that tell us exactly how far is too much. Many disciples of Jesus who have been on the streets and have known the hell of sexual sin know by experience what could violate their new life in Jesus. But it is also good to know that God has not left us in the dark here. The Bible has three words that exactly define where sexual problems begin, long before fornication or adultery or sexual perversion is committed. They are big words, which is why some Jesus people don't study them and why some preachers don't use them. They are the words *lasciviousness, concupiscence, and defraudation.* Now don't freak out over them. Each one is heavy with meaning and help. They tell us where wrong starts that winds up in actual acts of immorality. Here is what they mean and where they are found in the Bible:

1. *Lasciviousness,* used in a sexual sense, means to make a choice to turn yourself on sexually outside of God's limits in marriage. Any thought or action you deliberately make that stirs you up sexually when that desire cannot be rightfully expressed in marriage is the sin of lasciviousness. It is a choice of your will. The Bible tells us it doesn't come from temptation outside, but from the heart. No picture, book or sexually stimulating person can make you lascivious. If you are faced with a sudden temptation by seeing one of these, that desire is not in itself sin. The word lasciviousness means simply a *very strong desire.* It is used by the Lord Jesus when He talked about eating supper with His disciples, and by Paul when he talked of his longing to die and be in God's presence (Luke 22:15; Phil. 1:23). But strong desires become sin when we choose to turn them on.

How far *is* too far? The Bible gives us this answer in the word *lasciviousness*—anything that begins to turn you on sexually when you know you can't afford to be turned on. Too far is anything that stirs up sexual desire in your heart outside of God's ways. Necking has been defined as "an exchange of kisses and caresses, keeping both feet on the floor and all hands on deck." If necking turns you on sexually, necking is wrong for you. I know there are disciples of Jesus who can hug each other and not be wrong; but there are other kids who can't even look at someone of the opposite sex without sinning. God knows your heart. Remember, it is sin in the sight of God to make a choice of heart to stir up sexual desire when you know you can't go on with it and be right before the Lord. This is why masturbation is wrong before God; it is simply an expression of lasciviousness.

2. *Concupiscence* is another big Bible word that spells trouble in sex. It simply means to be caught in a strong physical lust for sex. It is an overexcited state of sexual focus; it is being so hung up on sex that you keep on going back to it again and again in your mind. It is being so turned on that you can't turn off. The Bible sometimes translates it "lust." It is this word that Jesus uses when He says, "But I say to you, Whosoever looks on a woman to lust after her has already committed sexual immorality with her in his heart" (Matt. 5:28).

Concupiscence happens when sexual fire begins to really burn out of control. It makes a girl parade her body before guys, and to wear a sign in her eyes, "For sale cheap. Slightly used." It makes a man give the X-ray treatment to every girl who walks past.

Concupiscence is no light matter before God. The Bible tells us it is one of the things He will judge in anger (Col. 3:5-6). We are not to let our bodies be bound by it, "even as the heathen who don't know God" (1 Thess. 4:5).

Lasciviousness leads to concupiscence. A little light necking can lead to a lot of heavy petting. And it will do you no good to pray and ask God to take away the desire for sex if you are doing all you can to keep it burning. God *made* sex. It is His idea. But He put its control under your will, and expects you to yield that will to Him. He can no more wisely take away sexual feelings from you than He can wish to make you a non-man or non-woman. Sex is like a time bomb with a long fuse. The fuse is lit by necking and it burns shorter by petting. Petting is a prelude to going all the way with someone—full sexual intercourse with them. That is reserved only for the love and responsible commitment of marriage. Long before actual sexual intercourse you can break God's law in lasciviousness and concupiscence.

Don't pet at all. Don't even start. If you have started, stop now before it gets any worse. Petting will add to your life, it is true. It will add guilt and shame. It will add dirt to your name. It can also take away. If you are a girl it can take away your boyfriend, because after you go further than you should he may decide you are too cheap and leave you. It can take away your virginity and so lead to pregnancy, break your parents' hearts and get you married too early, too soon or to the wrong person. God has reserved petting and sexual foreplay for one place— marriage, and marriage only. If you want to mess, go ahead! But be prepared to be part of tragic statistics. And remember this: no sexually immoral person will walk in white with God's new family. No true disciple of Jesus is a slave of sexual sin.

3. *Defraudation* is the last word. It just looks big with an *ation* ending on it. The Bible word is actually *defraud*. It defines the sexual sin that begins when you involve someone else. It simply means to turn someone else on sexually when you know you can't go through with it without getting into trouble. The original word means "to make a gain of" or passively "to be taken advantage of." Anytime you set out to capture someone's feelings of affection, when you deliberately choose to make them fall in love with you so that you can use them selfishly, you defraud. You don't even have to involve them sexually to defraud.

It is possible for a disciple of Jesus to unwittingly deeply hurt a brother or sister by giving them the impression that they are in love with them in more than a brotherly or sisterly way. Anything you do towards that impression is fraud.

But used in a sexual sense, defraud means to make choices and actions to turn someone else on, when you know good and well that it is wrong to do so. You cannot take advantage of someone else's trust and affection without getting into deep trouble from God. He says that no man should "go too far and defraud his brother in any matter, because the Lord is the avenger of all such, as we also have warned you before and testified. For God has not called us to uncleanness, but to holiness" (1 Thess. 4:6, 7).

Don't let the fire burn outside of God's controls and limits. You will not be able to stop it, and it will burn you badly and deeply. Sex without God is full of dangers. Do it, and you will not only get yourself and others into trouble, but you will also be in deep trouble with God. Sexual sin has terrible penalties. Ask any disciple of Jesus who has already been there once. Once you get into that, then only God can help you out of this fire, and even then it will leave scars that you might never erase.

43

Why Not Go All the Way Before Marriage?

"Can a man clasp fire to his chest and not be burned?" (Prov. 6:27).

"I came back to reality with a sickening thud. I wasn't drunk anymore. The party was over, and I felt sick, cheap and dirty. It didn't make me feel any better to hear him say, 'Why on earth didn't you stop us before things went too far? You should have known what would happen. You could have called a halt at any time. But you didn't.' "

"My mother and dad just found out that I'm pregnant. They were so shocked they just won't believe it. I'm only fourteen years old. They just stare into space and when they see me they break down and start crying. They say, 'It just can't happen—not to our little girl!' But it did happen. Now I don't know what to do or where to go. What future is there for me now? It happened so quickly; it just wasn't worth it. Could you please find a home for my baby when it comes and could you please give me some advice before I lose my mind?"

"It's not so bad if you've never loved anyone, because what you don't know won't hurt you. But if you're like me and have loved a guy before, what do you do when it has to end? I never used to have problems getting to sleep, but now I stay awake nights wishing I were back in some guy's arms again. And although I know it's impossible, I dream of all kinds of situations where he comes back and we make up and it's all beautiful again. But it never happens, and the memories never go away and leave me alone. If you really care, give me some answers quickly. Please help me!"

Sex is like an emotional hand grenade. It blows up so fast when the pin is pulled that lives can be shattered almost without warning and blasted forever. Necking and petting light a fuse of desire that will not easily go away. The trouble with petting is that it never just stops in one place. Thinking what is beyond makes it hard to be satisfied with less. It demands an ever increasing stimulation. Kids who once laughed at the Word of God and ignored the warnings of their conscience are now trying to put their lives back together because they allowed a fuse to be lit that cost them their purity. Listen to these burning words from David Wilkerson in his message, "Parked at the Gates of Hell."

Who but God could know what goes on in parked cars and secluded woods across this nation? Who but God could see what happens on nights like this when students test their moral courage and their codes; who but God could really know what sweethearts are allowing in their lives; what privileges are being demanded; what risks are being taken; who but God could see the whole picture? The Bible warns, "Can a man take fire in his bosom and not be burned?"

Young people break the laws of God and then excuse it by saying, "God made me this way; we're only doing what comes naturally; we're in love; God will forgive us anyhow; God knows our human weaknesses; He knows our hearts." It can happen so quickly; it can even happen on the way home from a religious service such as this. Too suddenly, in a frenzy of hugging and kissing and petting, the natural flame that God has put in the heart of every young man and woman begins to burn out of control before God's appointed time and without God's approval; and the devil keeps urging you on and whispering, "It's all right—you're in love, you belong to each other, you have a right—and even if you get into trouble he will carry you through, he'll stick with you, she'll stick with you—everything's all right!"

These stolen pleasures last only for a very short time, and then the roof caves in. One minute it can seem so right and pretty and so good because the devil can bring two young people together and make everything seem so pure and sweet and clean, when in actuality their lives are going through the filth and dirt and exceeding sinfulness of sin. Then as the pleasure ebbs away and the emotions are brought under control, it becomes dirty, wrong and sordid. One moment you thought it was real love, and the next you saw it for what it really was. It is then that these two realize they have parked right at the gates of hell and allowed Satan to deceive them.

The trouble with sex before marriage is that there is far more involved than just giving up your virginity. You can walk the streets and talk to kids who have really been around sexually —kids who say they know how to take care of themselves, kids who have grown up in the language and practices of the gutter who have learned to use sex as a weapon and a commodity and who have heard all the arguments against sex before marriage that they want to hear. But the problems that come into your life in premarital sex are not the usual ones that everyone talks about. No, you might not get pregnant. You might not be as dumb as the girl who took a birth control pill before giving in to her boyfriend, hoping that would protect her. You might have learned all there is to know about birth control methods so that you can trust your body to be chemically or physically blocked from its normal function. And, no, you might not get venereal disease either, although it is in runaway proportions throughout the world. The new virile forms of V.D. show no response to any known form of treatment, striking permanently and cripplingly at those who have played loose once too often to bring them disease, sexual debility and agonizing death or insanity. You might not have to have an illegal abortion, and die at the hands of some butcher who lives on girls who have lost the great debate and can't face it. These are all reasons, good reasons why sex before marriage is out for the disciple of Jesus, but they are not the basic ones. You may think that if you can only avoid these, sexual experimenting will be so cool you won't get burned, but you would be wrong.

God never gives His laws for fun. He always designs them for our highest happiness and holiness. Every advocate of sex before marriage adds three cancers to sexual happiness, three things that can never really be undone, three things that will destroy something beautiful. It will always happen no matter how careful people are and no matter what precautions they take. These reasons lie behind what happens with many young people who finally try marriage and just split up again; why many others no longer find ordinary sex beautiful or satisfying and turn to deviation, homosexuality or lesbianism. Have sex before marriage and you add three things to your sexual happiness that you can never get rid of:

1. *Guilt.* God has placed an alarm in your soul, a red light of warning to protect your integrity. It is your conscience. When you are about to lose control of yourself or hurt others it will sound, and you had better listen if it does. God made petting as a fuse to burn naturally down in marriage, with trust and love, to going all the way. You can't really give yourself to another until you feel free to give of your whole person to the other. Sex is not just physical. It is an investment of your life in someone else's. God made it to function in trust and love.

Experiment with sex before marriage and you will begin to learn about it in an atmosphere that is furtive, sly and secret, that is confined to wayside cabins, cheap hotels, out-of-the-way beaches and forests and parked cars. Sex outside of marriage is watchful, hurried, scared of interruption or discovery. And

here is the first problem: sex outside of marriage is always sex
learned with guilt. As the fuse burns down, you learn to feel guilty
with it. As you learn sexual surrender, you also learn to feel badly
about it. And what will that do to your marriage? You get used
to holding yourself back in fear, get used to being worried and
hurried, and you carry into your marriage guilty hands and
a soiled mind. The wound you give to your conscience may never
heal. Or if, instead, it hardens, you will join the ranks of the sexually sophisticated. That description means usually those who have
so burned out their moral sense and related nervous systems
that sex has simply turned into physical dexterity, and the other
person means nothing much more than a coke bottle.

2. *Fear.* Love means believing in the one you love. That means
trust. If you can't trust the one you love, you will hold back.
Fear and love are opposites in the Bible. You can't love someone
you are afraid of. Love without fear means to be able to fully
trust the one you love. And here lies the second problem with
going all the way before marriage.

Some people say, "Why not? We love each other. We're going
to get married anyway. If we're going to get married soon, why
not try out sex first? What difference does a scrap of paper make
anyway?" That philosophy is all right in its right place. But that
place is hell. Marriage is *not* just a scrap of paper. It is a public
declaration to each other before the watching world that you love
and are committed to each other. The waiting time before marriage
is just as important as the time after. It is important both to
you and to your fiancé. It says that you trust each other enough
to stay within limits, even when you want each other more than
anyone else in the world. It says that you trust yourselves not
to give in to temptation to indulge in pleasurable experience outside
of moral standards. If you both believe in real rights and real
wrongs, you have a chance to test it out before marriage. Give
in, and you blow your trust and your codes together.

So what? So then you add another ingredient to your future—
fear. If you have sex with each other before you've committed
yourselves publicly to each other in marriage, how can you be
so sure you'll stay trusting each other later? What guarantee
do you have in your heart that your partner will not give in to
sexual temptation with someone else later? You say you love
each other, but if you are not willing to keep faith with each
other through the pain of waiting before marriage, how do you
know you will keep faith after? What does that bit of paper mean
in marriage anyway? It means nothing—nothing but the public
point in time around which you prove to yourself, to each other

and to the world that you can be trusted to stay true. Jump the fence before marriage, and who is to say that you won't jump it again? And if you can't trust yourself or the other person enough to stay clean before you marry, you will always have doubt and fear, when some new sexual attraction comes his or her way, that that fence will be jumped again. And fear kills real love.

3. *Dilution*. Sexual love is such a deeply profound act that it is impossible to do without investing a part of yourself in that other person.

Rarely do the immoral realize the terrible price of sexual sin. The one obvious result of a dulling in normal sexual stimulation and a loss of excitement in natural forms of sexual intercourse seems to be deliberately ignored or justified away. The fact remains: Mix your sexual life with guilt by breaking God's rules and you will lose the power to have normal sexual satisfaction. You will be pushed by your own lusts into deeper, more bizarre forms of perversion until you find yourself doing things for sexual kicks that you never would have believed you would stoop to before you started in immorality.

This frustration is the source of hundreds of forms of sick sex that abound in our time—sexual involvement with groups, with animals, with machines; homosexuality, lesbianism, bisexual life-styles; sadism and masochism, hurt and torture, even murder—applied to sex in the name of "natural love." In sexual addiction, the wildest forms of insanity must be justified in a way that almost no other addiction could allow.

In some countries like Denmark, legalized pornography in books did not satisfy; dirty photographs were superseded by dirty movies, and that in turn by dirty live theater, and that even further by audience participation. Not enough. The latest has been films and plays making the holy and sacred bow to this perverse and poisonous addiction. Christ and the disciples are pictured as lechers and perverts. The masks are coming off; the true source of this insane drive towards hell is beginning to show itself as the demonic pressure it really is. Break God's rules, ignore His warnings, but once you choose the way of immorality, you are locked in absolute slavery to the consequences. And nothing or no one will ever get you out of lust if God gives up on you. You'll be hooked, and it will get worse, and that has to be the most damning addiction of them all.

44

Dealing With Sexual Hang-ups

"Blessed are the pure in heart: for they shall see God" (Matt. 5:8).

Perhaps you have already gotten into trouble with some form of sexual sin. Sex out of control is as addicting as drugs. If you really want to be free, deal with your heart, for the Bible says, "You shall love the Lord your God with all your *heart*." Take these steps to get right out and to be pure again before God:

1. *Be brutally honest with yourself.* Stop excusing what you did. Strip away all excuses that you have made for what you did. Don't tell yourself that it is "weakness," or, "God knows my heart," or, "I'm only doing what is natural." Reject the philosophies and moralities that have built a bridge for you to sin. Sin is not new. The same broken laws bring the same tragic results in every generation. Stop baptizing your sexual problem with any soft names. Call it sin, see it as one great habit of selfishness, and be willing to turn from the sin itself, not just be sorry for the trouble it has caused. No one can live a disciple life in the grip of sexual lust. God can free you only if you are willing to take sides with Him against it. Begin now, before conviction goes away and you start to feel cold and hard again.

2. *Make a gift of your love to God.* Ask God to forgive and cleanse you from the rotten things you have done. Let Him deal with the stain of your past through His blood. Ask Him for the courage to face up to what you have done, and get right. Ask Him for a new heart to love Him and serve Him as you ought.

Deal with your body. "Love Him with all your *strength*." You can do this by making a present of your body to the Lord. If you are a girl, you have taken that which is God's gift to you and wasted it. It was God's property that others used so cheaply. If you are a man, you took the temple of your body and used it like an animal. Misused sex has blown your purpose in life, bound you to a chain of mind and action habits that rise up against you whenever you struggle to break out. Now there is only one way out. Give up your life, give up your body. Give them back in their entirety to God. You have not taken care of them. Now give them to God as His rightful property. Let Him take ownership. From this time on, it will be not yours to use, but His. Take it part by part.

Begin now. Start with your hands. "Lord, take my hands. They have been defiled, and Your Word says, 'Cleanse your hands, you sinners.' Help me to keep them from doing wrong."

Then take your eyes. They have gotten you into trouble too many times. "Lord, here are my eyes. I am shaken by Your Word that says, 'If your eye offend you, pluck it out . . . it is better that you enter life with one eye rather than having two eyes to be cast into hell fire' (Matt. 18:9). I make a covenant with You and my eyes right now. I will not use them lustfully again. I will not look on that which stirs me up into sin (Job 31:1).

"Take my lips. I remember that Judas betrayed You with a kiss. I, too, have been Judas to You. Take a fire from Your altar of cleansing and touch my lips. Make them clean again to sing Your praises from a straight heart." Do this carefully. Give God everything (Rom. 12:1, 2). Deal with your relationships—"love your neighbour as yourself."

3. *Confess to the other person involved, and break off with him.* Write a letter, but don't tell him all the details of why you did. Sexual sin cuts so deep that everyone knows what was wrong. Do not go to see him in person unless you cannot help but see him, as this may only involve you deeper with him in your feelings, and that may start your problem all over again. You *must* break off with him unless you are engaged, in which case God may want each of you to really get right with each other and stay clean for His time in marriage. This will not be easy. It will be hard for you, especially if this has gone on a long time. But if you want to be free, you must do it (Matt. 5:28-30).

4. *Set up a prayer covenant with another disciple of Jesus.* If the other person doesn't know what you are going through, just relate that you have a great need for victory in your life and you would like support in prayer. If you are engaged, set up this prayer time with each other (James 5:16).

5. *Stay away from sources of temptation.* Avoid places where you will be alone together if that is a temptation, or stay away from the places where the person is who was party to your problem. Go out with a full crowd of disciples of Jesus. Stick together in a big family where you can have friends and learn to love without having to bring sex into it (1 Thess. 5:22).

6. *Get into some solid work and exercise.* Throw yourself into activities for God with all your energy. This will help channel the powerful drive of sex into more useful outlets. It will help release sexual tension and make your happenings more fun. Set yourself tough deadlines on all that you do. Don't waste time. Challenge yourself to meet everything in Christ with all your heart, mind and strength.

Section XI
The Disciple &
SCHOOL

45
Every School Needs Disciples of Jesus

"You are the light of the world. A city that is set on a hill cannot be hid" (Matt. 5:14).

If an angel came into your class and asked a sinner who was a Christian, would he point to *you*? Do your friends at school know you love Jesus?

Every school needs disciples of Jesus. There are a lot of things you can use later in the service of God if you will do your work in school well. Languages are useful if you are going to go to another country. Social studies will help you know how people think and live in other lands. Science subjects will teach you how to think clearly and test out what you believe. Classes in English and drama will show you how to speak and write so that people will listen to you. History can teach you what can happen to nations that honor God or forget Him. Biology classes will help you see what a wonderful world God made.

Of course, many of your teachers will not know Jesus. The books you are given to read will not talk about Him. A lot of your subjects will be given to you as if God had nothing to say about it at all. Some classes will really put down faith in Him. But you do not have to be afraid that these will make you lose your faith. If you will think harder, and spend more time asking questions of Christian friends, your faith will come out stronger. God is not afraid of being proved wrong. You will find that true faith really makes more sense than no faith at all and you will learn how to speak up for Jesus in a world that does not like to serve or love Him. What better place to learn than in school?

You must be clean. Paul sent out Timothy with faith and a clean conscience. Kids who hold sin in their hearts will lose their faith because it will not be real. The man or woman that really loves Jesus will find answers to the tough questions skeptical teachers can give them. Jesus will give you these answers if you will be faithful to Him and study His Word. "Keep a strong hold on your faith in Christ. May your heart always say you are right. Some people have not listened to what their hearts say." If you get into sin, doubt will slowly destroy your faith. You must set your heart to stay clean.

Do the best you can at school for His sake. This means school work, too. Set up a good place for study. Make it a habit to always study at the same place. Work hard, and work against the clock. Set yourself a time to finish in. Give yourself a race to see how fast you can do an assignment. Be neat. Take careful notes. Use different colors to help you see different parts of your study.

No one can really stop you from serving Jesus at school. You do not have to break all the laws of the land to share your faith. You must learn what you can do *in* them, and what you cannot do. If laws should be passed that really force you to disobey God, you must find a way around them.

Be on the lookout for newcomers to your school. The first ones that meet them should be disciples of Jesus. Look for the lonely, the hurt kids. If no one else is their friend, *you* be their friend. Some kids will stay away from you because they know you love Jesus. Some will laugh. But deep inside, most will really respect you. Set a good standard for others. Be known as one who sticks up for what is right. Don't follow the crowd. Be busy serving Jesus and you will not get into trouble.

There are many ways to speak for Jesus at school. Put posters inside your lockers. Put stickers on your bag and books. Wear buttons that witness for Christ. Buy good books that you can loan to friends. Meet a day a week for prayer with other Christians. Invite Christian groups and speakers in to sing or speak in classrooms or assemblies. Put up invitations to special Christian events on your school bulletin board. Have a good supply of effective tracts on hand in your locker. Carry your Bible with you and read it often.

46
Sharing Jesus in the Classroom

"Always be ready to tell everyone who asks you why you believe as you do. Be gentle as you speak, and show respect. Keep your heart telling you that you have done what is right. If men speak against you, they will be ashamed when they see the good way you have lived as a Christian" (1 Pet. 3:15-16).

You do not have to go to another land to be a missionary. Your own school usually has more people who do not know Jesus per square inch than heathen lands have per square acre. You do not become a missionary by crossing the sea, but by seeing the cross! Every person who knows and loves Jesus *is* a missionary; every person who does not is a mission field. And your school needs Jesus very much.

Most kids can hardly wait to get out of school. It is not always fun to go. A lot of subjects may seem boring, and tests can get pretty hard. If you asked some Christians why they wanted to leave school they might say, "So I can serve Jesus." If you have thought this, ask yourself these questions first: "Do the people in my classes know about Jesus' love?" Then think about this: not so long ago, a youth worker took a survey. He found that about 85% of all people who were getting saved were 18 or under. That means that only about 15 out of a hundred give their lives to Christ when they are over 18. He also found that about 90% of the kids who graduate from high school without being saved will never be saved—unless disciples of Jesus do something about it.

What are you doing about it in your classes? One young man gave his life to Christ in his senior year. He felt he had wasted so much of his life in not serving Jesus earlier that he actually talked his teachers into letting him come back an extra year in his senior class. It was hard to do it. It was humbling to study with the junior class he used to be above, while his friends all graduated and left high school. But that year he had time to win honors in many things through the school and lead scores of kids to Christ as well. You may not dare do what he did. You may not be in the senior class either. But you have the chance to share Jesus with one of the biggest groups of lost people you will ever meet in your life—your school.

Do these things if you want to count for Christ in your class. Take your studies to God. Treat each class like a hard mission field. Ask God, "How can I speak for You in this class, Lord?" Now take the homework and reports you must make for it. Look hard at each one. Let God open your mind to how they can be used as a tool for getting out the gospel to the kids and the teacher. Think of the classes where you can speak or write for Him! English (essays, free verse, poetry), speech (every speech about problems of the world being met by Jesus or His disciples), history (how God's people affected it for good), psychology ("Jesus is a soul man"), biology (there is another explanation of how life came here in the first place), art (pictures and posters that preach), music (new and old songs about Jesus), and any others you can think of.

Besides this, you can use your classes to train for later work in the world for God. Learn your languages well, and you will have different tongues to speak for Him in other lands. Study your society and its laws, and you will know what you can do to help put God's Word back in its right place. Use your physical fitness classes to train your body for His service. Think hard about other cultures and religions and you will see how the good news can go into the lands and customs of their people.

Do your homework—and do it well. Be someone who usually has good answers to problems your teacher sets. Be the kind of person kids can go to for help. Think of your class as a place you are trying to reach for God. Go slowly, and wisely. Walk softly before the Lord. Win their respect. Get through to your teacher by doing work well and cheerfully for Jesus' sake. Don't be phony, or try too hard. Relax in the love of God and show by your clean life and warm friendliness that you are not just some weird religious freak on some spiritual trip. Be natural so He can be supernatural in you.

Wait for questions or free rap times. Here you will sometimes find good chances to share about the Lord or His Word. Don't be a pest and keep on butting in at each class, but ask God each week to give you a good time for a well-placed word for Him. Jot down at home things that might open a witness in class. Think ahead, and try to guess the sort of questions you might be asked if you speak for Jesus on a subject. Above all, make sure you have your heart and your head ready to serve Jesus when He gives you the go-ahead in a class. Ask God for the gift of divine wisdom. You can tell what it is like by reading James 3:13-18: "Who among you is wise and understands? Let that one show from a good life by the things he does that he is wise and gentle ... the wisdom that comes from heaven is first of all pure. Then it gives peace. It is gentle and willing to obey. It is full of loving-kindness and of doing good. It has no doubts and does not pretend to be something it is not. Those who plant seeds of peace will gather what is right and good."

47

Witnessing to Your Teachers

" [Jesus] was sitting among the teachers. He was hearing what they said, and asking questions. All those who heard Him were surprised and wondered about His understanding and what He said" (Luke 2:42:46-47).

Teachers, too, need Jesus. Some teachers have problems that only He can take care of. Sometimes they may seem touchy or mad because they are hurt and lonely inside. Many have real needs in their own life. Many are teaching kids but do not have answers to their own problems. You do not know as much as they do in many, many things. But you do know the Lord Jesus. And God may use you to get through to a teacher how much He cares for them and loves them if you will follow the example of the boy Jesus.

You will see from Luke's account of Jesus' life here that He *listened* and *asked questions*. Teachers respected what He said because of the questions He asked. This is the way to witness to teachers. Your questions should show that you understand some things that not many people understand. Your questions should show that you do really listen. That means that you must show respect, and honor your teachers. Jesus did. Unless you do this, not very much you say will make a good impression on them.

How is your attitude toward your teachers? It is possible to be right and say the right things in the wrong way. We are not to try to do God's work in the devil's spirit. Don't be a smart aleck. Do not disobey God by trying to act as if your teacher is an absolute idiot in everything just because you disagree with him, or because he does not know Jesus. You are not a know-it-all. Don't act like one. If you have an argumentative, critical spirit, you will deserve it if your teacher makes you look like a fool in class.

It is not easy to speak for Christ in a classroom and to get both teacher and kids to listen. We cannot let ourselves get proud or try to put either side down. We must not do things that will make people resent us for the wrong reasons. If you want the class to be on your side when the teacher is teaching something against God or His Book, do it like Jesus would do it. Be honest, have good facts, show that you understand something of both sides of the question, and be willing to smile at yourself now and then. Be firm but teachable. Be willing to listen and also to admit your lack of knowledge when it is true. But don't try to turn your class against your teacher by prejudice or scorn. That is not God's way.

Make sure of your facts. Take time to get good ones. If you know you are going to get into a subject where you will probably have to speak up for Jesus, get ready early. Get some good books on it, and read up on it. Have facts from the Christian side ready. Wait and pray for a chance to put in your word for Jesus. You do not have to be bossy when you do this. If you have some words from qualified Christian men, say something like, "Dr. X is one of the top men in his field, and he had quite a different view. He said...." This means you will not speak strongly unless you are very sure of your facts. It is wise to say, "I may be wrong but I thought that..., " or, "Isn't there another side to this question?" Much harm can be done for the cause of Christ if you come on too strongly with something that turns out to be wrong. Have your facts backed up with reliable sources. The Bible says, "Prove all things; hold fast to that which is good" (1 Thess. 5:21).

You must *earn* the right to be heard. Make the class *want* to believe you by being the kind of person they can look up to. Always be kind. There is no excuse for the follower of Jesus to be biting and critical. God's Word tells us that we must "speak the truth in love." If you get some good facts that really put down something a teacher said, make it easy for him to back down. Give him the benefit of the doubt. Resist the temptation to make him look like a fool in the eyes of the class. Say, "I may have gotten the wrong idea on what you said. You didn't mean *that*, did you?"

Loan good books to your teacher that will help explain your stand. Ask older Christians for their advice on what you can give to him or her. Ask your teacher what his opinion is on the book, and challenge him in a nice way to read it. You could say something like this: "Here is a book that really has a lot of solid points for the opposite side of what you told us in class. How would *you* answer what this man has written?" Get good, factual tracts for him to look at that might go with one of the things you have mentioned in class. Wait until some person that is a Christian comes to your town, or is in the area, that knows a lot about a subject you have talked about in class. Ask the teacher if he could arrange to have that person speak in class to share his views so the class could see another side. Be honest about this. Do not lie or pretend just to get someone in, or you may get your teacher in trouble, and he will hate you for it. Finally, see if you can get your teacher in touch with an adult Christian more his age who could speak to him about Jesus. Invite him home for dinner if you have a real Christian family. Be ready to help in any way you can. And tell him you are praying for him. Then you *do* just that. He may be won to Jesus.

48

Sports and Sharing Jesus

"Do you not know that your body is a house of God where the Holy Spirit lives? God gave you His Holy Spirit. Now you belong to God. You do not belong to yourself. God bought you with a great price. So honor God with your body. You belong to Him" (1 Cor. 6:19-20).

We are told in the Bible that we are to take care of our bodies because they belong to Jesus. If we hurt them by being lazy or flabby we sin against God. To use sports as a way of making our bodies strong and healthy is one way to honor God's gift to us. We are to make the best use of the bodies we have in this life.

The Word of God uses a number of sports illustrations. Paul said, "We wrestle not against flesh and blood, but against the leaders and powers of the spirit world." In 1 Corinthians 9:24-27 he says, "You know that only one person gets a prize for being in a race, even if many people run. You must run so that you will win the prize. Everyone who runs in a race does many things so his body will be strong.... In the same way, I run straight for the place at the end of the race. I fight to win. I do not box the air. I keep working over my body. I make it obey me."

The Lord wants us to have strong, disciplined bodies. Jesus himself was a carpenter. A carpenter in Bible days had to be both strong and skilled. He was not lazy or sickly in health. The Bible tells us that He "grew strong in mind and body" (Luke 2:52). We are to love God with all our *strength* (Mark 12:30). If we use sports to do this, and serve Jesus with a better body because of our sports, God is glad. We must not, of course, take too much of His time with sports. If we spend too long a time just excercising our bodies, we can make it a god.

Charles Finney once said, "No amusement can be innocent that involves wasting precious time that might better be used for the glory of God and the good of man. Life is short. Time is precious. We have but one life to live. Much is to be done. The world is in darkness ... No time is to be lost." Sports, like any other way to amuse ourselves, must not become too important or too loved in our eyes. We must not let sports take God's place in the first seat of our lives. You can tell this has happened if you prefer a sport to some other work Jesus wants you to do. But if you have given your sport life to Jesus to do with as *He* pleases, you can use it mightily for Christ. Many men of God have been famous sportsmen before God used them. Billy Sunday was a baseball player. Billy Graham also wanted to be one. C. T. Studd, founder of the Worldwide Evangelization Crusade, was one of England's most famous cricketers. Jim Elliot, the missionary martyr to the Auca Indians, was a leading wrestler in his college days.

These men built strong bodies in their sports lives that were later useful in God's service. Every Christian ought to take up some form of exercise. Jesus and His disciples took long walks between towns in their ministry. Early morning running or brisk walks in the fresh air are good for you if you can do it. Tennis, swimming and other sports that give you a good overall workout for your body are wise ways to exercise, and are fun too. The true disciple of Jesus loves God with his body. He keeps it well with rest and good food. He does not eat foolishly. He eats the right things, and does not eat too much because he knows that he must "endure hardness, as a good soldier of Jesus," and that "no man that goes to war gets himself tangled up with extra things, so that he will please Him that has chosen him to be a soldier" (2 Tim. 2:3, 4).

He will not abuse his body with alcohol or drugs, or shorten his life and breath because he smokes. He does not party around until the early hours of the morning. He will not let himself get lazy because he knows he must not waste God's time. A true follower of Jesus makes a good athlete because he keeps his mind and body healthy for God's service.

The Lord Jesus will help you to play well. Peter Marshall said, "God is at home in the play of His children." The trials and pressures of sports will give you a chance to learn patience and forgiveness. You will learn to trust Jesus for grace when someone you play against is unfair or wrong. You will learn to choose right when it is hard. You can learn to earn respect both on and off the field or court by being tough in body and strong in faith. Team sports can teach you to get along with others and carry your share of the load. And many, many chances to witness to others can and will come in your sports times. Locker rooms can be places of witness. You will want to win, to play your best for Him. So when you go out on that track or field or court, go out for God! When you play, play for Jesus. Make each shot count for Him, put out your best because you are playing to the grandstand of heaven. And you will play the best games of your life because you will play for His glory. He will be watching you! And you will play to win.

49

Taking Your School for Christ

Begin an early morning prayer meeting with all who really want a revolution for Christ to happen on your campus. Do it at least once a week, preferably Monday. This will not be for *your* personal needs, but for the lives of other Christians in the school who are not yet on fire. Here you will claim people for Christ. Ask God to lay on your hearts one person that He wants you to talk with at school about Jesus. Spiritual revolution at school begins with one person at a time.

At the conclusion of this meeting, someone should hand out a new witness tool for the week. It may be a button, a poster, a ticket for a Christian outreach, a book like *The Cross and the Switchblade* or *God's Smuggler*, a new tract or modern language New Testament. This is what your outreach group will use during that week. Close this early; don't drag out the meeting or make people late. Keep it short and sweet.

At school, every revolutionary for Christ will pray that he has an opportunity to talk to that person who is on his heart, and that God will prepare his heart. And you will pray for the one God has laid on your heart every time the bell rings at periods! This will be just a sentence prayer, but it will serve to remind you of your responsibility. Then open your spiritual eyes and look for the opportunity to open for that one. Don't push for it—wait for God's timing. When it comes, use it to share whatever Jesus lays on your heart. That person must see that you really *care* about him even if he doesn't care about God or himself. Love him with the love of God so he feels it.

Every Christian must prepare to use that thing he or she is best at to influence others for Christ. All the sportsmen will go on the fields and tracks to play and perform for God. All scholars will work to be the most diligent and informed men and women in their classes on their subjects. All the talented will pray that

God will make them the most outstanding people in the school, and work for it. The one difference will be this. When you are asked the secret of your success, you will speak for the glory of God. When people make friends with you because of your gifts, you will use your standing to influence them for Jesus. Each revolutionary will use his gift to help others who do not know Jesus, until a growing nucleus becomes involved in this "magnificent obsession" for Christ and His kingdom.

Make available the best training materials you can lay your hands on for the new Christian task force. Let them understand that to love God with all their hearts does not exclude the command to love Him with all their minds. Challenge them to tithe their time—two to four hours a day for study, prayer and witness. Have them buy out of their own pockets the best follow-up material and tracts for new Christians so they will read them and use them wisely.

Do not hedge on the conditions of true discipleship. Lay it out straight to those who are interested in following Jesus. Tell them that becoming a Christian involves the surrender of *everything*. Do not try to make it easier than Jesus did. If you are too soft here, your revolution will never get off the ground. One person who makes an easy decision that God will not honor (who will discover that his profession did not work) will turn off at least seven others by his nonexistent testimony. Make it plain that they must give up everything to follow Jesus, or they cannot call themselves Christians. Nothing less is true Christianity (Luke 14:25-33).

So love the kids in your school and show that you are willing to *die* for them. They will feel it and respect your stand. It will put tenderness in your warnings, compassion in your counselling. Make sure that all you do flows from a genuine concern for the hurt God feels in His heart over the sin of the kids in your school. No matter how good your methods, how true your message, without God's motives your work will come to nothing. Why should you take your school for God? Because kids are overdosing on drugs, tripping out and becoming suicides, and they need help? Because someone must do something before the Church becomes a back number? Because all the teachers are unbelieving and agnostic? These may all be true but cannot be the basic reason why you should take your school for God. Because *God is being dishonored by the sin of your school!* When you let *your* heart break with the things that break *His* heart, you will see spiritual revolution on your campus.

Nothing less than absolute commitment to Christ and His cause will suffice. One of Lenin's opponents was asked why he feared him. He said, "Because there is no other man who thinks and dreams of nothing but revolution—twenty-four hours a day." And so must the Christian revolutionary. Every thought must be brought into captivity for Christ. Every class must be the opportunity for a word on Jesus' behalf. Every gift must be bent towards spiritual awakening, every sport made the vehicle of witness, every leadership position the target for takeover by a disciple of Jesus!

Section XII
The Disciple &
THE SYSTEM

50

Don't Live Like the World

"Don't copy the behavior and customs of this world, but be a new and different person with a fresh newness in all you do and think" (Rom. 12:2, The Living Bible).

What *is* the world? It is not the planet earth which God gave us to enjoy. Right through His word, God warns us to not live like the world around us. "Pure religion is to keep yourself clean from the sinful things of the world" (James 1:27). "He [Jesus] gave Himself to die for our sins. He did this so we could be saved from this sinful world" (Gal. 1:4). "Because of the cross, the ways of this world are dead to me and I am dead to them" (Gal. 6:14).

We see from reading the Bible that the world is the system of ideas and ways of living that are evil, against God, ruled by the devil and headed for hell. The true disciple of Jesus has been saved from it, and must refuse to live like it, keep clean from it, and to remain against it. There is no such a thing as a worldly Christian. God says, "If any man love the world, the love of the Father is not in him" (1 John 2:15).

Living like the world does not have to do with *things*. Worldly living is a heart attitude. It is a spirit of giving in to selfish ways of life. It is to copy the standards of lost people, instead of living like Jesus. The real disciple of Jesus does not live like the world around him. If you want to serve Jesus, you will not copy the fads and fashions of our selfish society. You will take your standards from the Lord Jesus and from His Book, the Bible.

Resist the temptation to do what is "in" at the time. The way of the crowd is usually the wrong way. The disciple of Jesus has been called to go against the crowd. The world is against God. If we want to follow the Lord Jesus, we must go against the world's ways. Remember, if everyone who is selfish is *for* it, God is usually *against* it.

Do not try to do God's work in the world's way. There are many things that we can use for Jesus to do His work in a better way. The tape recorder, television and film have all been used for Jesus to bring lost people to Him. No one thinks that in a modern world we ought to use oxen and carts instead of cars and planes to take us to places where God wants us. Some things can be used to make our task to reach the world more simple. But no new method can make the job of touching and changing people's lives in Jesus easier. It cost God His Son. It cost Jesus His life. To share Jesus will always cost us something too. Do not give in to the world's ways of doing things. We must not make God's costly gift of life cheap by worldly methods.

Sometimes disciples of Jesus follow the world's ways without knowing it. Whatever new thing is "in" they take pains to show that Jesus says the same things. If drugs are in it is easy to say, "Jesus will get you high too. Jesus can also put you on a 'good trip.' " It is good to speak in ways that the world will understand. We must always speak in words that lost people can grasp. But we are not free to put Jesus and His standards into someone else's mold. He is the standard by whom all lives must be measured. And serving Jesus is not a "trip," not just a way of feeling good or leaving problems behind. If long hair is in, everyone says Jesus had long hair without ever reading His Book first to see what it says. What will we do if *bald* heads come in? Do not tie the Eternal God to the changing fads of the world. He does not change. He is the same.

Now I know it is hard to be lonely. Many kids today would rather sell their souls than feel left out of the crowd. They would rather mix in with a crowd that is rotten than walk out if it means standing alone to do right. The youth culture shows constant change from idea to idea, a series of searches to bring kids together without God. About the only things most of these ideas have in common is that they all were things kids could do together. Most of these ideas became merely what was "hip" at the time and were not seriously practiced.

The need to belong can be a real addiction. It can be just as strong as drugs or sex. And Satan knows this. If he can make Jesus just another fad, if he can make the gospel just a cover to bring people together without their need to change their hearts, he will have success in using the gospel against the gospel. If kids can unite around Jesus, not because they really believe or act on His words, but because it is what is bringing people together, he can fool the world. Look around you. Jesus is being sold for the wrong reason and is being sold out. He is not presented as a threat to wicked living or to the hang-loose trip, but merely as the next step in the evolving drive to "get it all together." No, mark it down clearly. If we follow the Bible Jesus, we will not go the way of the crowd. The way of the crowd is the way to hell and death, and the disciple of Jesus is the one person against the crowd.

51

What About War?

"If God is a God of love, why doesn't He stop war?" Have you ever thought about that?

Wars are terrible blots on the pages of man's history. There have been less than 300 years of peace in the past 4,000 years. Why do men go to war? The Bible tells us where wars come from. "What starts wars and fights among you? Is it not because you want many things and fight to have them? You want something you do not have, so you kill. You want something but cannot get it, so you fight for it. You do not get things because you do not ask for them. Or if you *do* ask, you do not receive because your reasons for asking are wrong. You want these things only to please yourselves" (James 4:1-3).

The Bible says wars come from selfishness. If men were not selfish, war would not exist. God is very grieved over wars that men fight. Death, bloodshed and separation are not what He wanted for His world. But He gave us the power to choose, to know and love Him or reject and refuse Him. The way is always open for us to be bad if we are able to be good. If men insist on being selfish, wars are bound to happen.

"Why does God allow war?" One answer to that question is the answer to another one: "Why does God allow men to be wrong?" Both problems have the same answer. If we are really going to be free, we must be free to choose wrong as well as right. And we have done wrong, despite all the care and love and warnings God has given us about sin.

Why did God sometimes send a nation to fight against another one in the Bible, and sometimes tell them to wipe it out completely? Think about a famous surgeon who has a friend. He notices a small growth on his friend's finger. Tests show that the growth is cancer. The surgeon cares for his friend. He also wants him to keep his finger. He treats the cancer to make it stop growing, but it does not respond. Instead, it grows a lot bigger. What can the surgeon do? The cancer is now covering his friend's whole finger. The surgeon is faced with a hard choice. He must either keep treating the finger and hope the growth will stop, or he must cut off the finger. This will mean death, blood and separation for the finger, but it is the only other way to stop the cancer from eating into the whole arm and body. He must decide at last on what he thinks is best, and act.

Think now about how God feels. Sin is like a cancer. It is the awful result of something good God gave us that we have turned into evil. If a nation sins against God and begins to infect others, God must decide what to do about it. If the people will turn from sin, God can spare the nation. But if they do not, He must decide how He is going to stop the evil from spreading. He may use other nations as His instruments to cut off this growth of death from the rest of His world. One of the ways He allows is war. The awful results of man's sin are never more clearly seen than in war. Sometimes war wakes men up so they can see just how bad they have been.

No Christian should fight in a war unless he is convinced of two things: that war is the only possible other choice besides a greater evil; and that he can take part unselfishly, to do this for the glory of God, and to love his enemies. This does not mean he will be soft or feel good about wrong things the enemy he fights against does. But it does mean that he longs to find a way to show mercy wisely and to forgive those who hate him. Unless a Christian is sure of these two things, to go to war is sin for him. Each one of us must go to God and ask Him what He feels and thinks about a war which we may be involved in. Each of us must decide for himself as God shows us.

God hates war because He loves the people who are hurt by it. Nobody ever wins a war. But when people will not be wise and good, what can He do? He can only let them hurt each other, and hurt His great heart, or step in and stop them himself. Now if two people really wanted to fight, and you stepped in to try to stop them, what would they do? They would fight *you.* And if you were *God,* that would not even *be* a fight, if you wanted to use force. To fight against God would mean the end for anyone, no matter how big or how strong he was. So God has chosen to let himself be hurt rather than step in.

Why doesn't He stop war? He could. He could stop all war, and do it very easily. He could stop every war in the world in the next sixty seconds. He could do it just by giving in to His hurt feelings, and wiping out in anger every selfish person on earth.

But how many people would be left in sixty seconds to enjoy the new peace and quiet?

The disciple of Jesus believes God is going to stop war. He will stop all wars. But, as C. S. Lewis puts it, "When the Author walks on stage, the play is over." I wonder if people who complain about how long God is taking to stop war really know what it means. When He comes back to this planet in person, it will be the end of the world. The Bible tells us, "The Lord is not slow in keeping His promise as some people think. He is waiting for you. The Lord does not want any person to be punished forever. He wants all people to be sorry for their sins and turn from them. ... We are looking for what God has promised, which are new heavens and a new earth. Only what is right and good will be there" (2 Pet. 3:9-13).

52

God's People and Their Country's Government

"Every person must obey the leaders of the land. There is no power given but of God, and all leaders are allowed by God. The person who does not obey the leaders of the land is working against what God has done. Anyone who does that will be punished. Those who do right do not have to be afraid of the leaders. Those who do wrong are afraid of them. Do you want to be free from fear of them? Then do what is right. You will be respected instead.... You must obey the leaders of the land, not only to keep from God's anger, but so your own heart will have peace" (Rom. 13:1-5).

With these words God tells us how disciples of Jesus must live under the leaders of their countries. The world has many forms of government. God has not told us which one is best because it depends on the people in each land. But the Bible says to us here that God will give a nation the kind of leadership it deserves.

People cannot get together unless they can know the same facts and do the best with what they know. Unity is based on common knowledge and common unselfishness. Since we do not have all the same facts or knowledge, we need people to show us what is true and valuable. We also must do what is right, so people need someone who can make sure everyone does the right things. This is why we need government. There can be no true peace or freedom without it. God has His own government.

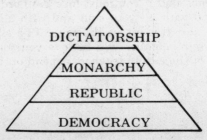

DICTATORSHIP

MONARCHY

REPUBLIC

DEMOCRACY

As long as people live together, there must be some form of guidance and information. Without it we cannot be happy together. Without it we cannot have peace.

When a nation has a lot of people that are both wise and good, God can let that nation have some form of democracy. In a democracy, people lead themselves by making laws that are best for all the nation. If people are less wise or good, God may allow a form of republic, where a nation picks some small groups to give them rules to live by. If a nation gets even less wise or good, God may let a king take control. We call this a monarchy. A king has a lot more power over the people, and less people tell him what to do. If a people get so far from God and from right, if they become both foolish and evil, God will let a dictator take over the country. He is a man with absolute power.

This is important. God gives a nation the leaders it deserves. In Proverbs 8:15, 16, God says, "By me kings reign, and princes decree justice. By me princes rule, and nobles, even all the judges of the earth." Because God allows our form of government, it is not for Christians to attack or seek to overthrow the form of government. It is the kind that God knows our country most needs. This does not mean that the person God allows to lead will always be good or wise, but he will be the kind of person God needs to hold the nation together. We must respect the position God has allowed him to have, even though we may not agree with everything he does. He may not be a Christian at all (like Nebuchadnezzar, in Daniel 1-4), but he is the one God has put into the place of a leader, and we must respect him for it.

Because of this, we are to obey the laws of our leaders—with one exception. If a leader passes a law that goes against God's laws, disciples of Jesus not only have the right but the responsibility to disobey. They not only *can* disobey, but they *must* (Acts 5:29). No law is a true law unless it admits that God has the final say in human affairs. No law is a true law unless it has its roots in God's love-law. We cannot and must not obey any order that commands us to be selfish and to sin.

The Lord Jesus said, "You must love the Lord your God with all your heart and with all your soul and with all your strength. This is the first and greatest of the laws. The second is like it: You must love your neighbor as you love yourself. All the laws and the writings of the early preachers depend on these two laws" (Matt. 22:37-40).

53

How Can Christians Change the System?

If our leaders tell us to do something that God has not forbidden, we must do it to honor God. If we disobey because we do not like it, or because we think it is too hard, we are really disobeying God, because we are not doing what He says to do.

If we feel that God wants us to do something differently than what a leader has asked us to do, and there is nothing God has said in His Book that can stop us, we must do something different. We must ask God to change our leader's mind so that we can both obey and do what we feel God might want us to do. The Bible says that God can do this when He wants to. "The king's heart is in the hand of the Lord, as the rivers of water: he turns it wherever he wants to" (Prov. 21:1). If we pray and ask God to do this and He says no, we must not go by our feelings but by God's written Word. We must do what He has said and obey our leaders, even if it is hard, for Jesus' sake. We must "give to Caesar the things that are Caesar's, and the things that are God's we must give to Him."

How can Christians change the system? Does the Bible teach any ways by which we can change the way people live, and make our rules more fair and our life more happy? Think of two men who came to Jerusalem. One was a trained revolutionary. He was skilled in violence; he knew the tactics of fear and war. He came because he wanted to change the system. It needed to be changed. There were a lot of bad things happening to his people. He believed he could change it. He even murdered people to do it. But his revolution did not work. He was caught and thrown into prison. His name was Barabbas. You can read about him in the Bible in Matthew 27:16-26 and in Mark 15:7-15.

The trouble with Barabbas was that in trying to change the system he forgot that *he* was in the system. He saw the greed, the injustice and the wrong in his nation. He did not like what it did to him or to his friends. But what *is* the system? The system is *people*. Barabbas had the same evil in his heart that he hated in others. And no system can be changed until you find a way to change the people in it. The trouble with his revolution was that it was not revolutionary enough. It tried to change the outside, when the real problem was the inside. It dealt with the leaves and branches of the problem, but not the root of it. And no one can really change the world for better until he himself has been changed that way. No one can make his world unselfish until he has solved the problem of selfishness in his own life. How could Barabbas think to overthrow greed, stealing from others, and the violent invasion of other people's rights and lives when he himself was a robber, a thief and murderer?

They put Barabbas in prison. They took the other Man who came to Jerusalem too. He had come to change people. His way was not the way of hate and fear. He knew how to change people inside, so that the world would become right outside. But they were more afraid of this Man than they were of Barabbas. It is always easy to deal with men like Barabbas. You just crush him with power and death. But you cannot do that with the message Jesus brought. So they let Barabbas go and crucified Jesus. No one ever heard of Barabbas again. But in less than fifty years, it seemed as if half the Roman Empire had become followers of Jesus. Now you tell me who won the revolution.

This is God's way of changing the world. We must deal with problems at the heart. Problems start with people, in their heads and their hearts. God has power to change people in both places. And when people really change, in both high and low places, the system will change. This is God's way of changing the world. The early Christians knew how to do this. People said of them, "These that have turned the world upside down have come here also." It is not easy to change people God's way. It cost God His Son. It cost Jesus His life. But if we pay the price, we can see our world changed.

Here are five things God has given us to preach about and do if we are going to see real changes in the world. We must do them. Think about them, and put them into action:

1. *Every-believer evangelism.* Every disciple of Jesus must be trained to win others for Jesus, and in turn train the others to do the same thing.

2. *Confession and restitution.* Society is ruined by sin. Confession and restitution is God's way of putting things back together, to undo some of the harm sin did.

3. *Reproof and rebuke.* This is God's way of stopping sin

before it grows. We must learn to speak out without fear against the things God has said are wrong.

4. *Social reform.* If we really love Jesus, we will love people. True love for men means we will work and sacrifice to meet their physical and spiritual needs. See what changes occurred in the lives of people when men of God like John Wesley and William Booth set out to bring men back to God and to set them on their feet again for Him!

5. *Prayer and fasting.* Earnest, concerned prayer makes it possible for God to pour out His Spirit and to work miracles in key places of leadership. Nations have been spared from judgment by Christians who cared enough to agonize before God. It is time we tried these things again. They are part of the good news of Jesus. (See chapter 79.)

54

Revolution, Revival and Reformation

Whenever God gets ready to change a form of government, He allows the country to come to the brink of *revolution.* If no repentance occurs, revolution will. There have been many revolutions in history, although not all of them have been violent or warlike. If God sees that a country needs to change, He will allow some form of revolution to take place.

Sometimes in kind sorrow God has given people new forms of rule when the people reject His leadership. The root of non-Christian revolution is a rejection of God and His truth. If people return to God and His Word, He can restore a land without judgment.

God says in His Word that He must judge a nation if it gets into sin. He has done this every time in history, although He always looks for a way to show mercy and spare it, especially if people are ignorant of His ways and His Word.

Do Christians have a way to help their country avoid revolution? Yes! God is looking for an important number of people to become *wise* again and an important number of people to become *good* again. If enough people meet these conditions He can spare the country from judgment. In 2 Chronicles 7:14 He says, "If my people, who are called by my name, shall humble themselves, and pray, and seek my face, and turn from their wicked ways; then will I hear from heaven, and will forgive their sin, and will heal their land."

To turn from sin, to begin to obey God again, to live cleanly and lovingly again, is what we call *revival.* Revival does not begin in the world; it begins in the church. Revival means to live again. You can only revive something that has lived before. The careless sinner cannot be revived; he has never lived! The world needs evangelism but this cannot happen until the church has revival. The divine order is revival in the church, then evangelism in the world. Revival is nothing more than a "new beginning of obedience to God." This is the first condition of social change without the violence of revolution, when Christians can unite in true love and can have a common unselfish concern for God, for each other, and for their world.

The second condition has to do with a return to true wisdom. This means knowing what God has said is true about our world. We call this return to truth and wisdom *reformation*. While revival has to do with obedience, reformation has to do with knowledge. Revival solves the problem of selfishness; reformation solves the problem of ignorance. Reformation makes people wise; revival makes them good.

This means it is not enough to just do what we now know God wants us to do, and to challenge our world to obey God. Both revival and reformation must come if a nation is to change to the Christian way. We must take steps to find out more of what God has said in His Book and spread wisely the knowledge of His Word across the land "till the earth shall be filled with the glory of God, as the waters cover the sea."

How many people must become Christians before God will spare a whole nation from judgment? If God was willing to spare both cities of Sodom and Gomorrah for ten righteous people, He is very, very merciful and kind. No one can tell the number for whom He is willing to hold back His judgment. But if a significant percentage—for example, 10% of a country—had a voice for God, it is quite probable that God could withhold His sentence.

We have had revolutions before. Yes, they do often mean agony, bloodshed and death in the land. But they do not bring lasting change, and they will happen again and again. All that a revolution can do is to change around things that already exist. What God offers is far more than revolution. Revolutions cannot change the heart. God does not merely reshuffle old orders. He creates a new order in society by setting up divine order in men's hearts. The gospel is not revolution, but recreation. It is God doing something that has never been done before.

There still may be time to claim this promise for the nation: "If my people, who are called by my name, shall humble themselves, and pray, and seek my face, and turn from their wicked ways; then will I hear from heaven, and will forgive their sin, and will heal their land" (2 Chron. 7:14).

William Booth said, "God loves with a special love the man who has a passion for the impossible."

Section XIII
The Disciple's
SOUNDS

55

Music Has Power to Get to You

The voice of youth is the voice of music. Music is the single biggest link of young people around the world. It has become the way young people of our time share all their fears, hopes and ideas. Many young people today do not read a lot of books. Kids brought up on TV have grown a taste for indepth feeling, although they know they can't always watch a screen. But music can go everywhere. You don't have to think hard to listen to it.

Youth music has seen very fast changes over the past twenty-five years. Rock music has become the number one means of young people talking to each other. Record sales in the U.S.A. climbed from less than 200 million dollars in 1954 to close to one billion dollars in 1968. About 70% of this was pop music. In 1955 most homes owned a radio, but by 1965 over half the 10 to 13 year olds had radios of their own! New hits are instantly spread over the world through radio, TV films and records, and groups appearing in person. The whole world is listening to music. The church, too, is writing new songs and creating new sound. Disciples of Jesus must take care not to copy the world's sounds without thinking.

There are some kinds of sound that God cannot bless because they can actually hurt our bodies or our minds. We must not let ourselves feed on such sounds or we will grieve God. Neither must we use these kinds of sounds as part of new church music.

This is not to say that any new sound must be a bad sound. Sometimes parents are not fair to young people who are trying to write new songs. Just because people are used to one kind of music does not make that sound the only one Jesus can honor. Some church adults have been unfair in this area. It might help if they could see that many of the hymns and choruses of today that they think are Christian tunes shocked the Christians of a century ago. They were used to another kind of Christian music.

A century before that, people were shocked even to hear organ music go with Christian singing. Jesus and His message never change, but times do. We must not mix up which is which! Each new song must be judged by itself, not by the standards of "Christian" fashion or culture. We must judge by the Bible, not by our own tastes or ideas.

Parents must be careful not to let culture get in their way of deciding what is Christian music or not. They can make mistakes here three ways: (1) By thinking only quietness in music is reverence; (2) by feeling angry at music being too loud; (3) by being put off because new musical instruments and forms are used.

There is a place for quiet. We need times to be still and wait on God. There are some kinds of soft music that help this mood. But there is other music in the Bible. There are sounds of praise and worship that are loud and bright with joy. Worship does not always mean quietness.

Kids today do not just like to _listen_ to music. They have learned to _live_ in it, be a part of it. They have a habit of making all their music loud. And often it is far louder than parents are used to.

Parents often put things like guitars and drums automatically into the bad bag. Yet forms of these were used in the Bible. God has not told us to outlaw new instruments.

No one has the right to say what new Jesus music will sound like. God has some sounds for His children no one has ever heard yet. The Holy Spirit is deeply creative and can make all kinds of new music that brings glory to Jesus. All over the world, wherever God is moving, people are writing new songs of praise. Every revival has brought with it two things: deep sorrow for sin and intense praise. That joy always comes out in song. When the Lord Jesus really saves from sin, He may give them a new song in their mouths. We do not know what these new songs will sound like. But we can to some degree say what they will _not_ sound like.

56

Don't Let the Media Be Your Master

"How shall we sing the Lord's song in a strange land?" (Ps. 137:4).

Music has great power to affect our lives. You know how easy it is to feel a little afraid when someone plays spooky music on a dark night. But a happy song in the same place can make the whole room seem different. Because there are many different ways of people giving you messages in music, you must be careful to listen only for the glory of God.

Most people do not listen to records or tapes just because they like the singer or the song. People get records because they feel what the singer is saying, or because they want the kind of feeling that that record gets across. This means that most people really like only songs they can identify with, the songs they themselves can sing. This is also often true about singers. People buy their recordings because in the back of their minds they like to pretend that they can sing like them. That is why not all of today's singers have good voices. If a kid can sound like the one he admires, he does not mind how that singer sounds. It is easy to make idols of rock stars.

This is one of the key dangers of the secular music world. It is so easy to grow to like a catchy tune and, by putting things together in the back of one's head, grow to look up to and admire the singer. And the trouble with this is, the singer may not be the greatest kind of example in the world to look up to.

The Lord Jesus warned us against taking our standards from the world around us. If we allow our admiration for a recording artist to lead us into sin, we are not followers of Jesus. If we spend more time in listening to records than we do listening to God, we are hurting Him. If we sing more about the world than we sing about Jesus, we can know where our hearts are really fixed. When the Lord Jesus is at the center of our lives, He is our life, He is our love, He is our song. He must be number one, or He is not our Lord.

Do not go to places where you know there will be sound loud or freaky enough to bend your head, or where there will be light shows and psychedelic displays that will affect your mind for evil. Stay away from media that you have no control over. If you let yourself get in a place where something begins to take over you, you have gotten away from Jesus. Paul said, "Think of yourselves as dead to the power of sin. But now you have new life because of Jesus Christ our Lord. You are living this new life for God. So do not let sin have power over your body here on earth. Do not give any part of your body for sinful use ... Sin must not have power over you" (Rom. 6:11-14).

The same applies to TV and the films. We must not deliberately expose ourselves to influences that will turn our hearts from God. We dare not let our hearts and minds feed on ideas that can take control of our thoughts. Some scene can be carried by a screen that can make a permanent mark in our memories for life. The TV and film media are more powerful than simple sound. To make sense of what happens on the screen you must be fully involved in what is being shown. Be careful what you watch. There is a knob on a TV screen that turns it off. Use it when God speaks to you in warning. You do not have to go to a movie just because everyone else has gone. You must ask God to help you in being careful about what you watch. If you just have to see something, it will be good discipline for you to not go, just to prove to yourself and to Jesus that nothing rules your life except His love.

Neither ought a disciple of Jesus think that just because he could sing or play before, that Jesus wants him to now. Jesus does not need our talent. Jesus wants *us*. If our talent takes His place, we are wrong. Every disciple of Jesus with talent must be willing to give it up forever if Jesus asks him. Until that has happened, we do not truly belong to Jesus. This may be hard sometimes. But Jesus did not say, "You shall have no other *bad* gods before me." He just said, "No other gods." And He meant it.

57

Ideas in Music

It is important that Christians stay in touch with what is happening around them. We must retain our sense of what the world is like so we will know how to reach it for Jesus. We are in the world, but we are not to be *like* it. Jesus said to His Father, "I have given Your Word to My followers. The world hated them because they do not belong to the world even as I do not belong to the world. I do not ask You to take them out of the world. I ask You to keep them from the devil" (John 17:14-15). We are to live holy lives but not be hermits. Living in a *hole* will not make us *holy*! We must know what the world is doing so we can speak in the language they will understand when we speak for God and right. But there are some things we must watch. The ideas which worldly songs get across can stick in our minds. If we are not careful we will mix these into our Christian thinking. Worse still, we may come to think that that is the way things really are and accept wrong things as right.

You have all heard ideas like, "No adult understands young people"; "Old people never know where it's at"; "Never trust anyone over thirty." Scores of songs over the past ten years have sold this idea. Bob Dylan's song, "Times Are A Changin,' " was one of the first with its "Come, mothers and fathers throughout the land; and don't criticize what you can't understand." Of course, there are a lot of adults who don't know where it's at. But there are just as many kids with the same problem. The Bible tells us to respect the advice of the old and not put them down. Some of us may even live to be over thirty ourselves. *Then* what will we say to our kids?

The "now" ethic says that only *today* is important, that we should forget the past, and no one needs to think about history. Many songs have wiped out faith that there will be any future, starting far back with songs like Barry McGuire's giant hit, "Eve of Destruction." (A lot of kids do not care about the past. Yet if we don't learn from it we will make the same mistakes people made before us. History is important. The Bible is a history book.) The future also means something to the Christian. God has a "new world coming." Christians will have new bodies. We are not to worry about the future, but we are to "lay up for ourselves treasures in heaven."

Other song ideas will hurt our thought life. The media is filled with music that says in so many words that sex outside of God's laws is natural and fun; that drugs are an acceptable means of reaching reality; that all adults are hypocrites; that God is rather irrelevant or Jesus was nothing much more than a misguided, middle-aged hippie. Even when songs are *about* Jesus, we must think and check it carefully against the Bible. All songs about Jesus or God may not be about the *right* Jesus or God. The real Jesus said, "Be careful that no one leads you the wrong way. Many people will come *using My name* . . . they will fool many people and turn them the wrong way" (Matt. 24:4-5).

(I'll say it again: The chief danger a young Christian person will have will come from his or her *music.* Guard your mind by guarding your ears. Don't spend God's money on the devil's messages, no matter how attractively they are packaged.)

Christian Music: What Is It?

Are there any rules for Christian music? Can we say anything about a sound that will be marked in any generation or any culture as Christian? Many say this is not possible; that all we can really say in any generation is that music should be conformed to reality and should be true to what actually is. This means that we have no guidelines in writing sounds that will be of honor to God; because Christ is Lord of all, anything at all can be used, including the hard and the acid sounds generated by the subculture in the early sixties.

But is this true? We know this about truth that will help us decide: (If something is biblically true, it will always apply in every culture, at every time in history, in its basic principles.) And while it is difficult to define the actual structure or chording and the harmony and consonance of a sound which will honor God, the Bible has not left us without guidelines.

All biblical music is music of worship. There is fundamentally no other form in Scripture. Worship can be generated from only two ultimate bases: a supreme regard for the glory of God, or an ultimate preference for ourselves. Music is a mobilization of the power of worship. And a principle we can analyze music by is this: What is its motive? Is it self-centered or God-centered? Does it point to man or to God? Is it the music of love or the music of selfishness? To find this we can look at 1 Corinthians 13 again and ask ourselves:

What Does the Music of Love Sound Like?

1. *Love's music is patient.* People resist change. Each new sound in Christian history has been firmly resisted by the backslidden dropouts of the previous awakening; and if new forms of music are brought to the church, they cannot be forced. Is *your* music patient? Music that demands its own way is not love's sound; love challenges without forcing.

2. *Love's music is kind.* It is not bitter or hostile, violent or vicious. In Romans, chapter one, Paul lists the characteristics of a society that has heart-rejected God; the end result of such a world is people without natural affection, without pity or mercy. Love's music is not ruthless; kindness is goodness and graciousness which gently breaks down resistance. The end of the music of hardness is a calloused conscience; does your music reflect kindness?

3. *Love's music is not envious.* It has no desire to copy or emulate the gods of a pagan world. Music can be a prop for acceptance; if it is your whole life, it is not enough! Groups that sing and play must ask themselves this: "Is this the overflow of my love and gratitude to God?" A music which seeks recognition is not a ministry but a mission field.

4. *Love's music is not proud.* It does not show off. It is not driven by desire to push its sound, its group, its talent. Love's music knows who it is; it doesn't have to talk itself up or talk itself down. It doesn't think much about itself at all, but its object is love, its focus is worship. Is that the Lord Jesus? Who do people think about when they hear your kind of sound? We must know the difference between vision and ambition.

5. *Love's music doesn't misbehave.* It does nothing deliberately to offend. Posture, display and affectation have no place in the music of God. It is not rude, unmannerly, or indecent. The Greek word *hyperion* means "actor" and is the word the New Testament translates in English as "hypocrite." In our quest for spiritual reality, are we real? For music to be a genuine expression of a life-style, there must be no acting. Your true self will be revealed in the music you delight in; what kind of person do you show the world?

6. *Love's music doesn't seek her own.* Self-centered music is reflected from self-centered living. The world is polarizing into

two groups who earn respect: the vile and the virtuous. The man who wants to walk between will never change it. Love doesn't seek its own way, insist on its own rights, chase rainbows that were never generated by the Son.

7. *Love's music is not easily provoked.* Christian music is not reaction but action. All of God's decisions come from the internal pressure of His wisdom and love; none come from external pressures or problems. Too much music is written in reaction: "Here is what people think or do; I'll write something relevant against it." But love isn't pushed into reply. Love generates her sound from the loveliness of her Lover; it keeps no score of wrongs.

8. *Love's music thinks no evil.* There is great pressure in the world of ideas. We must not give in to secular concepts; we must not surrender to the pressure of society. Remember this fundamental fact: the world is always wrong. According to the Bible, the world is forever against the true Church; and it will only court her to try to rape her and murder her. Any passing interest it displays will always prove shallow, self-centered and short-lived.

9. *Love's music does not rejoice in iniquity.* It finds no happiness in sin. Love's music will not glorify or magnify rottenness; no major time will be spent on the wrongness of the world—gloating over others' sin, being glad when people go wrong. When it touches sin, it will do so as God does—in sadness, in holy hatred, in judgment, and in brief.

10. *Love's music rejoices in truth.* This is her joy and delight—the truth of God; not just what He *does,* but who He *is.* All biblical music can be tested ultimately by this: does it center its excitement around God? Does it worship in spirit and in truth (John 4:23-24)? This tells us two things about the music of love: (1) It has a genuine *truth content.* It must be real and biblical; it must be filled with the great thoughts of the Word of God. It is this more than anything else that will focus the sound on reality, turn sentiment into love, add power to sweetness. Is your music real? Do you live constantly in the thoughts of God? (2) It must be *joyous,* even in sadness. There is no biblical precedent for hopelessness in worship; love's music has unquenchable faith, limitless vision, eagerness to dare for the best because of the greatness of her Lord. The cross is a *positive sign.* It was for the "joy that was set before him" that the Son of God gave himself in agony for the sins of the world. Love's music isn't minor; it majors on the power and the glory of the great God.

This must be the firm resolution of our hearts: to reject from our worship the music that does not conform to the gentle criteria of charity, the agapé love of the Bible. *Worship* is the sole function of music in Scripture and *love* is the only motive the Word of

God will allow for those that represent the Son. And will it touch the world with power? Will it reach out to those that do not know Him, speaking a language that is strange to their ears? Can such music really be used for anything else other than people who love and enjoy God?

"I have given them Your Word; and the world has hated them, because they are not of this world, even as I am not of this world. I pray not that you should take them out of the world, but that you should keep them from the evil; they are *not of this world,* even as I am not of the world. Make them holy *by the truth;* as you have sent Me into the world, even so have I also sent them into the world. And for their sakes, I set Myself apart, that they may be thoroughly dedicated in the truth."

"But I am not thinking of them only; but I pray for them also which *shall believe on Me through their word;* that they may all be one; as You, Father, are in union with Me; and I am in union with you, let them be in union with us that the world may believe that You have sent Me; and the glory which you gave me, *I have given them;* that they may be *one,* even as we are one; I in them and You in Me, that they may be made perfect in one and that *the world may know* that you have sent Me and have loved them, as you have loved Me."

(John 17:14-23, Combined Trans.)

58

What to Watch Out For

"You [the real King of Tyre—Satan] have been in Eden, the garden of God . . . the workmanship of your tabrets and of your pipes was prepared in you in the day that you were created" (Ezek. 28:13).

It seems from this scripture that Satan must know a lot about music. If this verse refers to him, as many Bible scholars believe, he is the only angel recorded in the Bible who had built-in musical instrumentation. Some forms of sound are dangerous. It is not enough just to watch out for the words or ideas of a song. Sometimes the sound itself can harm your spiritual life. It is possible to use music just like a drug. Some tunes can take you up, and others can bring you down. Some sounds recreate drug trips and can send you on a flashback years after you have done acid. Some forms of music stir you up sexually or turn your spirit from the things of God. There were men and women in the Bible who used drugs and music to turn them on. God says, "The harp, and the viol, the tabret, and pipe, and wine, are in their feasts; but they regard not the work of the Lord, neither consider the operation of his hands" (Isa. 5:11, 12).

There are three kinds of dangerous sound that Satan can use: (1) The *blue note, minor key* sound; (2) the *high energy, body-pulsed* beat; and (3) *distortion* and *psychedelics*. Avoid listening to these at all cost. Never expose yourself to them deliberately, especially at high volume levels; never use them for entertainment or to fill your home.

1. The *bluenote, minor key* sound is the least harmful and can even be used in some kinds of Christian music. The trouble with this type of sound is that it is "downer" music; it can make you feel sad, empty and lonely. It is suicide sound. I know that some disciples of Jesus have used it with effect to sing about their past of sin. It might be used also to describe trouble or

problems in life. But it ought never to be the basic mark of Jesus sound. The Lord Jesus told us to rejoice in trouble, not to complain or moan about it. He even went to the cross for the "joy that was set before him" (Luke 6:23; 2 Cor. 7:4; Heb. 12:2). If sad music takes a big place in our musical preference there may be something wrong with our souls. Sadness is not the mark of the disciple of Jesus. Minor music must take a minor place. Only the songs of the Christian faith are marked as a whole by major treatments among the great religions. They are notes of faith to a lost and hopeless world. The Bible says that the kingdom of heaven is in right living, peace and joy in the Holy Spirit (Rom. 14:17). The *joy* of the Lord is our strength.

2. The *high energy, body-pulsed beat* is the "heartbeat of hell," the most dangerous form of non-Christian sound. It is dangerous for two reasons: it can damage your peace and can teach your body to control your mind. The pulse-beat sound is not new; men have used it for thousands of years to psyche themselves up for love or war or pleasure. Today it is usually created by electronic bass and percussion. It is sound pulsed into the basic, primal rhythms of the body. It is dangerous because it is so exciting that you can let it control your soul.

Some groups are masters of the primal pulse. The Rolling Stones, Steppenwolfe and the MC-5 all knew how to build intense energy into their music. If you have ever heard "Satisfaction" or "Let's Spend the Night Together" or "Born To Be Wild," you have had firsthand experience with this sound. Using sound to train people is still a largely unexplored field. Studies by Ivan Pavlov (the Russian pioneer in this field who discovered the techniques of brainwashing) showed that sound could be used to make parts of the body react without directly telling them to do it. Certain sounds, repeated often enough, can make your body behave automatically in response.

Think of a lunch bell. Every time it goes off, you learn to think of food. Pavlov trained a dog like this. With one sort of sound he made the dog's saliva run by feeding it every time he played that tone. Next he taught the dog's juices to dry up by removing the food every time it heard another different note. Soon he had a dog whose saliva would run or dry up just by his making the right sound. Along with this experiment he found that sounds like a heartbeat could fool the body into thinking the sound was its own heart. (The heartbeat sound had to be deep, solid, and pulsed like a real heart.) People hearing a pulsebeat sound faster than a normal heartbeat would find their own hearts actually tending to speed up; the same sound run slower than normal would actually tend to calm or slow down normal heartbeat and body actions.

Put these together and you have a rather dangerous weapon in sound, provided you can have enough time to work on a subject. First, you can train a living creature to react automatically to a certain sound. Secondly, one type of sound can actually excite or calm a living creature, depending on its beat frequency. (A pulsebeat sound timed to be right on normal heartbeat has a hypnotic effect on a person.)

What if you taught a person to react to a pulsed sound until he automatically responded to the pulse, exciting or calming him, stirring him up or holding him down? Pavlov did this with his dogs. When the dog's saliva would "run" or "dry up" by sound alone he did something which can be done by anyone today.

What if your mind and body got two signals with exactly opposite responses at the same time? Think of how you would feel if someone (or something) tried to hold you down when another part of your mind was yelling to jump up. What would you feel like if a wolf grabbed your leg when the rest of the pack were howling after you, or if a table fell on top of you when you knew the whole roof was going to fall in within a minute? Did you ever get grabbed by someone when you knew they were really going to bash you, and they had hold of the back of your shirt? You know what feelings happen in all these situations; you would get both violent and desperate; you would fight anything that tried to hold you down or back, when everything else in you yelled to flee!

When one part of you screams "go" and the other part yells "stop," you are in trouble. Conflict and tension like this does things to your head; it clouds your ability to see or think clearly; it puts a wedge in your mind so that someone else finds it easier to tell you what to do. Say that you woke with your five-story apartment building on fire. You come to from a deep sleep and find the whole door and wall in flames. Panic and fear hit you— emotions so strong that they sweep your head clear of everything you ever read on how to behave in a fire. You rush to the window and if someone yells "jump" as the flames roar behind you, you might just do it to your death, even though there is a fire escape ladder right beneath you.

Pavlov built the "stop" and "go" reflexes into this dog until they were very strong. Then he did an awful thing. He played both sounds together! And what do you think the dog did? He tried to do two opposite things at once, both things that he had learned to do unthinkingly under the influence of Pavlov's conditioning sound. It tried to "run" and "dry up" at the same time. Its mind was simply overloaded. It suffered the doggie equivalent of a complete nervous breakdown, a total freak out. And precisely this state of mind opens the door to being told what to do by another with such force that it comes like a hypnotic command.

The primal pulse can do just that. It must be learned. It grows on you. It teaches you response by dealing with your body rhythms on a primal level. Play hard rock to a baby and it will probably cry. Play it to a little kid the first time, and he will not like it. But keep on playing that same sound, a little at a time, and he will learn to like it. When that baby becomes a teenager, growing up under the sound, he will later have to stop himself from moving with it. It will hook him like a drug. He has learned to surrender to the pulsebeat sound.

High energy hard rock screams "go" to your body. What if your mind and conscience say no at the same time? Give in to the sound and you may throw away something precious that your conscience warned you to protect. But if you refuse to give in, while still holding yourself under its power, you cannot stop happening in your mind what happened to the dog in Pavlov's experiment.

Dr. William Sargant, former President of Psychiatry in the London Royal Society of Medicine, said, "If subjected to excessive excitation or inhibition, the brain becomes incapable for the time being of its usual intelligent functioning. Under such conditions belief can be implanted in people after this function has been impaired by accidentally or deliberately induced fear, anger or excitement. Of the results . . . the most common one is *temporarily impaired judgment* (the ability to see and think clearly in a situation) and *heightened suggestibility* (openness to being told what to do by another).

No wonder Pete Seeger said, "The guitar could be mightier than the bomb." Any rock group understanding this power has at its disposal not only weapons by which an entire culture can be told what to do and how to do it, but it also has an audience of millions, thanks to rock's popularity.

If you expose yourself to constant conditioning from hard rock, you have a choice of reaction: give in to the sound, which breaks down mind control, opens the soul to attack from the enemy and creates internal anarchy; or fight it and begin the process of getting your head freaked. Either way, you lose! That's the main reason why informed disciples of Jesus know that hard rock is poison. Leave it alone!

Some kids have said, "If hard rock is such a powerful teaching tool, why not rip it off for the gospel? Why not play a steady wall of hard sound with a gospel message so that kids lose all their barriers over the message and buy it outright without thinking about putting it down? Why not create such a heavy metal sound that kids come running to get saved without even knowing why they are doing it?"

It is true that we can bend people's heads with sound, and then have them join in whatever religious trip we want to lay on them. Some have even done this and have seen large crowds swayed by sound. But never forget one thing: becoming a true disciple of Jesus is not a trip and does not happen as the by-product of a freaked head. Study the lives of those who have come to Christ under hard rock sound. We can do without most of these kinds of conversions. Jesus is not looking for decisions but disciples. He is not interested in crowds; He wants holy people—people who will stick with Him even when the music is not playing and the chips are down. He said, "Behold, I stand at the door and knock." He did not say, "Behold, I freak your head so I can kick in your door." That is the way of the world, the way of the devil and the way that leads to hell. And every true disciple of Jesus who has spent fifteen minutes in the awesome presence of the true God will never buy it.

One prominent rock group said, "Our program is cultural revolution through a total assault . . . which makes use of every tool, every energy and every media we can get our hands on. We breathe revolution. We will do anything to drive people crazy out of their heads and into their bodies. Rock . . . is the spearhead of our attack, because it's effective and so much fun. We have developed organic high-energy guerrilla bands who are infiltrating the popular culture and destroying millions of minds in the process. . . . You don't need to get rid of the honkies. You must rob them of their replacements. . . . We have more powerful weapons. Direct access to the minds of millions of teenagers is one . . . their belief in us is another."

God says, "Don't let the world around you squeeze you into its own mould" (Rom. 12:2, Phillips). Be a new and different person in the way you act and think.

3. *Distortion* and *psychedelics,* commonly called acid rock, was introduced into the music scene through the drug culture. Mastery of electronics, deliberate distortion and rerecording techniques made it possible. In acid rock, sound is bent, twisted, distorted and rechanneled through the senses. Regular timings and rhythms are upset, forced into dissonant and unpredictable, chaotic patterns. Psychedelic sound was first popularized by the Beatles in their "Revolver" album with the song "Tomorrow Never Knows." In "Sergeant Pepper" they used it again and built a new era in rock with it. Jimi Hendrix, Eric Clapton and other

masters of guitar extended the acid sound into complex levels of genius. It marked the music of a new generation.

But no one can listen to acid rock for long without spiritual damage. Psychedelic sound is spirit music, but it is a different spirit and has a different sound from the songs sung in heaven. Acid can play havoc with the soul. It can create fear, unrest and tension. It is an accurate reflection of the madness of our world, of chaos trying to find order, of the mystic and spirit worlds breaking into man's being. But it is sound that opens the door of the mind to occult attack. It is illusion music, and Satan's game is with the mind. It not only recreates drug trips but also creates its own trips into the dark worlds of the enemy. This is not the sound you hear "near to the heart of God." This is not the music of the Good Shepherd who leads beside quiet waters. No angel from the realms of glory ever used this sound to announce the birth of the Messiah. But it is possible that acid sounds will usher in a new "Jesus" to a world of waiting, deceived disciples who have sold out their souls to false worship in music. And only the informed disciples of Jesus will know the real Jesus well enough to stay away from it.

59

Sing a New Song for His Sake

"Sing to the Lord a new song, and his praise from the end of
the earth . . . let them shout from the top of the mountains, let
them give glory to the Lord, and declare his praise in the islands"
(Isa. 42:10-12).

Every spiritual awakening has brought a new sound for God
to the nation it happened in. When people fall in love with Jesus,
they are so happy they want to sing. The good news is *joyful*
news. When Jesus was born, all the angels sang (Luke 2:13, 14).
Music can carry God's Word across the land like a flood of happiness. God has told us to worship Him in song and to sing about
His goodness to the whole earth.

How can Christians write songs that will hit home for Jesus?
Here are some ideas about new Christian songs. Of course, they
must all come from a heart that really is deeply in love with
the Lord. No one should write Jesus songs just to show off talent
or to make money off people, and no one should sing songs like
this for the same reasons. God will not honor songs from selfish
hearts. He will not bless them.

They should, of course, be songs about the Lord. They can
be songs of worship sung to Him. They can be songs of happiness,
to sing because we are happy serving Jesus. They can be songs
to sing to others who do not know Christ, telling of His love for
them.

I love to tell the story
Of unseen things above,
Of Jesus and His glory,
of Jesus and His love. . . .

They should be songs that are true pictures of lost or saved
men and the Bible God. We should make sure our words and
thoughts come from the Bible and not just things we think might
be in the Bible. Be careful that the words you write are true.

Many people may sing them. They must not learn the wrong things from your songs.

I love to tell the story
Because I know 'tis true,
It satisfies my longings
As nothing else can do.

Good songs will be simple. It may have heavy words, but they will be little words. The best songs put big ideas into small words that everyone knows. Write songs so that even a child can understand and sing them. And keep the songs as short as you can. Three verses and a chorus are about all most people can remember at one time.

Being simple also applies to the melody. A song should have such an easy tune that anyone hearing it for the first time will be able to remember at least two lines of it. The gospel is simple. What Jesus said was simple. Being simple gives it power. You can use all kinds of musical backing in your songs, but never get too complex. If it is, no one will remember it, and no one will want to sing it. Go over your songs ruthlessly. Cut out every long word, every vocal or music line that clutters. No big words. No super-fancy arrangements. Stay simple.

Good songs also repeat themselves a lot. If a song has a chorus, use it at least three or four times. If it has a catchy title or theme line, use it as many times as you can. When a thing is repeated a lot of times people remember it better. A song is a powerful teacher. We want Christians to remember what Jesus has done. We want lost people to think about what Jesus said.

I love to tell the story—
'Tis pleasant to repeat
What seems, each time I tell it,
More wonderfully sweet.

The same repeating idea also applies to the music. The basic melody should be heard often for a song to be known and loved. Many all-time hit songs have had both verses and choruses almost alike. People ought to be able to hum the basic tune right through on about the third time they hear it. If a song changes its tune too often, no one will want to sing it.

Many popular songs have had catchy chord progressions that climb to a high climax note, or scale down to a low one. Remember, these climax notes should not be too high or too low because you want a song that almost anyone can sing, even people who are not good singers. Avoid sameness in your songs. You do not have to make a song sound flat or without life just because you repeat its words or lyrics often. Instrument fill-ins, backing vocal choruses, silence breaks of both music and words make good sound colors to paint with in your tunes.

Finally, people are hungry for songs that will remind them of things that most of the world has lost—love, affection, friendship, faith, brotherhood. Almost every all-time hit in the last twenty-five years has been on one of these themes, or a song about the loss of these. The world yearns for such things, but does not know what they really are or how to get them. The disciple of Jesus does. That is why we must sing new songs for His sake.

And when, in scenes of glory,
I sing the *new, new* song
'Twill be the old, old story
That I have loved so long.

Section XIV
The Disciple & SCIENCE

60

Is Blind Faith Real Faith?

"Now faith is the substance of things hoped for, the evidence of things not seen" (Heb. 11:1).

A young man caused a stir in a major university some time ago. On graduation day he walked out with others to get his degree. Everyone waited for his short acceptance speech. He took his degree. Then, in front of the shocked crowd, he tore it to bits. "This is useless to me," he said. "My education has not prepared me to answer the deepest questions of my life." Then he walked off stage.

A lot of kids feel the way he did. Many left school for the streets of Haight-Ashbury and Telegraph Avenue in San Francisco when the whole hip scene began years ago. It seemed to a lot of kids that all they had learned was a lot of irrelevant garbage. Facts hadn't come through for them, education didn't have the answers they wanted and needed. Some just dropped out totally. Youth are in revolt today against machine thinking, against the sterile, computer type way of living and thinking that has no place for beauty, art, love or human dignity. Across the world you can find young people with deep distrust of a logic that has stripped from them their meaning, their feelings, their humanity.

It is important to see that it was not Bible thinking or Bible facts that took away their human values. Science has left its Christian base and has put nothing in its place that leaves room for the humanity of man. Only in the Bible do you find the way to fully think through your lives and your universe without losing your value or worth. The Bible revelation is perfect. Everything fits inside what God has told us. We can think without losing our feelings; we can feel without losing our minds. This is Bible faith. It is facts and it is beauty. It is sensible but it is spiritual. It is profound in wisdom and just as deep in meaning and value.

In the Bible we find answers to who we are and why we are here.

However, today's world is filled with funny ideas. Non-Bible thinking made people think they were only accidents, the lucky end result of a freak mutation that began in mud without a mind. It is no longer in fashion even to think of man as an animal; today, he is nothing more than a machine, without meaning, hope or value in an accidental world. This unbiblical thinking brought fear and death to the hopes of many people who did not believe in God; but they did not return to the Bible's facts. Instead, they got scared of thinking. They became like the man who read that smoking causes cancer so he gave up reading! They tied reality in with experience and feeling instead of facts and logic. They threw out thought as a worthwhile test of reality. Their answer to life was an experiment, a leap in the dark with a hope that they would feel again their value and meaning by tasting the stuff of life as it came. Religious trips of various kinds seemed to offer hope; those that were religious felt that faith was basically a lovely feeling one experienced. Their jump was one of blind faith. But it must be said again: Bible faith is *not* blind.

It is true that God asks men and women to do things for Him when they don't really know what will happen to them when they obey Him. Abraham left his fine friends and home to obey God and found a new nation. He went somewhere he had never been before just because God told him to. But Abraham's faith, though strong, was not blind. He had seen God keep His every promise before. God had given him enough proof of His love and wisdom for Abraham to not be afraid and to trust Him for the unknown future. and that is Bible faith. It is based on promises backed up by a trustworthy person who will prove the kind of God He is. Bible faith is nothing more or less than a loyalty of love to the Word of God, both living and written. The Lord Jesus is called the Word of God (Acts 4:31; 8:14; 13:7). When we trust them both and obey them both, we have Bible faith.

There have always been people who either want to put down Christ or throw out the Bible. Skeptics and scoffers will fill every generation until God stops all scoffing by the second coming of His Son. People who ought to know better have listened too long to words of doubt. They have become afraid that perhaps the Christian life or the Scriptures will not stand close study. They follow the way of the world and say, "Well, it doesn't matter if it doesn't make sense or stand up to close examination anyway. The important thing is not whether the Bible is true or not.

The only important thing is what you feel when you read it. You can't disprove it by logic because it isn't logical."

It sounds nice to say that and looks like a good answer. No one can argue with it or you if you don't care whether it is factually true or not. It is "immune to being disproved." Except for one thing. If you can't think of the Bible as true or as fact, there is no way you can say "one way" either! How can you say that the Bible is better than any other religious book, or that what it says is more true than another saying the opposite thing? If it can't be proved wrong, it can't be proved right either. If it can't be trusted, there is no way we can say, "Jesus is the only way." But Bible faith is not blind faith.

God encourages us to think. Repentance is a change of mind that leads to a change of heart, and God doesn't expect Christianity to stop there! We are to love the Lord with all our minds (Mark 12:33). He puts His laws into our minds (Heb. 10:10). He opens our understanding of the Scriptures (Luke 24:27). We are not to be children in our thinking (1 Cor. 14:20) but to gird up our minds (1 Pet. 1:13) and be fully convinced in our own minds (Rom. 14:5). The Lord Jesus was called teacher or its equivalent over sixty times in the New Testament; His disciples (or followers) were learners because the word *disciples* means "learners." They were called disciples over 243 times. We see them preaching with power and also see them reasoning right through the book of Acts (Acts 4:13; 6:10; 17:2, 17; 18:4, 19; 19:8; 24:25; 26:25; 28:23). We are to know the Scriptures which are able to make us wise to salvation through faith (2 Tim. 3:14, 15). We are not to be conformed to this world but to be transformed by the renewal of our minds (Rom. 12:1, 2). Bible faith is a thinking faith that gives us a reason for the hope that is within us (1 Pet. 3:15). God is not afraid to let His Book stand in the arena of logic and fact. The Bible is a history book. The Lord Jesus actually came about 2,000 years ago to this planet. If you had been there you could have taken a movie film of Him on the cross and rising again from the dead. Every calendar that says A.D. or B.C. is a record of that visit. The Bible deals with real people and real events so that we could make audio and video tapes of their voices and actions.

The Bible is not just a set of pretty words and inspiring stories to help people feel better when they read it. It has its roots in space-time reality. It is full of facts. And as far as scientific facts are concerned, although it is not a book on science it can be tested up to the limits of science.

No, "Blind Faith" was just the name of a rock supergroup.

The faith of the Bible and the faith of the disciple of Jesus can be tested by facts. We believe in a faith that makes sense. And we are willing to stake our lives on it.

> For feelings come and feelings go,
> And feelings are deceiving,
> My warrant is the word of God—
> Naught else is worth believing.
>
> Though all my heart should feel condemned
> For want of some sweet token,
> There is One greater than my heart
> Whose word cannot be broken.
>
> —Martin Luther

61

Does Science Disprove God?

We can only use the scientific method to prove some things. For other areas it does not apply because the scientific method, like other methods of analysis, has limits. Science can help put together evidence for God's reality, but it cannot do what it was not designed to do. The tools of science can check out what is actually happening now and give us clues on whether or not something else once took place. There are some things we can use to check statements of the Bible. Science can help us in archaeology, seeing if the Bible record is true when it speaks about history. It is amazing just how much the Bible has to say about our world. When it touches on things of studied facts, it has surprises for the man of science.

The God of the Bible is the God who created the universe that science studies. True science and true Scripture will always agree; one is God's demonstration of power and glory in the universe, and the other is His revelation in word for man. We have had some centuries to examine facts in the Bible. Although opinions of men about nature and the opinions of men about the Bible have sometimes clashed, no real fault has been recorded in the Scriptures. The Bible does not tell fairy tales. Its statements are true, able to stand the closest tests that language and description allow. It is a matter of history that science has never developed significantly anywhere except where there was first a Christian influence or base. The scientific method and motivation for study is really a child of Christian concepts; the universe is the orderly product of a rational, divine Mind. We can discover some of these secrets because we are made in the thinking (but finite) image of our Maker. Science began in the areas where the Bible God was honored. Western technology has forgotten its roots but still uses the fruit of this Bible idea.

Before Columbus sailed around the world, Scripture records the spherical nature of earth (Isa. 40:21, 22). When science as a baby thought that the world was held up by three elephants on the back of a tortoise, the Bible factually established its free float in space (Job 26:7). The moon is shown to be a reflector, unlike the radiating sun (Job 25:5; 31:6). Modern precision telescopes charted the runaway "Arcturus." Drifting with all its planets in tow it travels silently through twenty-seven and one-half miles a second. The Bible recorded its wanderings centuries before the invention of the telescope. The Bible record of creation is a masterful example of the harmony of geology, biology and genetics to the scientist who has studied it from a biblical viewpoint. Three hundred years ago it was discovered that physical life was resident in the human blood; the Bible recorded that 3,500 years ago (Lev. 17:11). Principles of meteorology, aeronautics and geology are hinted at in Scripture (Ps. 135:5, 7; Job 28:5; 38:4). Atomic energy is old stuff with the God of the atom (2 Pet. 3:10-12; Isa. 4:1; 13:12; Joel 2:30). The word *dissolve* in Peter is the Greek word *luo* which means "to untie"; the word *pillars* in Joel is the Hebrew word for "palm-trees."

Science can tabulate for us the "what," analyze the "how" and probe for the "why" of things, but it cannot tell us the ultimate "where from" nor give any reason for why the universe exists that leaves man with meaning. It cannot say who you are or why you are here; it can tell you what you are able to do but not what you ought to do. And here are some of the limits of science. It is not an all-knowing oracle. God has given us more than His universe to study; He has given us a Book to tell us why and what we ought to be doing. One shows His power, the other shows us His purpose. And both are valuable for knowing more about Him (Ps. 91:1; 8:3-6; 19:7-14).

Science just studies the patterns of existing reality. It finds out what things are like now. It measures, weighs, compares. It can make informed guesses about how things could have happened if no one saw them happen. Its job is to tell us how things hang together and how they work. But science cannot tell us what to do with that knowledge we learn. That is not its job. It can tell us how to release atomic energy but not what to do with it. Science gave us a secret; with it we can warm up a city or burn it to radioactive ash. Science can say how our bodies work but cannot say why we have them or even if we should continue to stick around on this planet. Those are the limits of science. A man speaking as a scientist cannot answer moral questions as a scientist—only as man. Science cannot answer moral questions any more than you can use a hammer to cut down a tree. It is the wrong tool.

Now when a scientist speaks today, he speaks with great weight and authority because our generation worships technology. He may speak on anything and carry that same weight of opinion. But he may speak just as a man and he may be very wrong. He can sound as if he leaves nothing to chance or guess by saying, "Nothing is real unless I can weigh or measure it." But what if his instruments are limited in range? How do you put on paper ideas not made of matter or energy? What microscope can analyze poetry or what test tube isolate the essence of art? What would a gram of justice look like, or a millimeter of love? When a scientist talks about values or morals he is not talking about science and is not speaking as a scientist. If he wants to throw out morals or dignity or freedom or value in the name of science he is not speaking for science either. No scientist has a right to say all-knowingly that the only things that are true and real are material things.

No scientist worth his salt makes his own knowledge the measure of his wisdom. That is small minded indeed; no one can speak with absolute authority simply from logic or studied reason without assumptions because everyone makes some. The man of science knows that he always has to work from some ideas he holds as true but cannot prove. He *assumes* that reality exists, that if something is there he can find it. He just starts as if it might be true and discovers more as he goes along. And who is to say that God's man or woman cannot also make some assumptions? We assume God is there and that *He* can be known. We assume that His Word is true when it tells us He is the same, yesterday and forever. And if the man of science speaks with authority on what he has found by experiment and experience, so can we. Let him do his thing. His work is of great value. But let us not talk about science disproving Christianity. It will and can do no such thing.

62
What About Evolution?

"Keep that which is committed to your trust, avoiding foolish and unthinking babblings, and oppositions of science falsely so called" (1 Tim. 6:20).

Life covers our earth in myriads of complex forms. There are thousands of creatures great and small on our planet, from germs to man. How did it all get here? We have only two possible basic explanations. Here are both of them.

1. "In the beginning *God* created the heaven and the earth. And the earth was without form, and void; and darkness was upon the face of the deep. And the Spirit of God moved upon the face of the waters" (Gen. 1:1, 2).

2. "Once upon a time, perhaps 2 1/2 billion years ago, under a deadly sun, in an ammoniated ocean topped by a poisonous atmosphere, in the midst of a soup of organic molecules, a nucleic acid molecule came accidentally into being that could somehow bring about the existence of another like itself."—Isaac Asimov

Now whichever of the above explanations we take for the start of life on earth will mean a great deal for our future. It may even help decide whether we *have* one. Some people talk today as if smart people can only believe that life came from time, chance and matter. That is not true. There are many questions that idea doesn't answer. Think, for instance, about this problem:

Suppose the universe is about ten billion years old. (That is a big "suppose" to begin with.) Think how long it would take for a watch to put itself back together if you first pulled it totally to bits from the strap to the springs. Drop all its parts into a frying pan. Pour in some cooking oil and boil them. How long do you think it would take for these parts to bump into each other long enough for the watch to properly join itself together and *wind itself* up? Probably quite a long time! Then, if you pulled a car to bits and did the same thing with it, one thing is certain:

it would take even longer. And how long would it take to fill itself up with gas and drive off on its own down the road? Now a watch has only about 200 parts. Even a car has only about 200,000 parts. And these examples are nothing compared to how complex a man or woman is. Now how on earth did this complicated creature called man put himself together (without knowing what he was supposed to be like) and become alive?

An average man is made up of literally millions of parts. They work together and depend on each other. A human body alone has about 10^{14} cells in it—that number is a one followed by fourteen zeros (100,000,000,000,000). A brain has about another 10^9 cells in it. And that is not the end. Each cell is incredibly complex. It has in it nearly one million molecules. And each molecule contains between one thousand and ten thousand atoms, all in the right place. You can see that it is going to be hard, to say the least, to make a man by chance. Think about it again. Suppose we took just a human body *without* a brain. This brainless body would have in it 10^{14} x 10^6 x 10^3 atoms in it, or 10^{23} atoms, all arranged in just the right way. This is a very big number. The supposed ten billion years age of the universe we talked about earlier turned into seconds is only 10^{17} seconds. If all the right atoms joined together in the right places, at least one a second, there would still not be enough time in the whole age of the universe to even make a mindless man. You can see it is not fair to say that people are foolish who believe in a wise God who created life as a product of His infinite knowledge and genius. It is actually *easier* to believe the Bible way than any other way with the facts we have.

Disciples of Jesus do not worry about evolution. They can afford to take the simple Bible statements just as they are. Even if man (with all his genius in biology and chemistry, sided by the most modern fourth-generation computers) could finally make something he could call life, it would simply underline what the Bible says: Life did not come by accident. It takes a very high order of intelligence and knowledge to make it, and it had to be put together intelligently. That is why Murray Eden, who worked for some years at M.I.T. with high-speed computers, got an interesting answer to his question, "Given only time, chance, and undirected matter, what is the possibility that life now exists on earth?" The answer he got at the end of his complex work was "zero." There is nobody here! Life could not have happened by chance. To use such infinite concepts of chance and time is to make probability a worthless concept. By such logic we could prove anything. No, man is not an accident. It took a creator, a genius of immense power and wisdom. The Bible tells us His Name.

If you have studied or been taught false concepts of evolution, do not be worried that they will shake your faith. Many men of science are writing today on the subject. Some of their new findings actually throw out ones that people previously used against the Bible position. There are many books written on this problem by Christians who are men of science.

If you are bothered, don't just avoid it. Make it a special study if you can. Ask God to help you find answers to people's questions. And, remember, discovered facts can be interpreted different ways. Check the facts first as best as you know how to see if they are wholly true. If they seem to be, then see if you can find a different way to explain in the light of the Bible what has been found. But don't make the Bible try to say what it doesn't say to science; and don't fall into the trap of trying to show that *every* new idea of science is proved by the Bible. Science makes mistakes too. The God who made the worlds and us also gave us the Bible. He knows both what His Word actually says and means, and what is actually true about His world. We can rest assured that He can defend His own position. He has all of eternity to show us what He actually meant.

63

What Do Disciples of Jesus Believe About Creation?

"In the beginning God created the heaven and the earth" (Gen. 1:1).

Disciples of Jesus have three main ideas about how God created the earth and what the things we have found about the rocks of the past mean. God does not tell us *how* He created the world; that is up to us to guess about or study if we want to. The Bible is not made to be a scientific textbook; it is simply a history of what actually happened. To find the "hows" we must match, as best as we can, what we know from the Bible records with what we find in science. Here are the three basic ideas that Christians have had concerning the making of the earth and concerning the fossil records:

1. *The day-age theory.* This idea fits the long age some men of science think are the record of our past with the days of Genesis. It says that God created each distinct species in each era, then watched over their growth and changes as they spread through all the world. Because the Bible word for *day* is sometimes used for ages, or long periods of time, the day-age theory simply thinks of each Genesis day as a long age, as long as needed to fit into the concepts of our time as interpreted by one group of scientists. The Genesis record is thought of as being put in a logical rather than chronological order; it is simply an account of what happened back there, not necessarily in the right time order. It gives a divine reason for the origin of life without challenging assumptions of our supposedly super-ancient planet and its history.

2. *The gap theory.* This idea was popular especially in the last century. It says that there was an original creation, perhaps millions or billions of years ago, which in some way was wiped out by terrific destruction that turned our planet into ruin and waste. Then, on these ruins, God created our modern world's ancestors in six literal days. That long time between the original creation

and the one we know today is explained by the silence between two verses at the very start of the Bible. Under the gap theory, Genesis 1:1 and 1:2 would read something like this:

"In the beginning God created the heaven and the earth" (creation of the ancient fossil world, perhaps millions of years ago). Then, the gap, an awesome wipeout of that first world, possibly connected with the fall of Satan and the dark angels in a war in heaven. Then, verse two: "And the earth was [became] without form [*tohu*, a Hebrew word which can mean 'confusion, desolation'; see Isa. 45:18], and void [*bohu*, 'an indistinguishable *ruin*']; and darkness was upon the face of the deep." From this point, the Spirit of God begins a recreation work. The original wipeout may have been in the form of a flood, which was followed much later by Noah's flood.

This theory gave some answers for these problems: some fossils are found in very hard rock like those from the Archaezoic to the Cretaceous layers; but fossils dated from the Paleocene to the Pleistocene era seem quite young, with soft surroundings that can be dug out with only a pick and shovel. Also evidence points to a sudden destruction of the reptile age and the equally sudden appearance of mammals and men.

3. *The apparent age theory.* This is more modern, holding to a literal six-day creation but challenging the idea that the earth really is very old. This theory says that our planet is actually quite young, but was formed under such totally different conditions than those existing today that some major scientific techniques we trust have to be rethought for the birth of this planet.

Basically, this idea says that God made in six literal days a full grown planet, just as He made Adam a fully mature man. In other words, in one day God created Adam as a, say, thirty-year-old man; He created the world with an apparent age of, say, many thousands or millions of years, but in a few literal days. If we believe in the supernatural in creation, it is certainly hard to disprove this theory! There is no reason why God could not do it this way; again, the Bible doesn't tell us how, but only that He did do it.

All three of these theories are studied and held by different disciples of Jesus. There are others to think about, but these three are the only current Christian ones. The idea that God created the earth through a process of accidental evolution is the same as saying that God didn't even have to be there, either then or now; and true disciples of Jesus don't buy that.

Some scientists who are Christians believe that the flood(s) were judgments sent on our planet, possibly by bringing an ice moon through our solar system and collapsing it over our magnetic poles. This giant "ice-dump" created an unearthly deep-freeze over the poles and total flooding of our world, wiping out all life. The fossil record, then, is not a history of life's growth, but a record of death, with creatures that were buried by floodwaters loosely arranging into layers by their size and density after being mixed by tides from 5,000 to 10,000 feet high. Of course, some small fossils would be found in upper layers, just as a few larger ones would be found in lower ones. This is what is actually found when we look at the fossil layers. Much study is going on in this area. The important thing for us to understand as disciples of Jesus is this: the Bible account has better answers for life and earth's origin than any others. And we have answers not only for earth's creation but also why we are here on it.

64

Can a Christian Be a Scientist?

"The fool has said in his heart, There is no God" (Ps. 14:1).

Believing in God has nothing much to do with being intellectually clever or not. A good many clever scientists in history have chosen not to believe in God, and a large number on the other hand have acknowledged His handiwork in their studies. Many men have been Christians and scientists too. It is not hard to find words of faith from men like Galileo and Copernicus (whose works on the solar system, incidentally, went right against popular religious tradition in their time). Louis Pascal was a devout lover of God, and his work still forms the basis for much of our studies in fluids and hydraulics today. Possibly the greatest genius who ever lived was Isaac Newton. He invented the calculus at twenty-one because he couldn't solve a problem with existing mathematics; he formulated a base for modern physics to build out from. What many people don't know is that Newton wrote more about God and faith than he ever did about science, although none of his religious writings were published until after his death. And what shall we say of the brilliant Christian chemist, Francis Bacon, or the humble George Washington Carver, the black biochemist whose ideas came from his talks with God in the woods and began two industries?

And not just past scientists were disciples of Jesus. In our century there have been many men, like Dr. Werner Von Braun, the pioneer in rocket research, or Robert Milikan, the man who first measured the charge on the electron. The American Association of Science lists hundreds of men who are firm believers in the Bible God, who occupy some of the top research positions of western technology. Some took part in designing the equipment and patterns that planted man on the moon.

It is certainly no shame just to acknowledge the reality of God. No man could call Albert Einstein a fool. At the time of his death less than a handful of men could even follow some of his mind-blowing equations about energy, matter and gravity. Yet Einstein was a Jew with a quiet faith in the God he had seen in his study of the universe.

I hope you can see that faith does not depend so much on whether we are clever or not, or on how much we know, but what we *do* with what we know. Two men could live in the same house, go to the same college, win identical honors in identical fields. Both could do significant research; both could add greatly to the sum of human knowledge. Both could be highly honored by men. But one could be a true follower of Jesus and the other could be the very opposite. The difference comes in the way they look at their world.

Both of them must assume some things. All science does, and so do scientists. Just wearing a white coat and having a degree or two doesn't mean you always think and speak like a computer. Both have some personal questions to answer for their lives as well as the ones they face in research. One of these is, "What is man?" Others are, "Where does he fit in the universe? How did he get here? Where is he going? Does he have any purpose here? Does he mean anything?"

And here is the critical difference. What each one believes *man* is, and what should direct his life on earth, will govern not only his study and research conclusions, but, to some extent, his own personal life as well. And it is our personal lives, the things we actually do as a result of the way we think, that will alter the destiny of nations. The real issue is, who or what is *man?* To this question there are only two basic answers. The one we give to it will determine how we live and treat others.

One answer begins by saying, "There is no God," no personal, infinite creator. There is no person behind the universe able to speak and guide; man and all of life is simply the freak result of a fantastic chemical accident. Man has no soul, no spirit; he is just the product of conditioned responses, chemicals, organic machinery. There is no life after death, no heaven or hell. As a result, things like love, value and morals mean nothing; man and all the universe means absolutely *nothing—zero.* He is totally made what he is by impersonal forces around him; everything about him can be explained like a machine. And that is the result: Man, as a person, is dead. He is only a machine. As a matter of fact, he never really *lived* at all. All we call value, love, beauty, art, faith, dignity are meaningless; we have just given them meaning without reason. Man is a machine—nothing more or less.

With this philosophy Hitler fed two million Jews and Christians into his gas ovens. Thinking this way, Lenin, Stalin and Mao murdered millions. Because of this idea, hundreds of thousands of kids dropped out for good and joined the hip subculture. Man cannot live as if he is only a machine. If he is only a meaningless nothing, why go on? Why not just drop the bomb?

The other answer says, "There IS a God," a personal, infinite Creator. He is big enough to take care of us, but because He is a person, the universe is not just a big runaway mindless machine. Life is not just a cosmic accident; it is the loving creation of a wise and powerful Father. Man is not a thing. Beauty, love and communication all really do mean something. Man is far more than just matter-energy. He is important. Being a person means something. God made us; we are valuable whether we are weak or sick or old or helpless. Life after death is real and so is our responsibility to others and to God. And the good thing about being a scientist who loves God is this: you know not only *what* you can do, but *why* you can or cannot do something. You know what you *could* do, and what you *should* do. You have two limits: your technology and the Word of God.

Disciples of Jesus can be and have been scientists. It is harder to do this today as more and more people are rebelling against what they know of God. But it is possible. After all, science assumes two things: truth exists unchanging, and it can be known. And that is all that God asks of us in faith—that we will be willing to live in the fact that He exists with all that it means. And we must admit that He can and must be known and obeyed for His happiness, ours and that of the whole universe. He says, "He that comes to God must believe that he is, and that *he will reward* those that diligently seek him" (Heb. 11:6).

Section XV
The Disciple &
SPIRITISM

65

Don't Talk to the Dead

"The Holy Spirit tells us in plain words that in the last days some people will turn away from the faith. They will listen to spirits who deceive and follow the teaching of demons" (1 Tim. 4:1). "Why do you look for the living among the dead?" (Luke 24:5).

God has given us a spirit. Our spirit can put us in touch with a spiritual world. God gave us our spirits so we can talk with Him and worship Him. Through these He can speak to us. He can tell us inside whether we are doing what He wants or not. He can talk to us by using intuition and our conscience. We can worship Him with our spirits. They are like a radio or TV set; with a radio you can hear music that is all around you, but no one would know without it that the music was there in the air. Our spirits can contact the invisible God who made the whole universe and talk to Him as well as hear His voice. The Bible says that God's "Spirit himself assures our spirits that we are the children of God."

Science tells us something eerie. If it were possible to change the basic atomic frequencies of matter so that one set of things was out of tune with the rest of the world, those solid things could pass right through the rest of matter as if it were not there! As a matter of fact, if this were possible, two worlds could co-exist. Each could be in the same place at the same time. But each could pass right through the other without either knowing that the other was there! Two worlds, with real people in each, could exist together in the same place in space, but in different dimensions.

The Bible tells us there *is* another world. It is parallel with ours. It is as real as this one, and as close to us as this one. Spirit beings live in this world that in our time reckoning would be at least 6,000 years old. But they are at war. There are two main divisions. One group is the spirit beings who love and remain faithful to the Bible God and serve the Lord Jesus. They are called

the angels. Angels are a created race of spirit beings who serve
God and help His children in times of difficulty. There are dif-
ferent kinds of angelic beings recorded in the Bible (Gen. 3:24;
Ezek. 28:14-15; Isa. 6:1; Rev. 4:6; 5:1; Ps. 84:1; 103:20, 21; 148:2-5;
Col. 1:16).

Then there is another group of *rebel* angels. They serve the
devil, and are called demons. They hate man because he is made
in God's image and they are in rebellion against God. Because
they cannot hurt God directly, they try to hurt or kill us to bring
grief to His heart. The Bible reveals that these spirit beings are
not just figments of our imagination. They are real, personal spirit
beings that have great power and intelligence. They have knowledge (Mark 1:24; Acts 19:15; Gen. 3:1; 2 Cor. 2:11; Eph. 6:11;
Matt. 4:6; Rev. 12:12), emotions (James 2:19; Rev. 12:12; Mark
3:11; 5:7; Luke 8:31), and the power of choice or will (Matt. 12:44;
Luke 3:31-33; Isa. 14:12, 13), and other signs of personality like
having personal names (Mark 5:9). They can speak, act, and by
every other accepted standard of judgment behave as persons.
This is vital. Demonic and angelic beings are not states of the
mind, but persons.

Because the members of the demonic and dark angelic race are
at war with the minds and souls of men, we must be aware of
their tactics and tricks. Remember, they are very cunning. They
are not wise, because sin is never wise. But they are clever at
fooling people. They know how to play games with people's heads.
Unless you learn to stay away from their traps by staying close
to God and to His Word, you can get into real trouble with them.
They fight dirty. And they kill. Even some very clever people
have been taken in. They no doubt think they can use these spirit
beings' powers for their own purposes. They sometimes learn some
of the occult secrets and even get power over other lost people.
But these secrets are just bait for the trap. Satan does not care
what he gives as long as he can get people to serve him and
not the true God. He will promise a man or woman anything
as long as he will worship him. The real God is not selfish like
the devil. He is all wise. He knows that power is deadly if it
is given to selfish people. God has begun the hardest way, but
the best. He first tests men to see what they will do with power
and responsibility. He does not give His power to people He cannot
trust with it. This world is merely our decision and testing-ground
(Rev. 2:24-27; 21:7). All of God's people will have tremendous
powers in His new world (1 Cor. 2:7-9; 13:1-12). But they can
be trusted with these powers because they have given up their
selfishness and given their love to the true God.

Our spirits can put us in touch with the Lord if we know and love Him. But if we do not serve the Bible Jesus, we are open to attack from the side of the enemy of our souls. Spiritists are the most tragic example of this. They are people who have, knowingly or unknowingly, given themselves over to contacts with these horrible creatures, who often come in disguise as "angels of light" (2 Cor. 11:14).

Demons like to trick people who are hungry for power or curious about the satanic realm. Sometimes kids will experiment with the occult for the thrill of the forbidden. More often, demons attack people who are sick or who have lost loved ones in death. They set traps by copying the voices of dead friends or relatives. They can even put on shows to prove that they are good spirits! But no spirit is good that contacts people in a way that God has forbidden in His Word. We are to have no contact with mediums, spiritists or the fortune-teller. We must stay clear from all attempts to foretell our futures by party games or by friends who want to try out an occult art as a new kick. The Bible is gravely clear in warning us of the deadly dangers of these practices (Lev. 19:31). No one on earth is wise enough to tell the difference between the true and false in the spirit world on their own. God has ruled that we learn about spiritual things only through His Son the Lord Jesus. He is the only One who has never lied, who knows both our world and theirs. He can tell between the real and the counterfeit. We are not to try to talk to or contact the dead. This can only lead into the occult world. Jesus said, "I tell you the truth: the man who does not come into the sheepfold through the door, but climbs up some other way, is a thief and a robber ... I am the door of the sheep. All who came before me are thieves and robbers, but the sheep did not hear them. I am the door; if anyone enters *through me,* he shall be saved" (John 10:1, 7, 8).

66

The Stars, Séances and Satan Worship

"And the soul that goes after those that have familiar spirits and after wizards that make themselves prostitutes to them— I will set My face against that soul and cut him off from among his people" (Lev. 20:6).

Another false teaching to fool people into being involved with the occult is astrology. Astrology is the occult art of using star and planet motions to try to predict the future. The zodiac is the basis of this sytem. It is a "pretend" ring that goes right around a set of stars that is cut up into twelve parts. Each part has a name or label for its star clusters, like Leo or Virgo or Cancer.

People born under the signs of the zodiac are said to be alike in many ways. Astrologers use the stars to try to advise people on what to do in life, in everything from love affairs to big business decisions. There are at least 10,000 astrologers in the U.S.A. alone. They make over $200,000,000 a year casting horoscopes or star maps of life for people. God is wholly against astrology because it causes people to look to stars instead of to Him. We are not to turn to the things God made for guidance when God longs to show us how to run our lives wisely and wonderfully. God has given us good laws and told us how to seek Him for help in every decision in life.

The Bible warns us to not seek to be guided by the stars "lest you lift up your eyes to heaven, and when you see the sun and the moon and the stars . . . should be driven to worship them" (Deut. 4:19). God says the astrologer or his horoscopes have no power to tell you what He will do to a land if He has to judge it for the sin of astrology (Isa. 47:10-14). To study astrology, even in fun, is to learn about an evil thing that God hates. No true disciple of Jesus lives under a sign or reads a daily horoscope when God has warned us against this. No stars can guide. No sign is the real thing; it only points towards the real thing. The stars were placed in the heavens as a testimony to the power and great glory of their mighty Creator. They point only to Him as our help.

The séance is another deadly tool of the devil. It is usually held around a table with someone who is a medium. (A medium is a person who claims to have a spirit guide.) Often the séance poses as a religious (or even Christian) service. Religious prayers or hymns may be used as long as they do not hold up in love and glory the Risen Lord Jesus or talk about His blood shed for our sins. Through the lips of the medium, the spirit guide can speak when the conditions are right, and pass on information about dead relatives or give direction to those participating in the séance. Sometimes strange apparitions are seen; the table may rise, or voices may speak from the darkness.

Although many times séances have been shown to be clever fakes for the deception of a gullible audience, some spirit contacts are real. It is about these that the Bible warns us so strongly. Being a true medium is something that God deeply hates. It is one of the things for which He has allowed judgment to come to a nation which practiced this by letting the land be put to war. You can read about it in Deuteronomy 18:9-12. The Bible words for mediums here are "necromancer" (medium who consults the dead) and "consulter with familiar spirits" (a medium with a spirit guide or advising angel).

The medium's spirit guide is revealed in the Bible to be really a demon from hell. Demons apparently keep records of all people who live on earth. They can copy their voices and looks just as easily as you or I could use a videotape recorder. People who have had loved ones die are easy prey of these creatures of Satan. They trick these sad people into thinking they are their dead friends come back to speak with them. God hates so deeply this horrible deception (Lev. 19:31; 20:27). He had people put to death who kept talking with these demons that pretend to be friends because they led hundreds of people into the clutches of hell. No true disciple of Jesus would willingly attend a séance and put himself in the way of enemy attack any more than he would think of sleeping in a pit of angry rattlesnakes and black widow spiders to see what it would be like.

67
Ouija Boards and the Occult Movement

God forbids all forms of spiritual knowledge outside of His truth. Many people today do not care about Him but still want to explore the spiritual world. There are many practices and tools that can be used to connect people to the spirit world, but it will not be God's world. It is both foolish and dangerous to use or be involved with any of these kinds of things. Often they are sold as games for kids. But Satan never plays for fun.

There are three bridges that can build a doorway into the occult. No true disciple of Jesus has the right to build any of these bridges. If you have done any of these before giving your life to God, you must take steps to destroy them. Any of these can open you to occult deception and demonic attack. Continuance in any of these is an open invitation to invasion.

1. *Sin.* Any person who lives as the slave of sin can also be blinded by Satan (2 Cor. 4:4). Any form of sin can be a platform for demonic attack. The real base of the devil's invasions are the twin roots of pride and unbelief. (Pride is the refusal to be known for what we really are; unbelief is the rejecting of what God has said to be true.) To protect ourselves from these, every Christian must be open and honest before God. We must trust God's Word as our guide. But out of the roots of pride and unbelief, there are another three sins that stem from these and lack of self-control. These three forms of sin especially lay the ground for occult attack: anger (violence), sexual sin, and bitterness. Disciples of Jesus must be meek, with yielded rights. They must be clean from sex sins. They must always be willing to forgive those that hurt them. To do this will help guard our lives against enemy attack.

2. *The blank mind.* Almost all of the devil's attacks have to do with the mind. He makes thoughts his battleground. We must think of our minds just like a field of war. On no account must

we let thoughts from his side stay there, once they are recognized as from hell. They can be recognized by some of the following signs: flashing thoughts that inject themselves into the mind suddenly, that are unclean or blasphemous to God; ideas that pop into the thoughts without any relationship to the train of thinking; a continual commentary in the mind; thoughts that depress or puff up the believer into forms of depression or pride.

Such thoughts must be rejected in the power of Jesus. We must check all new-coming thoughts with care, comparing them to what God has said in His Word to be true. And we must never allow our minds to go blank without control. This is the flag for enemy attack. God never told us to stop thinking. Only the devil tries to get us to do this. We are to love God with all our minds (Matt. 22:37). This rules out for the Christian every practice or tool that asks us to turn off our minds or thoughts, or surrender our thinking. This will include the use of the Ouija board, drugs, preparations for telepathetic experiments, astral projection, levitation and hypnotism. Only God has the right to guide our thoughts.

Under this rule, you will see that the disciple of Jesus can have nothing to do with any forms of guidance that do not come by our minds and wills and by the Bible. This includes many so-called innocent games like I Ching, Tarot cards and other fortune-telling cards or devices. It also means we will not take part in divination, wear lucky charms, or let ourselves be hypnotized (Deut. 18:10; Jer. 27:9; Hos. 4:12).

3. *Ignorance.* We will not be kept from the enemy only by being sincere. God has promised safety only if we walk carefully in His Word and humbly before His eyes. Some people have thought that guidance and protection from deception comes automatically with being a Christian. But the Bible does not tell us that Christians are immune to deception without conditions being met on their part. We are told to "prove all things; hold fast to that which is good" (1 Thess. 5:21). Jesus did not just say, "The truth will set you free." He said, "If you continue in my word, then you are my disciples indeed; and you shall know the truth, and the truth shall set you free" (John 8:31, 32). We must read the Bible which warns us against doing wrong things. We must not be ignorant of the ways of the devil. Paul could say, "We are not ignorant of his [Satan's] devices" (2 Cor. 2:11).

Here we must say a word of warning. The word *occult* means "mystery" or "secret." There are some things which God cannot show a man until he is proved trustworthy. It would not be wise for God to give people secrets until their lives are truly loving and good. No one is truly loving or good until he has given his life to the Lord Jesus. When a man begins to obey God and live as God wants him to, God will show him everything he needs to know to live happily. To search for spiritual knowledge or power outside of God or His Word is both deadly and wrong. Only God can tell us what we really should know. Only He is qualified to give us the true facts about the spiritual world. Only His power will not harm our lives or that of others. That is why we are not to learn from the occult.

The disciples of Jesus may want to learn something about the devil's tricks. If you pick up a book about things you know are satanic, you must be very, very careful. On no account should you ever read about the how-to of occult arts. It may be all right for the mature and spiritually strong Christian to do a little study about the extent of modern witchcraft—how widespread it is, some of the major doctrines or practices of the occult as far as what they are. But you must never read books on the how-to of the occult—how to cast a spell, become a witch, or run a black mass or black sabbath. This knowledge is occult and forbidden by the Scriptures. We are not to expose ourselves to it. It will infect our minds and spirits. It will hurt our faith and make us afraid. If you read up on the practices of occult powers, you will be affected spiritually by them.

68
Drugs and the Bible

Drugs are not a new problem. They have been used by man for thousands of years. The East has always known and used drugs as a part of some of their religious rituals. People have always known about plants or chemicals to eat or smoke that would do things to their feelings or thoughts. What is new is that people all over the world have turned to drugs to find answers to problems that are too big to handle. Science has made it possible for us to make drugs by the millions. And people who have not given into the real God have tried to find the key to life in another God: chemical consciousness. What has happened to our world from this?

The drug abuse explosion has had terrible results. Millions of people have become addicts and cannot give up their drug habits. Multiplied thousands have died from bad chemicals or overdoses, and thousands more from bad trips that led to suicides or accidental death. The drug scene began in Haight-Ashbury with people smoking grass and throwing kisses and flowers. The apparent beauty ended within a few short months with people burning each other and throwing rocks, bottles, and knives. Today the terrible results of misused drugs can be seen everywhere. The pleasures of sin are only for a short season; the end of that season is all too often insanity, disease and death.

But the great problem with drugs is not just the bad trips. It is the good ones that cannot be brought down to real life. Here is a young man who goes up with a cap of acid. In his trip he feels artistic as colors and texture seem alive in his head and fingers. He grabs a brush and oil paints, and covers his canvas with what looks like a perfect masterpiece. He has never done anything that looks so beautiful to him. Then, many hours later, he comes down. He sees his painting as it really is without a chemical to color his mind. It is then that the shock hits him. It is here that the empty promise of the drug vision shows itself for what it really is. His picture is nothing but a scribbled scrawl of smeared paint. His masterpiece was an illusion. It was all in his mind, and is now gone forever.

This is what really hurts in the drug scene. The expanded mind is so unreal and unnatural. The colors and scenes really come from chemicals. Your world is only pretty when your mind is the slave of a drug. When it wears off, it is the same old world with the same old problems. You are still the same person that you were before, or sometimes worse! And often it takes bigger doses to get the same levels of experience the next time. Nothing is different. Your guilt, your loneliness and emptiness is still there waiting for you.

How different it is with Jesus! "Heaven above is softer blue; earth around is sweeter green; something lives in every hue Christless eyes have never seen." Someone who knew the reality of God's Word and God's Son wrote those words. The whole earth becomes beautiful when you know the love of Jesus. Your soul becomes clear, and your inner eyes of the spirit open to see the loveliness of His creation, when your heart is at peace with the Bible God. The loneliness is gone. The world seems no longer empty when your heart is full of Christ.

Listen to what one young man, Samuel Logan Brengle, said about the difference the power of God's Holy Spirit made in his life: "He gave me such a blessing as I have never dreamed a man can have this side of heaven. It was an unutterable revelation. It was a heaven of love that came into my heart. My soul melted like wax before the fire. I sobbed and sobbed. I loathed myself that I had ever sinned against Him or lived for myself and not for His glory. Every ambition for self was now gone. The pure flame of love burned like a blazing fire would burn a moth.

"I walked out over Boston Commons before breakfast, weeping and praising God. Oh, how I loved! In that hour I knew Jesus and I loved Him till it seemed my heart would break with love. I was filled with love for all His little creatures. I saw the little sparrows chattering. I loved them. I saw a little worm wriggling across my path; I stepped over it; I didn't want to hurt any living thing. I loved the dogs, I loved the horses, I loved the little urchins in the streets, I loved the strangers who hurried past me—I loved the whole world!"

No one who has ever lived and loved the Bible God ever needs drugs again. His joy is real!

The Bible mentions four powerful drugs, three that are stronger than L.S.D. They are wormwood, hemlock, gall and myrrh. None are ever used to induce visions of the Bible God. No prophet of God ever used drugs to speak or to listen to God in the Scriptures. Anything that takes away the conscious control of our minds or feelings is a sin against our souls. No one has a right to put himself at the mercy of a chemical that opens the door of the mind to the spirit world outside of Christ's loving protection. No true disciple of Jesus uses drugs. The use of drugs to put us into contact with the spirit world is something that God hates with a holy anger because it brings such deep spiritual damage to the souls He has entrusted to us. It is worth a note to see that Jesus was offered a drug mixture only once in His life—and He refused it.

It is silly to say, "God made pot or peyote (or some other chemical) so it is holy." God made poisonous toadstools and spiders, too, but no one has started a movement to eat these. We are not to eat or drink anything that will confuse our minds or bring spiritual darkness to our hearts. Drugs that break the mind free from conscious control by the will open the dimensional door to the occult world. Over this blank mind bridge, Satan and his dark spirits can invade the cities of our souls. The Bible specifically warns us here. It absolutely forbids the use of drugs. In Revelation 18:23 a special word is used. It is *sorceries.* The word is in Greek "pharmakeia." It is the word we make use of in the English word *pharmacy* or druggist today. It means "to make religious trips by the use of drugs." God says this will fool all the nations in the last days. God warns that no man who uses drugs or sells them to others for a trip will be in heaven (Rev. 21:8). Beware that you do not get fooled by the tricks of the devil. Many false Christs are coming (Matt. 24:3-5). Only the Jesus of the Bible is the real one. He has told us how He would show himself to us, and it is never by drugs. Jesus said, "If anyone loves Me he will *keep My word*; and My Father will love him, and we will come to him and make our home with him. He who does *not* love Me does not keep My words; and the word which you hear is not Mine, but the Father's who sent Me" (John 14:23, 24).

69

Breaking Free From the Dark Dimension

"Give yourself to God. *Stand against* the devil, and he will run away from you" (James 4:7).

Have you been in the occult? If you have had contact with any occult powers, you may have built a bridge into the dark world of hell. Check your life with care. Have you had trouble with your mind? Have you felt you were losing it? Do you feel afraid many times without knowing why? Do very strong feelings to do evil things keep coming back to you? Are you hung up with some funny ideas about food, or marriage, or certain days of the week? Do you have voices that keep speaking to you? Do you have real trouble with doubt? Have you had in your thoughts either the idea that you are nothing or that you are God himself? Do you think about killing yourself? All these can be signs of mind attacks from the powers of hell.

If you have had even a short contact with any occult method or practice, do not pass it off as harmless. It may have been in fun. It may have only been one time; you may not even have thought much about it at the time. But many times Satan can put a hook into your soul through just one contact. He will pull on that hook when you really need God. Do not laugh this off! God is terribly serious about this. If you know of any time that you did something or studied something occult, you must do this to be sure you will be free from its power:

1. *Give yourself wholly to Jesus.* Call His name aloud! Call on Him to help you. Tell Him you really want to serve Him. Tell Him you really want to be free. If you cannot call on His name, your mind may be in a fight with the powers of hell. Take your Bible. Make yourself read out aloud some verses that talk about the power of Jesus. Use verses like Luke 10:17 where Jesus said He has given His followers power over all the power of the enemy, and that nothing will hurt us; and 1 John 3:8 which tells

us Jesus came to destroy the works of the devil.

Believe that He can do what He says. He has never told a lie. He has power over all the power of the enemy. Yield yourself to the Lord Jesus! Give your whole self to Him. Submit your being to Him. Let His holy strength hold you up in your heart. Cast yourself on the living Christ. He is the only one who can help you.

2. *Confess all sin to the Lord.* You must be willing to say good-bye forever to a life of hate and anger, sex sin and bitterness. These are the key sins that open a mind to demonic attack. No disciple of Jesus can hold onto such things. You must see how much they hurt God. You must hate what they have done to you, to others, and to Him. And then you must give them up forever.

Confess to Jesus all that you can remember about the occult things you took part in. Pray something like this: "Jesus, I have hurt you and broken your laws by my sin. I have done many sinful things. I have learned about things you have forbidden. I have done wrong in seeing a fortune-teller; I have done wrong in using a Ouija board, doing divination, reading a horoscope." Put in all the things you can remember. Tell Him you are really sorry for what you have done. And make a solemn promise that you will never do or study any of these things again.

3. *Renounce the devil and all of his works.* You must say a firm and final good-bye to everything you learned from him. You must say this *aloud* and *openly.* You see, the word occult means "mystery." For Jesus to break its power, you must bring the secret sins of the occult studies into the open, into the light of God's justice. Speak to the devil with firm faith that Jesus is with you. Satan is afraid of Him. Use the Word of God. Say, "The Bible says, 'Submit yourself to God.' I have done that. It says, 'Resist the devil, and he shall flee from you.' *God* said that. He does not lie. In Jesus' name, Satan, I *resist* you. I *renounce* your hold on my life. I *reject* you and all that I learned from your world. Jesus is my Lord. Jesus is my King. Jesus is my Master."

Do this with faith in the Lord Jesus. He has promised to honor His Word. Do it with firm heart. Do it, if you like, with a friend who has strong faith in Jesus. Let him pray with you until you know you are free. You will be able to tell by His peace. "For God did not give us a spirit of fear. He gave us a spirit of power and of love and of a good mind" (2 Tim. 1:7).

4. *Destroy all objects, books, records and materials that had any connection with your occult involvement.* Nothing must re-

main, or you will not be delivered. Do this, no matter how much these things cost you or how much sentimental value thay had to you. Burn them all. This is what the men of Ephesus who had been involved with occult arts did (Acts 19:19-20). You must also break off with all of your friends who still continue with these things. If you have relatives who go on practicing magic or occult arts, stay away from them as much as possible. As a matter of fact, it may be dangerous to pray for them on your own until you are built up in the Lord and are stronger in His love.

When all this is done, take by faith the promises of the Lord Jesus. If you have met His conditions, you have the right to claim His promises. Rest completely in His forgiveness and peace. He has said, "If we confess our sins, he is faithful and just to forgive us our sins, and to cleanse us from all unrighteousness" (1 John 1:9; see also James 5:16; 1 Pet. 5:7-11; Eph. 1:17-23; 6:10-18).

Section XVI
The Disciple &
SELF-CONTROL

70

When People Hassle You

It's a rotten world. As long as we live in it, we will meet people who hassle us. There's no escape from it. Every week, no matter how close we get to God, we will always run into someone or something that gets on our nerves.

Some time ago I picked up a little tract. I can't remember its title or its author. But what he said is worth saying again to every disciple of Jesus in the world. His message has stayed with me and I want to share it with you. Here is the heart of his message for you to think about and to practice when people hassle you.

"The Son of man came not to be ministered to but to minister, and to give his life a ransom for many" (Mark 10:45). This "coming to be ministered to" is the spirit of the world. It is at the bottom of fights in the nursery, arguments at school, quarrels between people and wars among nations. Isn't it true that we are too often cross, angry, hassled? Sometimes we show it by blowing our cool. Sometimes we keep our cool outwardly but the rotten feelings are still there. And why? Most probably because we have come to be ministered to and have been disappointed.

The fact is, we are *always* wanting to be ministered to by people, by fortune, by circumstances, even by the weather. It is so natural, so needed, so "right." If we are crossed or frustrated (as we often are), we are apt to get uptight and sulky, and we usually wind up making ourselves and others miserable.

You are slighted, ignored, brushed aside. Your boss doesn't show you the proper consideration. Your brother doesn't treat you with the respect due to your awareness, your wisdom, your talents. You feel it very much; in fact, you are really very hassled by it. It is because *your* feelings, *your* rights, *your* gifts, *your* position, *your* dignity, *your* importance were not recognized. *You* were not ministered to. Perhaps you are *jealous*; another is praised and put before you. He does better than you. She is luckier than you. The honor, the success, the popularity, the reward went to the others. They got what you thought *you* ought to have. You wanted it for yourself. You came to be ministered to. And because they have been ministered to in your place, you are jealous.

Think about it: Have you been hassled lately because someone slighted you or put someone else before you? Can you see now that your feelings were hurt because you were expecting to be ministered to? Confess your part in the situation.

Have you ever been treated like dirt? There is no excuse for people who have rotten attitudes and who deliberately put you down. But you are a follower of Jesus. I ask you, if you had come, like your Master, "not to be ministered to, but to minister," would you be feeling so sore and angry?

Think about that for a minute. How would your attitude be different if your main purpose were to minister rather than be ministered to?

Not praised? You have been kind to someone. You did him a service. It cost you something to do it. Naturally you thought he would appreciate your good deed. But he didn't, at least not the way you thought he should have. You expected warm thanks, a little fuss made over it, but your friend took it quite cooly. And now you are disgusted. You feel in your heart that you will never help anyone else again. Why? You have ministered to another. You helped someone in need. But *you* have not been ministered to by his thanks and praise, and perhaps by a little flattery, too.

After all, what is the real reason for doing something for another person? Is it to receive thanks and praise? Or is it because disciples of Jesus are called to minister to other people? And if Jesus tells us to do something, should we then stop doing it because some human being doesn't respond just the way we like? Ask the Lord right now to show you how your attitudes need to change in this matter of expecting thanks and praise.

Not consulted? You have great taste, sound judgment. Your head is together. You really have what it takes to give advice. But no one asked you. Or when they did ask, they ignored what you said even though you really felt you knew what you were talking about. You can't understand it. You feel rubbed the wrong way. Your spirit is ruffled. What is the trouble? Is it that you came wanting to minister to your friend, and by not taking your advice he is now in a real mess? Not at all. As a matter of fact, he has done very well without your help. The trouble is this: *you* have not been recognized. Your reputation as an authority has not been ministered unto. You came not to minister, but to be ministered unto.

You may speak in public. A good crowd comes out to one of your rap times. You see with satisfaction that Mr. X, a famous and important Christian, is there too. You have a great subject and you wax eloquent. At the end you feel very pleased with yourself. You naturally expect Mr. X to come up at once, grab your hand and thank you warmly. But he walks out of the hall quietly without a word. How disappointed you feel! And why is this? You ministered to a lot of people. But this was not quite what you wanted. In your heart you wanted that sermon to minister to *you*.

Think again about your gifts and abilities. Who gave them to you? In whose service are you called to use them? Does it really matter, then, if mere humans appreciate and recognize you? Ask the Lord to help you have the right motives as you use your gifts and abilities.

Perhaps you are bothered about your job. You are doing fairly well. Your needs are met. But you want great things, and circumstances just haven't lived up to what you expected. You feel down constantly over it. What is really at the bottom of all this? You want to make a bigger show, to be thought more of. You want to be rich, and you covet things God doesn't want you to have. And when your desires are not granted, when your love for success is not ministered to, you are discouraged or angry.

You went in for a race, a game, a competition. You failed; you were beaten. How horrible you felt! To this day that feeling haunts you. Do you play golf? Have you ever seen a full-grown, well-educated man stamp wildly up and down on the ground because a poor little golf ball did not minister to his conceit by going where he wanted it to? You say, "But we're supposed to do our best and to win." Yes, of course; but after all, it is only a game. And a disciple of Jesus must not take games too seriously. Even on the playing fields he can minister. When he is beaten he can enjoy the satisfaction of knowing that in losing he has ministered to the winner.

Think it through. Whatever we do in life, you will be surprised to find how much of your unrest and how many of your troubles arise from this same cause: coming to be ministered to instead of coming to minister, even in the little things. You want a wet day but it turns out fine; you want it to be sunny and it rains. A visitor calls when you want to go out. You are asked to sing, but your voice is husky and fails you in the middle of the song. The answer to the letter doesn't come. The phone rings. The phone doesn't ring. The pen won't write. The dress doesn't fit. The fire won't burn. Something is wrong with the meal. There is no meal.

There is nothing big, nothing we can really put our finger on, but we are always coming into the world with our likes and dislikes, wishes and wants; and if we are not ministered to in these little things, we get bothered and uptight and hassled with ourselves and with everyone else.

There is a better way to live! Instead of having the spirit of being ministered to, we can have the spirit of ministering to others. We can remember that Jesus said, "Whosoever will be chief among you, let him be your servant" (Matt. 20:27).

This doesn't mean that we won't feel badly when hassles happen. Annoyances, disappointments, rotten things that happen—of course we feel them! They would be no use to us if we didn't. But they don't have to make us uptight. If we come to be ministered to, we hold our hurts. We blow them up big in our minds, we nurse them in our hearts, we give in to them; we let them build their nests and hatch eggs. But when we come to minister, we don't hold grudges; we give hassles no major attention, no welcome. We are too busy with our Father's business to bother about them. Let us be like Jesus. He was always too busy thinking of others and ministering to them to concern himself about being ministered to. One remedy for being touchy is this; get busy caring for your brothers.

How have you been spending your time lately? Nursing your grievances, or serving the Lord by caring for others? Think back over the last three days. How much time have you been nursing grievances, and how much time caring for others? Do you see any changes that should be made in the way you spend your time? Ask the Lord to help you find practical ways of caring for others. Think of all the people you know who could use some kind of help, such as babysitting for a busy mother, personal Bible study for a new Christian, tutoring for a floundering high school student. After making your list, put a check mark beside those things that you are best able to do, and ask the Lord to show you what He wants you to do about helping in these and other ways.

"I send you my best wishes for your birthday," a girl wrote; "I hope you are dead." She was right. When this happens we can welcome disappointments, hardship, thorns, slights. They may all be turned to excellent account. To fail in getting what we want may be good fortune; to have our wishes crossed may be a positive blessing. A person who snubs us may be counted a friend instead of an enemy. As self dies, Jesus lives! And we in our own tiny measure may sacrifice ourselves for God's glory and the good of others.

Paul said, "I am crucified with Christ: nevertheless I live;

yet not I, but Christ liveth in me; and the life which I now live in the flesh I live by the faith of the Son of God, who loved me, and gave himself for me" (Gal. 2:20).

He expanded on this theme in Romans 6:1-10. Look up this passage and study it carefully.

Each time we experience a hurt or a hassle, we are really being given an opportunity to make real in our lives this truth that we are crucified with Christ. God uses these experiences to make us into the people He wants us to be. Look up Romans 5:3-5 and meditate on the qualities that are developed by tribulation as listed there. Take a moment right now and ask God to take your current hassle and use it in your life to produce these qualities.

A practical help in living the crucified life is found in Colossians 3:1-4. Look up this passage and study it carefully. If you learn to avoid setting your affection on things on earth, you will find that hassles won't hassle you so much. And if your mind is busy thinking about God and Christ and the Holy Spirit and all that they have done for you, you won't have time to spare for brooding over hurts.

71

What to Do About Anger

Every disciple of Jesus should get angry. Did you know that you can be angry and not sin? The Bible says, "Be ye angry, and sin not" (Eph. 4:26).

The Lord Jesus Christ, who was completely sinless, showed anger more than once. Matthew 23:13-36 records a long denunciation He made against the hypocritical scribes and Pharisees. He was angry with them because they had utterly missed the point of God's law. Read the passage and notice things Jesus said against them.

On another occasion Jesus went into a synagogue on the sabbath and noticed a man with a paralyzed hand. He called the man to Him, intending to heal the hand. But He noticed something in the attitude of those around Him—something hostile to himself and to the idea of healing on the sabbath, a day when Jewish tradition decreed no work was to be done. He asked a question that should have pricked their hearts, but they stood there in stony silence. Scripture says, "And when he had looked round about on them with anger, being grieved for the hardness of their hearts, he said to the man, Stretch out your hand. And he stretched it out; and his hand was restored as whole as the other" (Mark 3:5). Jesus was angry because those Jewish leaders were less concerned with a suffering human being than they were with their own interpretation of God's laws.

Holy anger is not for our own sake. It is for God's rights and for others' hurts. We ought to be angry over sin or injustice to others. Also, in holy anger you actually care about the one who causes the wrong. You don't condone the wrong, but you do not reject the one who does it. Because you care, you take practical steps to right the wrong, and also to befriend and help the one who caused it.

How can you love anyone that you are angry with? C. S.

Lewis points out that you know one person you can be mad at without rejecting him altogether. That person looks back at you from the mirror every morning. When you get sore at yourself for doing some dumb thing, you are angry because you really do care about yourself. The day you don't care is the day you start thinking about suicide. If you really love yourself in the biblical way you will be angry with things you do that are wrong and take steps to change them. This is biblical anger. Learn from this how to treat others who do wrong.

The Lord Jesus never showed anger over His *own* rights. We have no record that He ever spoke in anger when people put Him down or cruelly wronged Him, even around the cross. And although the disciple of Jesus has a right to be angry at himself over his own wrongs, he does not have a right to be angry with someone who abuses him. The only time he can be angry is when others' rights are being jumped on and others who are weak and helpless are being hurt.

Think for a moment about the last time you got angry. Or maybe you're angry about something right now. What was the cause of that anger?

Were you angry because another person was hurt or wronged, or were you angry because you yourself were hurt?

What do you do about feeling angry when someone does something rotten to you? Understand this: no one can help feeling angry when he is hurt or put down in some way. God does not forbid us to feel hurt. He, too, feels hurt like this, only on a much greater scale than we could ever imagine. It is not our feelings that God wants to control; no place in the Bible are the feelings of anger or hurt called sin. God only tells us what we must *do* with those feelings.

Feelings are very useful. They are like level meters on a tape recorder or the mercury in a thermometer. They measure our response to what happens around us. They tell us something about our values. God will not take away your feelings. Being a disciple of Jesus does not mean that you feel less and less hurt or angry if wrong things happen to you. But it does mean that you will learn more and more about how to *deal* with those feelings and how to react the right way toward those who caused them. Love is not a feeling, it is a wise choice.

Angry emotions can come from one big thing or from a whole lot of little things that niggle away at us during a day and build up to the point of explosion. Sometimes we are irritated by things: the roof leaks, the car won't start, the nail won't drive, the pen won't write. Other times we are put out by people who always do things wrong, and by others who always do things right when we do them wrong. Sometimes we just get mad at ourselves because we don't feel we are making it as we should.

Be glad for irritations. You can't change them or make them go away; as long as you live in this world you will have irritations. But God can use them to help you grow up fast in your Christian life. You can thank Him that because you are His child nothing will ever happen to you that He has not filtered through His loving hands. You can thank Him for these irritations. Ask Him to show you what wrong attitude of yours that irritation has brought to light, and how He wants you to change.

Think of two barrels. One is filled with honey, the other with acid. If I kick the barrel filled with acid, what comes out? Acid. If I kick the barrel filled with honey, instead of getting scarred I get sweetness. The point is that the kick doesn't *create* what is in the barrel; it just *reveals* it. The last time that you were kicked by someone, what came out—acid or honey?

An old goldsmith had his flame on a sample of gold. His friend asked him why he kept peering closely at the gold. He said, "When there are still impurities in it, I keep on the flame. The impurities come to the top and form a scum that I can skim off. As long as it is not pure, the gold is dull. But when all the dross is gone, the gold is like a mirror. When I can see my face in it, I turn off the flame." God has us in His fire, and He will not turn it off until we are pure. Welcome irritations; they are not enemies but friends. Used rightly, they can carry us closer to God than blessings. The secret of dealing with anger is to use it to correct your own life if your anger is directed at yourself or at irritations in your life; and use it to help others correct their lives if it involves other people.

Read the following scriptures and make a careful study of them for your benefit: Job 23:10; Zechariah 13:8, 9; 1 Peter 1:6-9; 1 Peter 5:10.

Apply these scriptures to yourself. Perhaps you have been suffering some trial or some irritations. Perhaps people have been treating you badly, or things have not been going well in your life. Talk to God about it; tell Him about the things that have been troubling you, and then use the scriptures you have just studied to help you come up with a commitment to cooperate with God in the work He wants to do in your life.

What can you do about angry feelings? Don't blow up. If you are right, you don't need to lose your temper; if you are wrong, you can't afford to. Check out Proverbs 14:29 and Ecclesiastes 7:9 for some of God's words on anger.

Don't defend your own "rights," for a love slave of the Lord Jesus has given up all personal rights.

Don't try to shift the blame for your angry feelings onto someone else. It's too easy to make others mad, too, by yelling at them when we are angry (Prov. 15:1; 29:22). That only results in another Viet Nam in your home. It is not Christian to go around like a volcano with a cork in it. Some disciples of Jesus think the proper way to deal with anger is to hold it in, so they go around silently fuming or suffering. No, that is unreal. We are not to let the sun go down on our wrath. The one who nurses anger is called a fool in Scripture (Eph. 4:26; Eccles. 7:9).

If you get angry, do these things:

1. *Examine* what happened. Look hard at yourself. Remember that God let that thing happen! Do you believe that He loves you? Do you believe that "all things work together for good to them that love God" (Rom. 8:28)? Do you believe that if we are "faithful over a few things" (like dealing properly with small irritations) He will make us "ruler over many things" (Matt. 25:23)? Do you believe that Christians will one day judge the world and even angels (1 Cor. 6:2, 3)? Then you can thank Him for it, can't you? Take a deep breath, then *do it.* "Thank you, Lord, for this rotten day. Thank you for this rotten friend."

2. *Expose* your heart to the Holy Spirit. Let Him run His plow over your heart. Ask God, "What is happening here, Lord? What have I got in my heart that shouldn't be there? Is there something I am still hanging onto that is Yours, and I'm mad because I think it's still mine?" Let the Spirit of God show you what needs changing.

3. *Empty* your life of these wrong habits of selfishness and anger by the basic steps of honesty, repentance and asking God's forgiveness. We do not know how blind we are to our own faults until the Lord brings things or people across our path to show them to us. Whatever comes up, turn to God with it to get it straightened out. Let God skim you of dross again and again and again. He will not stop until you are as clean as you can be. Let the Holy Spirit show you through these things what kind of man or woman you ought to be. He will make you that man or woman. From now on welcome those miserable days. You will learn more from them about being a real disciple of Jesus than you can learn in a week of blessings.

Through the pen of Paul, God tells us, "In everything give thanks; for this is the will of God in Christ Jesus concerning you" (1 Thess. 5:18). Have you learned to give thanks in every situation? Perhaps knowing something of God's purpose in our life will help you learn this lesson. We already looked at Romans 8:28, but now let's look at it again, and along with it, verse 29: "And we know that all things work together for good to them that love God, to them who are the called according to his purpose. For whom he did foreknow, he also did predestinate to be conformed to the image of his Son, that he might be the firstborn among many brethren."

Did you get that? We are to be conformed to the image of God's Son, Jesus Christ. That's why God works all things together for good in our lives—the _good_ being our conformity to the image of Christ.

Take some time right now and think about what it means to be conformed to the image of Christ. What is Christ like? What are His qualities? What areas of your life need the most change if they are to become like Him? What areas of your life are already very close to being like Christ? (Don't be lured into false modesty here: if God has been working in your life, there should be some areas that He has brought into conformity with the image of His Son.)

Then think about some of the things that make you angry or irritated. How can God use these things to make you more like Christ? Perhaps you have begun to notice Him doing so already. What must be your part in cooperating with God, allowing Him to use these problems to make you more like His Son?

Before His death and resurrection, Jesus promised His disciples that when He departed from them He would send the Holy Spirit to be with them. And He indicated that the Spirit would teach them further truths. Read this promise in John 16:12-15. The Holy Spirit can work in your life to show you what God wants changed, and then to change it as you cooperate. God even helps you _want_ to make the changes: "For it is God who works in you both to will and to do of his good pleasure" (Phil. 2:13).

Part of making changes in your life is recognizing that certain things are sinful, and then confessing and turning away from that sin. God's Word says, "If we confess our sins, he is faithful and just to forgive us our sins, and to cleanse us from all unrighteousness" (1 John 1:9).

Take some time right now to confess the things that God has shown you are wrong. Ask the Holy Spirit to teach you what God wants you to be like and to work in your life to make you both will and do God's will.

72

How to Get Rid of Worry

Do you worry much? Do you know that God says you shouldn't worry at all?

The Bible says, "Be anxious for nothing, but in everything by prayer and supplication with thanksgiving let your requests be made known to God" (Phil. 4:6). That phrase, "Be careful for nothing," really means, "Don't worry about anything!"

Why do people worry? Sometimes it is hard to put your finger on any one cause. It may be a whole lot of things that never get dealt with, or it may be one big problem that threatens you. Worry is a form of fear—fear of the future, fear of death, fear of failure. But no disciple of Jesus can afford the luxury of worry. It is a foolish and destructive habit that can kill people like a slow poison. Only a true disciple of Jesus has the power of complete freedom from worry. God is your Father; the Lord Jesus is your friend; the Holy Spirit is your comforter and strength. The triune God is on your side. You don't need to be afraid of anything.

Being worried or afraid comes from lack of faith. If we really trust God, we don't have to worry. One cure for worry is to spend some time reading about who God is. The more we learn about Him the more we can trust Him.

Try it right now. Look up each of the Scriptures listed below, and carefully meditate on what that scripture tells you about God: Genesis 1:1, 27; Deuteronomy 32:4; Psalm 90:2; 145:3; Matthew 19:26; John 3:16; 17:3; Ephesians 1:3; James 1:17; 1 John 1:5; 4:8.

Another step in conquering worry is to give your problems to God—lock, stock and barrel. Sign them over to Him with no hesitations or holding back. If you want to get rid of worries, give them to God and let Him take care of them. Remember Philippians 4:6! That's a good verse to memorize. Then when worries come you can recite it to yourself as part of your campaign to get rid of worry.

Here's another practical idea. Let's say you have trouble getting to sleep at night. It's not because your conscience is troubled, but simply because you are worrying. Take a piece of paper and write all your worries on it. Then go to God in prayer. Tell Him, "Father, here are all the things I am worried about. I am Your child. This is too big for me to handle. I can't take it. But I know a little bit about how big You are. You can help where no one else can help. Here are my worries. Take them tonight. I give them to you as a child gives his father a toy he can't fix or a problem he can't solve. Please undertake for me. I claim your promise in 1 Peter 5:7 that says, 'Casting all your care upon him, for he cares for you.' "

Then go to bed. And if your mind starts to dwell on those worries, chase them out with scripture that you have memorized. Try Philippians 4:6 and 1 Peter 5:7; try some of the scriptures we just studied that tell what God is like. As you fill your mind with scripture, you will leave no room for worries.

What do people worry about? You only worry about things you have never given over completely to God. You have two choices to make about your problems. Either you can try to solve them on your own, or you can give them to God. You can't give them up for a little while and then grab them back to worry about. Have you ever tried to watch a seed grow into a plant by digging it up every day to see how it is doing? It doesn't work that way. You have to leave it alone. You have to trust it to the ground. You can deal with your own needs in the same way. Give them to God. Rest your case in His strong hands. Let Him take total charge.

God will let you get into situations that you can't handle by yourself. You should be glad about them rather than worrying about them. This is a chance to prove for yourself how faithful God is when we give Him everything. What is there to worry about? If the problem is so big that you can't think of an answer, it will be more wonderful and amazing to see how God can solve it. Our needs give Him a chance to show himself strong on our behalf.

Try it right now. Use the promises in Philippians 4:6 and 1 Peter 5:7; or use some other scripture that has become meaningful to you. Give your biggest problem to God and claim His promises to take care of it. And then leave the problem with God.

Only the man or woman who doesn't know Jesus has a right to worry. If you run your own life, you have good cause to worry. You really have to insure yourself against everything when you run your own life. But all the money or caution or defences or protections in the world cannot guarantee the life of a selfish man.

Only as a disciple of Jesus do you know you are immortal until your work is finished. Only the disciple of Jesus knows the One who guards and keeps better than armies, the One whose security is stronger than castles. Whatever things we need for living are in His hands to provide for us as He sees we need them.

Jesus spent a lot of time teaching His disciples to trust God rather than worrying about their own needs. One example of His teaching is Matthew 6:25-34. Look up this Scripture, and then answer these questions: What is God's person *not* supposed to be worried, anxious, or concerned about? What *is* God's person supposed to be concerned about?

People feel they have a right to some things in life. The disciple of Jesus has no rights because he doesn't belong to himself anymore. He is the Lord's. Thus, if some right of life is threatened, he can simply say to Christ, "You know my needs. I have done all You have asked me to. If I can still serve You to the best of my ability, You must supply all that I will need for Your work." Working for Jesus is far better than just working for an earthly boss. If we do what He asks us to do, if we are obedient and faithful, He must supply our needs. We have an ironclad guarantee of His faithfulness. But we are men and women who have no rights of our own, and to whom the word *rights* means only that which is borrowed from God.

Are there rights in your life that you have never given to Jesus? If there are, you will worry every time those rights are challenged. God will show this to you. He will keep on arranging things to bring the situation to your attention so you can see what you need to give up. People worry about five basic rights:

1. *Acceptance*—a sense of belonging, being thought well of, feeling loved and cared for. Everyone wants to be loved.

2. *Accomplishment*—the right to do something worthwhile with our talents, time, and abilities.

3. *Possessions.* All of us need certain possessions—food, clothes, shelter, or money to meet needs and to pay bills and taxes. We need to have things that we can call our own.

4. *Safety.* Everyone wants the right to have safety—to be protected from hurt, danger or disaster, illness or disability.

5. *Security* is an important need. We want to be confident about tomorrow, to feel safe about whatever the future holds.

All of us have "rights" to these five things. When we give our lives to the Lord Jesus, our rights become His. We become love-slaves of Christ. Everything we own or have rights to are transferred to His ownership. We are "bought with a price" (1 Cor. 6:20).

Let us say you sell a car to a friend. You liked the car but felt you should sell it, and your friend pays a good price to get it from you. You sign the papers, and he gives you the money and takes away the car. Will you then worry day and night whether anyone will scratch it or steal it from him? Not if you really have turned it over to him.

If you insist on worrying about something, that says one thing: you have not yet given up some right to God. There is still one area that is not wholly given up to Christ, one thing that you are willfully holding back from His loving Lordship. Worry means you are taking back the ownership of something that no longer belongs to you.

If you need to be delivered from the bondage of worry, do these things:

1. Ask God to show you what thing it is that you are holding back. It may be your right to be thought well of by someone. It may be the right to be healthy or wise or happy. It may be the right to be sure of everything. Ask yourself: Why am I worried? What is it that I am afraid of? What is that right that I still hold onto and have not given to God?

2. Write out your right. Put it on a piece of paper. Let that slip of paper represent your ownership of that thing. Then take a red pencil and write across it: "*Sold* to the Father, Son and Holy Ghost." Then take your slip of paper to God. Ask His forgiveness for holding back that which is rightfully His. Then take a match and burn it. Offer it to Him and in your mind's eye see it taken from you, destroyed, done away with, forever if need be.

3. Thank God for taking back that which is His. Then expect Him to test you. Believe that within the next two weeks He will put you on trial over that which you have surrendered. When it is challenged, remember that you have given it to God so it is no longer yours to worry about. If you want to have anything, you can only borrow it from the Lord, and He can have it back any time He asks for it. That must be your attitude; that must be your stand.

In winding up this study of worry, I want to add one important thought: Do not give God your *responsibilities*, the things He has told *you* to do. He does not want you to be a puppet, and He will not do for you the things that He told you to do. Give up only your *rights*. Rights are those things that you feel you deserve because they are things everybody needs. Responsibilities are duties that must be done and that sometimes are hard to do.

Do not say to God, "Oh, God, I now surrender my right to be a holy man. I give You my right to pray and read Your Word and obey it. Take it, dear Lord, because I don't want to worry about it." That is not surrender; that is sin. You can only be delivered from worry that is caused by some unyielded right. Worry that comes from sin must be taken care of by honest repentance, forgiveness and restitution. No private surrender of rights will accomplish that for you.

73

How to Fit More Into a Day

Part of the problem of not successfully using your abilities is what seems to be another problem: not having enough time during a day. Here are some hints to help you get more into your day.

1. *Plan a schedule for yourself.* You may have never done this before. Try it now. Some men who really changed the world for God found time because of their solid self-discipline. John Wesley said in the 24 hours of a day that he had eight hours to sleep, eight ·hours to work, eat, and study, and the other eight hours he could give to God. Jonathan Edwards disciplined his life so that he often had 13 hours a day to spend in study! Self-discipline is one of the parts of the fruit of the Spirit.

Pick a time when you *have* to get up. Set it according to your responsibilities. Then set another time when you *ought* to get to bed. You can find out how much sleep you need by going to sleep in a perfectly dark room for a week and averaging out the time it takes for you to wake up naturally, by yourself, without an alarm. Most people need between 7-8 hours, some a little longer or shorter. Set your night limit by this time.

Then plan out your day. If you have a job or school, you know how long it takes to do it each day, what time you will have to leave to get there, what time you can expect to be home. This gives you your second big division in time. Leave that until later.

Take the first block of time—that between waking up and leaving for work or school. How many hours do you have here? Write down, in order, the things you usually do after you get up—make your bed, wash, dress, eat breakfast, etc. Write them out and beside each one put the shortest time you can do each job properly in. Time yourself next to see just how long it has taken you to do these things. Go into the rest of your day in the same way. Divide it into big blocks and then subdivide each block up with rough times for each small part of the day. It may help you to put things in a "must do," "should do," or "could do" category. This will help you to put priority on the things that *have* to be done and the good things that *might* be done if you have time. You can use this same idea, by the way, to make a list up the night before if you have a whole lot of things on your mind to do the following day and you're worried about them. It will help clear your mind and give you a priority list to tack in order of importance.

2. *Have a race with yourself.* Now the fun begins. You should have a rough time for each thing you have to do in your day. Tomorrow when you get up, spend each small section having a race with yourself. Compete with your own time. How long does it take you to make the bed? Today you will see if you can do it just as well with a minute knocked off the time. How long did it take you to wash and shave or get your face ready for the day? You will do it faster today. Race yourself! If you have a five-minute timer like an egg timer or kitchen timer, you can use that to race against the clock. Do it in fun, but work as fast as you can. Race yourself against yourself. Win from each day a minute here, a couple of minutes there. See just how much time you have won before your next fixed responsibility time arrives!

3. *Use the "nothing" times to do something.* Often during a day we have times when we are inactive: waiting in line for a bus or train, traveling to and from work, waiting for a kettle to boil, a bath to run, someone to come home. How many hours can be used of these "nothing" times! Read a helpful book, do a little study; or, if you have nothing else to do, spend some few moments in prayer or in quiet meditation on the goodness of God. Make it a practice to carry your Bible with you everywhere you go. When you wait for someone or are doing nothing of profit, break it open and read until your time is up.

4. *Learn to select.* You can't read *all* books, so make sure the ones you *do* read are ones directly related to your goals. You can't go to all meetings, so go only to those that will best help forward what God is doing in your life. Select! The *good* is the enemy of the *best.* Learn to reject things that you could do which would take time away from the more important things.

5. *Do the hard things first. Make* yourself do them. Don't get into the bad habit of putting off the worst things until the last. Tackle them early when you are fresh. Begin all the worst tasks first and get them out of the way as soon as you can. This is one secret of discipline. It will help make you a man or woman who can really make the most of your time. Tackle the hard jobs first and finish with the easiest ones.

6. *Learn to be punctual.* Stick to your schedules. If you have an appointment, get there on time. It is a bad testimony and poor stewardship of God's time to arrive late everywhere. It will help if you keep a diary of appointments. Consult it often, plan ahead, leave plenty of time to get there, and don't leave things until the last minute. If it helps, set your watch forward five to ten minutes; sometimes it helps to get you there earlier, especially if you forget it *was* set forward!

7. Finally, *avoid all sidetracks.* There are many fun things you could do, but you are a child of God and are in training for the King of kings. Avoid all petty interferences with God's goal for your life; don't fret, worry or brood over others who interfere with this; leave it in His hands. Keep resolutely at what you are doing. Take the chance to discipline any area where you are wasting too much time, money, or energy; carefully think through things like eating, dress, relaxation, or entertainment. Get to bed before you get too tired; give the next new day to God and rest the one that has just passed in His loving and understanding hands.

74

Fasting Is Not Old-fashioned

Before any big, important event in your life, when you really need to do your best with God's help, there is a Christian secret you might like to try. For an important speech, prayer, message, or game, *fasting* may be a real help. It is an indication that you are earnest, that there is something you want so greatly that you will put everything aside to get it. It's honestly, sincerely—sometimes desperately—reaching out for God and His will. We put Him first—above food, water, friends.

Fasting for the Christian is simply the voluntary missing of a life need. It is not always food; it can be rest, sleep, friends, or drink. But in the Bible it usually means not eating food for a certain time. It can help you in two ways: it can rest and clean your body by not weighing it down with food; it can draw your heart close to God since you are spending the same time you would usually give to eating in prayer instead. You can fast from anything that you are willing to temporarily sacrifice for God.

It must be voluntary—something you choose to do yourself. There is no value in doing it because you are told to. God will not force you to fast, but if you really need that extra intensity it is there to help.

It must be private. If you tell anyone you are fasting so they will be convinced of your spirituality, God will not bless you for it. Fasting must be done for Him. If you go around boasting about it to others, you already have your reward. Of course, you may have to tell parents or friends who know your eating habits so as not to worry them; but this is different. When you fast, don't go around looking haggard, dead-on-your-feet, and wiped out. That is not fulfilling the fasting conditions laid down in Matthew 6:16-18.

It must be sensible. You won't want to fast for weeks as a teenager, or if you have a demanding or strenuous job to do. Holidays, or weekends are best; you will be able to control your activity better. If you want to go on a long fast, start with a few smaller ones and then work up with rests in between. Long fasts need longer rest periods both during and after the fast.

It must be thoughtful. Don't inconvenience parents or friends by being difficult. On a long fast, you must drink much water, at least seven glasses a day. If you want a real fast, don't drink anything else, especially coffee or tea. Long fasts can last from two to three or even four weeks. The most difficult part is the first five to six days. You may feel headachy, sick to your stomach, and tired as your body poisons are emptied out. Keep flushing your system out with water. After the worst peak is over, you can go many, many days without real appetite for food. One important precaution: stop the fast if hunger returns. This is a sign that the body has used up all its reserves. If you go on any longer you will begin to starve. Be *very careful* in breaking a long fast; take as long to break it as you did to take it. Use juices, clear, non-milky soups, etc., until you come gradually back to normal diet.

Use your normal action time—eating, pleasure, company time —for prayer instead. Talk to Jesus during this time. Read the Bible. You'll be richly blessed.

Section XVII
The Disciple &
SOCIETY

75

When the World Hurts You

"See to it that no one comes short of the grace of God, that no root of bitterness springing up cause trouble, and by it many be defiled" (Heb. 12:15).

The trouble with the world is that you don't find in it many people you can trust. Maybe you know what it is like to have someone you really looked up to let you down—maybe badly. If you are a girl, maybe it was some guy you really trusted when he said he loved you. That was when he found out you were pregnant, and then split, saying, "Too bad, chick. It just wouldn't work out." Maybe your dad is a hopeless drunk, or your mother runs around with so many guys that you wonder who your real father is. Or maybe you come from a church crowd where your parents are high officials, and you have seen their phony lives when they get home and let down their religious masks. Yes, there are a lot of ways to get hurt today—none of them quite the same, and none of them nice.

The rotten thing about being hurt is that the ones who really have the power to hurt are the ones you love and trust most. No stranger can really hurt you with words half as much as someone you want to love or call your friend. And you got hurt in direct proportion to how well you know and love the one who hurt you. The more you trust them, the more you look up to them, the deeper and more agonizing the hurt you feel if they turn against you or fail you. If you are a girl, you especially know what I am talking about. You feel far more deeply than most of the guys you've ever broken off with. You are more sensitive, more aware. And that means hurt, terrible hurt, if you have bared your heart and had it stabbed right through by someone you loved and trusted. But no man is exempt from that same kind of hurt either. Whoever it happens to, it happens as if it has never been so bad with anyone else in the world.

What do you do when the world hurts you? One thing you can't afford to do is the one thing almost everyone does: get bitter, and say in your heart, "I'll never forgive that rat again; as long as I live, I'll never forgive him!" Bitterness begins when you really get hurt but refuse to forgive. It is a deep disappointment that leads to resentment and hate out of your hurt. And when you live in the kind of world God has called us to speak to, there are an awful lot of people around who can hurt you.

The number one problem bugging disciples of Jesus from the street, experiencing broken homes, smashed marriages, lying politicians and phony churches, is bitterness. It is the most deadly sin affecting the growth of the Jesus movement. Left to fester and swell, it can totally destroy your spiritual life. Unless you deal with unforgiving hurt, you can be ripped off by any religious deception or ego-trip that is against something in the name of God going around.

Bitterness is a deadly sin. It doesn't enflame you like sex, or affect you quickly like a fix of "dynamite," but it gets you in the end. Just like a slow acid going "drip, drip, drip, drip," it eats away at your soul. Mel Tari, in his book, *Like a Mighty Wind,* says, "The more I have travelled . . . the more aware I have become that many people . . . have a brokenness or a wound because of past experiences. In the hearts of most Americans there is a bitterness, hurt or something. The result is that they feel bad inside and have no power or joy.

"In consoling many, I have discovered that this is something from the past, sometimes from their childhood or teenage years. Even when they become Christians and they have forgiven, often the bitterness and hate are still there. Many never think of giving it to the Lord for healing. Many try to forget their injury by trying to be spiritual. They struggle and grasp to find more of God and satisfy themselves. What they need to do is open their hearts to God so He can minister to their needs."

If you are like most disciples of Jesus reading this book, you have been hurt before. It is never the same, and it always hurts as much if not worse than the last time. Some kids try to handle hurt by just shrugging it off; others put on a tough front and play "rock-heart." But you wish the thing that happened to you had never happened. I feel for you. We all bleed the same way, and our worst wounds are inside where no one but God can see them. We all know what it means to cry in silence, no matter how brave a front we manage for the world. But there is one really bad thing about being hurt and not forgiving: it takes our thoughts off Jesus and off life and sends us to brood over the one who hurt us. And something will happen. As we center our thoughts on their ugly attitude and wrong, *we* will begin to change. As our hearts focus, so our lives will change until we will become like the ones we are thinking about. We will change, step by step, until we actually start living and acting like the very ones that hurt us.

In the film, *Ben Hur*, the central character forces himself to stay alive, hoping to get revenge on his Roman former friend who had betrayed him, imprisoned his family and sold him as a slave to the Roman galleys. After a miraculous deliverance and a spectacular chariot race, Ben Hur finds and beats his enemy into the dust. He returns to the jellied, bloody, Roman who is dying in agony. But the Roman grabs Ben Hur's tunic and manages to croak as he dies, "The race, Judah. The race. It goes on. The race is not—over!" He dies. But because Ben Hur never *forgave* Messalah, the enemy that Messalah had been still lived. He lived in Ben Hur's heart and blood and mind, until with fear and anger his girl friend sees the fearful changes bitterness has made in his life. She says something every disciple of Jesus should remember: "It is as if you had become Messalah!"

Hear it well. *You become like the one you despise.* Keep on thinking about him, keep on living in the hurt he has brought to you, and step by step you will change until you become just like him. And you will never be free from what he did to you, even if he is dead, buried and in his grave and ploughed under a hundred tons of rock. He will live on in your life and soul until you finish him off as an enemy in the only way God will let you: by forgiving him.

Stop right now and think hard. To forgive does not mean to stop feeling the hurt. No one in his right mind would try to say that a disciple of Jesus should not really feel hurt if people do rotten things to him. Of course you feel hurt. But stop to think also about this: *So does God!* As a matter of fact, no one in the whole universe can feel quite as hurt as God. Remember, we said you are hurt by as much as you know and look up to the person you trust. There is no one in creation who loves you more or has invested more in your life than God. When you hurt Him, you have power to hurt Him more than any other being in existence. And for every hurt you feel, He also feels it. And He feels not only your hurt, but also the hurt of every disciple of Jesus. He feels the hurt that the whole world feels from their own and others' sin; and on top of all this, the heartbreaking hurt of having his whole planet refuse His love and healing. Yes, God knows hurt, more than we can ever imagine. Never do we read in the Bible that Jesus laughed; but three times it tells us that Jesus wept. So to forgive does not mean to feel good about wrong or rotten things people have done.

To forgive means to come to God for His healing grace. The Old Testament gives us His promises: "The Lord is near to the broken-hearted and saves the crushed in spirit" (Ps. 34:18). "He heals the broken-hearted and binds up their wounds" (Ps. 147:3). The One who was bruised and crushed and broken for our sin understands our hurt. He knows how it feels because He has borne it before us. To forgive means to give your tears and hurts to God, and to pray for the one who hurt you. It means to unload your pain to the Lord Jesus until you can feel a little of the terrible hurt in His own heart, until you can feel your sorrow beat with His, until you join the "fellowship of his sufferings."

Whenever someone hurts you, at that moment God will flood you with special help. He will be very, very close to you. Take that moment to call out in your heart to Him. Remember that He himself has felt what you just felt. And learn what it means to say through your tears and pain and anger, your ruffled and hurt feelings, "Father, forgive them. They don't know what they are doing."

Two thousand years ago, they stood around His cross. There were stupid, evil people there, little ratty people with vicious faces who mocked and cursed and jeered as the Prince of life hung stripped and naked before the crowd, pegged up in blood and agony between earth and heaven by spikes of iron. He had come to save; they cried, "Crucify!" and the cross had almost done its deadly work. In front of Him was a sea of faces more animal than human, more demonic than natural. Here He hung, the King of kings, and the Lord of lords, at whose word the angels bowed in serried ranks of reverence across heaven. These people screamed at Him who was God made flesh, He who before time had made the stars and upheld galaxies by the word of His command, He who holds in His hands the life and breath of every creature on earth. As they spat and ranted, screamed and laughed, no being on earth could really fathom what He was going through— hurt more than any human being has ever felt on this planet. It was not just the physical hurt of His whole body being an aching pulse of pain; it was not just the mental shame of being stripped naked before this leering world. No, this pain and hurt was only a very little of His agony. His was the hurt of a world that had turned its back upon its Maker, the hurt of the One who had come to His own but His own did not receive Him. Watching the sea of filth and degradation, He could have gasped out, "You filthy, ungrateful, stupid little worms!" One cry was all that He needed to give—one cry to the serried ranks of angels with drawn lasers who watched with shock, horror and anger at what was happening. He could have cried, "That's it! I can't take this any longer. Legions three, four and five, all systems go. This is it; this is the finish; this right now is the end of the world!"

He could have said it. He didn't. All He said was, "Father, forgive them. They don't know what they are doing."

When the world hurts you, stand with Jesus. Say what He said. He did it first. And because nothing that has ever hurt you could ever be worse than that awful day, you can be strong in your hour of need. He will not fail you. He has been there before you. And the Day of Judgment will show men and women who are in His kingdom because of His choice and yours to forgive. Do it. No one else but disciples of Jesus can or will. When the world hurts you, forgive. That is the only way to be really free from its power.

> I think that God is proud of them who bear
> A sorrow bravely. Proud indeed of them
> Who walk straight through the dark to find Him there,
> And kneel in faith to touch His garment's hem.
> Oh, proud indeed of them who lift their heads and shake
> The tear away from eyes that have grown dim,
> Who tighten quivering lips and turn to take
> The only road that leads to Him.
> How proud He must be of them—He who knows
> All sorrow and how hard hurt is to bear;
> I think He sees them coming, and goes
> With outstretched arm and heart to meet them there;
> And with a look—a touch on hand or heart—
> Each finds his hurt heart strangely comforted.
>
> —Author unknown

76

Taking Revenge on Sin

"Now I am happy, not that you were made sorry, but that you were sorry enough to repent; for you were made sorry in God's way, that we might not hurt you. For godly sorrow works repentance to a salvation not to be repented of, but the sorrow of the world works death. For see this very same thing: you were made sorry in God's way. What carefulness it wrought in you; yes, what clearing of yourselves; yes, what indignation; yes, what fear; what vehement desire; what zeal; yes, what revenge" (2 Cor. 7:9-11).

Here is one of the most interesting verses in the New Testament for street people. It tells us how to handle hurt and how to use this hurt to take revenge in God's way. There are two ways to respond to hurt. One is the world's way, and it always leads to death. It means bitterness, despair, violence, and leads to taking away your reason for living. Perhaps you have known what it means to be hurt and go the way of the world in sorrow. What happened to you made you either so smashed and broken that you felt like killing yourself, or so deeply bitter that you vowed you would get back somehow, somewhere, at the one who hurt you.

There is a Christian way of taking revenge on people who do real wrong to you. We are not referring to the hurts we feel in the ordinary tides of life. We are not talking about hassles and irritations now. We are referring to the hurts from real sin done to you by others, or by things you have done to hurt yourself that were really wrong. When you are hurt by others' sin, take these steps:

1. *Learn to be careful.* Jesus gave three parables about lost things. The first was about a lost sheep. The sheep got lost simply because he was careless. He didn't stay close to the other sheep or the shepherd. He got so far out that when night came he wasn't

with the rest. Being hurt by sin gives you a clear warning: be careful how you live. Let the hurt teach you the lesson that sin always hurts. It hurts God so much that He cannot let a man who lives in sin into His kingdom.

Never treat sin lightly. God doesn't. There will be people who will be lost because of carelessness, lost because they didn't walk softly before God, even people who called themselves disciples of Jesus but didn't bother to be careful about God's conditions for salvation. The Bible does not say, "How shall we escape if we *reject* so great a salvation." It says only *neglect* (Heb. 2:3).

Think about the hurt that sin makes. Learn a lesson from it. When you see the grief it has brought to you, know what it has done on an infinitely larger scale to God. And you will never want to do that same thing again, or ever do what was done to you by others. The first thing that godly sorrow does is work carefulness.

2. *Learn to clear yourself.* If someone hurts you, use that hurt to drive you to your knees before God. Ask the Holy Spirit to show you if there is something in your life that attracts trouble. Sometimes we carry bad habits or attitudes around with us that we just don't see at all. They are blind spots to us, but others see them. Being hurt often can pinpoint what is wrong with us. Take a spiritual checkup when someone does something wrong to you. If it was in a friendship, ask yourself, "Did I really seek their highest good before God? Did I really have God's mind about this person?"

If you are a girl and have been used by more than one boy, you may have been projecting lustful attitudes that attract the wrong guys. If it was a betrayal of trust, ask: "Did I seek the Lord about this? Did he give me the green light on this matter?" If the hurt came from your own sin in part, the Holy Spirit has spoken to you already. Use your hurt to break before God, and humble yourself so that He can restore you. Clearing yourself means also the willingness to confess and restore to others.

Here are some ways you can clear yourself with others. If your problem is not covered here, ask God what to do. He will show you the best way the moment you are willing to do it.

1. *Stolen things.* Perhaps you have been a thief, a shoplifter, burglar or con-artist. If God speaks to you about certain people and their stolen property that you have, you must clear yourself by being willing to make restitution. This is the expressed teaching of the Bible: "If a soul sin, and commit a trespass against the Lord, and lie to his brother in that which was given to him to take care of, or in a deal, or in a thing taken away by violence,

or has conned his neighbor, or has found something lost and has lied about it—in any of these things that a man does, sinning in them—then it shall be because he has sinned and is guilty that he shall *restore* that which he took violently away, or the thing which he got deceitfully, or that which was given to him to take care of, or the lost thing which he has found, or the thing he has lied and cheated about; he shall even *restore* it in the principal . . . " (Lev. 6:2-5).

Make a full list of the things God speaks to you about. Put down all the things that you have at home that are not rightfully yours. Purpose to take them all back with an apology to the persons involved and a willingness to take any punishment. If the thing you took is used and is no longer returnable, begin to save up money for its value and determine to pay that back instead. If you did it the Old Testament way, you would be adding 20% interest as well! Sin—your sin of stealing—has helped wreck the world and trust between people. Restitution is the act of helping put it back together.

List everything the Holy Spirit speaks to you about. What you should have on your list are the things that have been bothering your conscience. Under each person's name or store or house, list what has to be restored or paid for. Then ask God to help you raise the money for that which you should pay for first. You may have to sell something you own, or lose a great deal of what you have, to do it, but you will have a clear heart when it is through. Ask the Holy Spirit to help you know what to fix up first. In some cases it may be best to get all the money together and then go; in others it may be better to go first and offer to pay things back on a weekly basis. Watch God move to help you do this. He may work miracles of financial provision to help you. And think of the thrill of knowing you can walk down the road perfectly free of all guilt over the past!

When you go to apologize, remember that you are going now as a new creature in Christ. You are not the same person as the one who once stole and lied and cheated. God has made you different and clean. Ask Him to help give you favor in the eyes of the person you stole from. Work out what you are going to say and how you will try to make restitution. Then go to see them.

You might say something like this: "I wanted to see you about something that has been bothering me for a long time. Just a little while ago I gave my life to Jesus Christ. Since then, He has been speaking to me about things I did wrong in the past. One of the things He brought to my mind was the wrong I did you in—(name the sin). I realize my wrong, and have come to tell you that I am sorry for it and to ask your forgiveness and to be willing to face up to whatever you want to do over it."

This may mean a total forgiveness, a clearing of the debt; on the other hand it could result in some penalty. I know young people who have gone to prison because of their wrongdoing as non-Christians, and who felt God wanted them to pay their debt to society that way. Put your whole case in God's hands.

I am thinking of a friend of mine who went back to own up for some crimes he had committed before he was saved; he was jailed for four years. During that time he had plenty of time to study his Bible. He also had time to evangelize the whole prison. He led numbers of prisoners to Jesus, witnessed to his jailers, and began a Bible study in his cell block and grew strong in the Lord. When he was released, he said that something beautiful happened. In previous times he had felt a sense of freedom and release when he was finally let out of jail for serving his time. This time, when the gates closed behind him as he left, he felt nothing. The Holy Spirit spoke to him. God said, "Son, this is my way of telling you that you have always been free." Prison is not captivity to the man who has been imprisoned by the liberating love of Christ. Today he has a great ministry to prisoners in jails. Don't be afraid of going to prison for some time. Jesus was put in prison for His walk with God; the apostles went to prison for their faith; many of them were even executed for the same reason. You will be in good company.

In court cases, get a Christian friend who can pray with you and possibly go with you. I have seen God work many miracles in the hearts of a judge and jury. The Bible says, "The king's heart (the one in authority) is in the hand of the Lord." God can influence their minds and decisions, and reverse them by prayer if that is what He decides is best. But do your part. Obey Him, whatever the cost.

2. *Criticism of others*. If you have bitterly put people down, you must take steps to go about building up their reputation after a true confession and restitution. Find some good things to say about them. Make a point of holding up their good points before others. If you have been envious or jealous of someone, don't apologize for saying rotten things about him. *That* wasn't your real sin. Apologize for what *caused* you to say rotten things: envy regarding their good life or fame. Your envy *led* you to say bad words about them. Don't confuse the *results* of sin with the sin itself. No one can forgive the results of sin. If you just apologize for saying rotten things when they didn't even know you did it,

you will only succeed in widening the gap between you.

3. *Indignation* is another important part of taking revenge on sin. Get mad enough to finish with it once and for all. How do you get delivered from sin? You must first *see* it for what it really is. The blood of Christ does not cleanse excuses. The way to see sin, to know Holy Spirit conviction, is not to try to just *feel* guilty. To see sin, ask the Holy Spirit to help you. Ask Him to show you just how awful it has been. Ask Him to show you what your sin has done to hurt God, to hurt others, to hurt yourself.

The next steps are to *hate* it and *forsake* it. To really get mad about sin, think through what each one has done to your life. What a waster of time and energy and beauty sin has been to you! Do you see your sin? Then hate it; ask God to really open your eyes and to give you such a loathing and anger over that sin that you really despise what you have done. Then you will have the power to forsake it for all that is lovely in Christ's love.

This is part of what it means to fear God. The Bible tells us that the "fear of the Lord is to hate evil" (Prov. 8:13). And taking revenge on sin means that we will learn to really fear God. We will not be scared of Him as someone who is infinitely spooky, but have such an awe and reverence of Him that we will do what He asks us to do, whatever people think of us. The fear of the Lord will help you set yourself against wrong with a perfect hatred.

Here is one thing you can do to take revenge on sin. Get really angry over all material avenues of your temptation. Destroy all sources of sin that are still lying around to tempt you. Take out all your dirty books, rip them up and burn them. Be merciless. Don't take out the anger and hurt you have felt over your wrong on other people or yourself; take it out on these objects of temptation. Get your acid and hard rock records that you used instead of drugs to take you up and bring you down without God. Break them into bits, make frisbees out of them over a fire. Flush any drugs you have left down the toilet. Smash your needles, pipes and fixings. Throw away or destroy every instrument of sin, everything that reminds you of wrong in your past. Tear down your occult posters, your horoscope charts, your peace symbols. Burn all clothes that remind you of your past life. Give away anything valuable that still reminds you of a guilty past.

4. *Vehement desire* is another part of taking revenge on sin. Being hurt by sin can give us power to speak against it when we are clean. Who knows the hell that sin brings better than the man or woman who has been delivered from it? Who can speak

with greater passion against drugs or sexual immorality or bitterness than the man or woman who has been its slave? When sin hurts you, use that hurt against the kingdom of hell. Vow before God that it shall not hurt you again, and that as long as you breathe you will do all in your power to stop others from being hurt like you were.

Abraham Lincoln saw the slave markets in New Orleans. He said to his friends in anger, "Let's get out of here, boys. If I ever get a chance, I'll hit this thing hard." When you are clean, something begins to burn in your heart for God. This is part of the zeal that comes from godly sorrow. What a thrill to be on the attack for God! What a thrill can happen in your heart when you are His soldier of love, when your reputation is in the trash can and you are out to burn a hole in hell! The Lord Jesus said, "I will build my church, and the gates of hell shall not prevail against it" (Matt. 16:18). When I first read that shallowly, I thought it meant that although the devil would really hit disciples of Jesus hard, God would see to it that they didn't cave in and give up the fort that they were holding. I could see all the Christians scared stiff, hidden inside a fort, yelling for the Lord to come back and save them out of their plight. I could see white flags being waved all over at the devil's crowd as they advanced.

But I read that verse wrong. That's not what it says or means. Look at it again and see what will not be able to stand. The gates of *hell* will not stand! Against the stronghold of hell comes the church militant, terrible as an army with banners, filled with fire and glory, smashing into hell with the battering rams of the gospel of God! C. T. Studd said it best:

> Some wish to live within the sound
> Of church or chapel bell;
> I want to build a rescue shop
> Within a yard of Hell.

This, then, is the way to take revenge on sin. We must learn what it is to be God's angry young men and women—angry over what sin has done to His world and His heart. Amy Carmichael put this power into poetry when she said this:

> What though I stand with the winners
> Or perish with those that fall;
> Only the cowards are sinners,
> Fighting the fight is all.

> Strong is the foe who advances;
> Snapped is my blade, O Lord;
> See their proud banners and lances,
> But spare me the stub of a sword.

Put right all you have ruined, as far as is in your powers. If you have enemies, there is even a Christian way to get rid of them. Go out of your way to do them *good!* Render good for evil (1 Thess. 5:15). Use the weapon of love, against which there is no earthly defense. If they hate, you love them back more deeply. If they criticize, praise their good points to others; if they slander your name, look for something nice to say about them. If they are thirsty, give them drink; if they hunger, feed them. Never stick up for yourself; defend only the Lord. Let Him do the defending. Kill your enemies with kindness. If you win, you have another friend who may also be God's friend. Take revenge on sin—but do it God's way.

77

Making Things Right With Others

Every disciple of Jesus must ask the Lord for courage to confess and restore to those they have wronged. If you hurt God, you know you must get right with Him. But if you hurt both God and other people, you must also put things right with them. God has made your memory to store your past. If you have done wrong, your mind will keep that memory, and when you get tempted you will think back to the last time you did wrong. If it is not put right, you may give in again. Until all wrong has been put right, you will always have trouble from a guilty conscience.

Not putting right all things from the past can give you deep problems. You will always find it hard to have faith or overcome temptation. You will not be bold in witnessing because you will always be afraid that someone somewhere will accuse you of being phony for not getting things right with them. Besides, a dirty conscience makes it hard for you to meet new people and make friends easily. And you will not really live in the joy of full forgiveness. You *must* put right things with others. God says, "He that covers his sins shall not prosper; but whoever confesses and forsakes them shall have mercy" (Prov. 28:13).

Restitution has already been dealt with. Confession is basically to humble yourself, admit your wrong to the other person, and ask for his forgiveness. Here is what to do to make things right with another:

1. Apologize to God. Make a full list of all the things still bothering you. You should get right what the Holy Spirit talks to you about. You will not have everything brought to your mind by Him. It may be only a few, but these are the things that block your happiness. Ask the Holy Spirit to show you them. Put down everything He brings to your mind. Don't leave out anything you know that ought to be on the list. Ask God to forgive you

for those things. Then ask Him for the courage to put them right with others.

2. Find out what the basic sin was in each case. No one can forgive you for the *results* of sin. What was the basic wrong that you did? Which one of God's laws did you break? Don't write down the results of your wrong because they can't be changed. Ask the Holy Spirit to search your heart and show you the basic sin in each case.

3. Set a time with the other person that will be all right with him. Make some place where you can be alone with him for a few minutes and where you will not embarrass him. If you can't do this, write a letter instead. Try to apologize in person unless it could be either dangerous or embarrassing to the other person.

4. Work out beforehand what you want to say to him. Don't apologize without naming the basic sin, telling him why you are doing it and asking his forgiveness. Here are three sentences to help you apologize: "God has been talking to me about something I did against you. I've been wrong in—(name the sin). I know I've hurt both you and God in this, and I want to ask you, 'Will you forgive me?' " Don't say too much, and don't preach. You only have to say a few words with a truly broken attitude to be effective.

5. Take time first to get the right attitude. If you can't go humbly and take full blame over what you have done, you need to spend more time before God. Think of all the hurt and loss your selfishness has caused. Think of what that sin has done to others. Think of the lives that same wrong has ruined and sent to hell. Think of the heartbreak it has brought to God's world. Think of the trouble it has caused in your own life, the sleepless nights, the guilty memories. Then think of this: that sin nailed the Lord Jesus to the cross; that sin broke the heart of God. Don't go until you have really let the Lord break you and show you how much you were wrong.

6. Be prepared to take all the blame. Even if the other person was really wrong, too, *you take all* the blame, just as if it were all your fault. Don't expect anything from him at all—even for-giveness. If you go in the right spirit and take full blame, you could start a chain of good that may bring salvation to many others. But even if the one you ask forgiveness of never forgives, go in the right attitude so that before God you have done all you can. It is your conscience that needs to be cleansed. Let God deal with the other person over his wrong. You do your thing and let God do His.

7. Before you go. ask a friend to pray for you during that time. If you are writing a letter, have a friend pray when you mail it. Ask God for wisdom as to the right time to apologize. You need His help to prepare the way for you and to prepare the heart of the other person. Deal with the big things first, and save the little ones until last. If you have restitution to make as well, work out what you are going to do about it before you start out.

8. Don't use any words that will take full blame off yourself. Don't involve others; you are not apologizing for them. Don't underestimate either your own wrong or how much they have been hurt by it, and don't wait too long in doing it. There is only one time that it is unwise to name the basic sin—when it is a sexual offense. A good phrase to use would be one like this: "I haven't set a decent standard for you"; or, "I haven't been a good example of a Christian before you," if you were a Christian at the time you committed your sexual wrong.

When you have gone through your list as thoroughly as if you were about to meet God before the throne of judgment, and have determined to get right everything you can, begin at once to do what you must do.

Remember this simple rule: The circle of *confession* must fit the circle of *committal.* This simply means that you only confess to the ones you have wronged. If your wrong is only against God, apologize only to God. Only He needs to know. If your wrong is against God and one other, apologize both to God and then to that one person. No one else should know. If your sin was against God and a number of people, you must put things right both with God and then with the group of people in a public apology.

Don't confess private sins in public meetings; it rarely helps anyone and is embarrassing to some. Don't confess public sins privately; if everyone has been wronged, it must be made right before everyone.

When you have finished getting clean, you will have the joy of burning your list and knowing that you are right with everyone that you know in the world. Think of your excitement and peace when you can walk down the road and can hold your head high before the world. If the enemy should bring back to your mind the bad memories of what you once did wrong, you can say to him, "Satan, you're right. I did once do those things. But there was a day when I got those things right with God, and I remember the day when I put those things right with those I hurt. And that's the thing I'm happy to remember. You can remind me only that now I'm clean."

Get those things squared away with God and with others. You need it. They need it. God requires it. There are thousands of other young people who need your example to give them courage to follow in this. This is Christ's way of triggering social change.

78

Stopping Others From Sinning

Perhaps the most disobeyed command in the whole Bible is found in Lev. 19:17: "You shall not hate your brother in your heart; you shall in any wise rebuke your neighbour and not allow sin on him." Many disciples of Jesus just do not reprove or rebuke sin. Yet God expects it of all of us; to fail to do it is to disobey God and to bring greater hurt to the world.

The life of the Lord Jesus was pure love in action. Yet He aimed rebukes in all directions. Jesus was not comfortable to have around if you held onto sin. He rebuked it, no matter who you were.

Most people have a funny idea of love. They think that it is just some kind of warm emotion, and that fellowship or compassion is a lovely feeling between two people. In this dream world, the arrow of rebuke is the very opposite of love. Nothing could be less true. To truly love or fellowship we must give ourselves, share ourselves. This means telling the truth about ourselves. This is not some sensitivity training trip. It is the Bible. We have a general idea that love and unity are wonderful, but can we pay the price for it? The price can be the pain of either taking or giving the corrective of reproof.

We *must* reprove. God teaches us to obey His authority by reproving. Family discipline, the backbone of divine order in both the church and the nation, is based on reproof. The most critical test of your growth as a disciple of Jesus is your ability to both give and take reproof. If you give it but don't take it from anyone else, you will be bossy, critical and will be nothing but a hassle to everyone else. If you will take reproof but are afraid to give it, you are gutless before God and are a partner to sin by letting it go unchecked, breaking God's world and His heart even more than it is already. The man who is unwilling to either take or give reproof is probably a phony; he fears man more than he fears God. Disciples of Jesus become "one in the Spirit and the Lord" in only one way: being truthful and honest with each other. We are not to be either dictators or doormats, but are to "speak the truth in love," taking correction from others even when it hurts, and daring to speak out for right even when it costs us to do it.

To avoid rebuke is evidence of a people-pleasing heart. No radical is ashamed to defend his platform. Where are the Christian radicals of today who are not ashamed of the Lord Jesus? No one likes to stand alone, but sometimes the disciple of Jesus must stand. He must stand for the rights of God, no matter what it costs. Someone must stop sin! God has given us a tool to limit sin. That tool is reproof and rebuke. If we do not learn to rebuke sin, what will we say to God when the hooker, the acid-head, the professional assassin and the witch stand before God in judgment? "We lived in all these things," they will have to say. And what will *you* say? "I let them go on without saying anything because I was afraid they wouldn't like me"?

The Lord Jesus had something to say about excuses like those. "Whosoever therefore shall be ashamed of me and of my words in this adulterous and sinful generation, of him also shall the Son of man be ashamed when he comes in the glory of his father with the holy angels" (Mark 8:38). "Whosoever shall confess me before men, him shall the Son of man also confess before the angels of God; but he that denies me before men shall be denied before the angels of God" (Luke 12:8). And Jesus always means what He says.

Love for God tells us we must reprove. Sin is His greatest enemy. To be holy means to love the things Christ loves and to hate the things He hates. The more we love God, the more we shall hate sin. Rebuke really tells how much we love God. The more we care about Him, the more we will get angry over sin.

Scripture gives only four times where it is best not to reprove. Don't reprove the scoffer (Prov. 9:8; 15:12) as it will only make him more hateful and bitter. Don't rebuke the rebel, the one that you know hates God and authority, as your words may only provoke violence (Ezek. 3:26-27; Matt. 7:6). Leave also the self-deceived heretic who has deliberately rejected what he knows is truth and has begun to teach others the same (Tit. 3:10; Eph. 5:11). He is to be warned twice, then left to the judgment of God. Lastly, don't rebuke the extremely self-righteous who are on such a pride and conceit trip and are so satisfied with their own wisdom and goodness that all your reproof will only bring argument (Matt. 15:14; 27:12).

In all other cases, you are to firmly follow the direction of the Holy Spirit by rebuking what is wrong. He will give you a clear nudge to speak out and the courage to do it at the same time. If you disobey, you will experience a deep sense of loss. It will never be easy, especially if the one we have to speak to is a friend, but we must have the courage to put God's principles above personalities (2 Sam. 12:1-14).

How do you do it? For fellow Christians, the proper Bible method is to first go to the sinning party, filled with the love of God. You must go wanting only to help him back to a good place with God. The secret of all rebuke is this: rebuke has nothing to do with how you feel. It is what *God* feels that is important; it is what *God* thinks that you care about.

Don't go and say, "Brother, this bothers me!" What does that have to do with it? A much better way to rebuke is to wait until you can first find something good to say about that person. Let him know first what you admire about him. Go as a friend; go in real love. Then word your rebuke so that you can get across what God says without giving off judgmental vibes. When the Holy Spirit opens the door, just quietly say something like this: "Brother, did you ever think that —— might be hurting God?" You must do it on God's behalf, not out of personal displeasure or as a complaint of injury against yourself. If he listens, you have gained a brother. Show him what to do to get it right. Share, if you can, your own past if Jesus has helped you with this particular sin. If you didn't have this problem, share that of a friend's experience of deliverance. And don't go until you think you can help him get right and unless you yourself are really clean before the Lord. Any known sin in a person who tries to rebuke will disqualify him from authority and holy conviction.

If he doesn't listen, get another concerned friend and go with him to see him again. Both of you must come in concern, not pointing fingers, but only with humble willingness to stand with your brother to help him get it right. You could say, "Brother, we may be wrong in what we feel, but we have come because we really love you and care about you. Now, if these rumors are not true, we will help you clear away the things that have been said about you; but if they are true, I want you to know that we are here to stand with you and to help you in any way that we can." If he listens and repents, you have gained a brother. If not, his sin must be brought up publicly in his presence before the whole church (Matt. 19:15-17).

This last rebuke is the hardest of all, but it must be done if we are going to keep God's work clean of infection. Again, there must be no bitterness or critical, judgmental attitudes. You could say, "Brothers and sisters, something very difficult has come up for all of us. We have a matter to bring before you all in prayer. Our brother here has had a problem for some time, and it has been hard for him to give this up. We have brought this up together now for your own love and concern. We feel this hurts God and His work, and is something that our brother must take care of before more damage is done to God's reputation. We want to give him this opportunity to have us as a church pray with him now."

If he doesn't repent even then, he should and must be treated as a heathen. This means he must be treated as away from God, out of the safety and security of God's care. And how does God feel over a lost man? He is not filled with resentment; He doesn't have an "I give up" attitude. God has only grief and deep concern over the sin that caused the separation, and has a willingness to forgive and forget at the least sign of repentance. Always reprove in the Holy Spirit so that the offender will feel as if the reproof came from God himself. And you will never learn how to reprove until you are willing to weep for the one in the wrong. Are there tears behind your reproof?

Be stronger in your reproof according to a person's relationship to you. If you know him well, rebuke can be more frank and direct. If he is older, you must treat him with the respect due to his age or authority (1 Tim. 5:1, 2, 19). Other things that will modify your reproof will be how much they know or how often they have sinned this way; if they really don't know how bad it is, reproof should be more in the nature of instruction or teaching rather than a "telling-off." Be sharper with someone who has kept on doing the same thing, especially when they have been warned before and still do not repent. A good thing to remember regarding sinners is that all you have to do to rebuke is to bring Christ into their wrong words or actions. If someone swears, you can say, "Do you really think God will damn it? I think He loves you and your work more than that." Or, "Jesus Christ? Did you know Him once? He is a Friend of mine." Always say it with a gentle but friendly smile so that they know that you really mean what you say but are not putting them down as persons. Let the Holy Spirit give you words to say. He will make them right on for each situation you face. All you have to do is to take the courage from Him at the right moment, and step out in faith to speak up for Him against sin.

> So he died for his faith. That's fine—
> More than most of us do.
> But say, can you add to that line
> That he lived for it too?

In his death he bore witness at last
As a martyr to truth;
Did his life do the same in the past
From the days of his youth?

It is easy to die; men have died
For a wish or a whim—
From bravado or passion or pride—
Was it harder for him?

But to live—every day to live out
All the truth that he dreamt,
While his friends met his conduct with doubt
And the rest of the world with contempt—

Was it thus that he plodded ahead,
Never turning aside?
Then, we'll talk of the life that he led—
Never mind how he died.

—Author unknown

79
Promoting Spiritual Revolution

You didn't ask for it, but here it is: the most awesome years in the history of the world! Never before has there been a more strategic hour. Never before has there been such a need for radical changes in the system we live in. Only two questions remain as we move into the last years of man. Can the tide be turned? And can the Church of the Lord Jesus see one last great awakening before He comes?

The answer to the first question is *yes*—yes, if *every* Christian is mobilized for the work of national awakening; yes, if there is immediate involvement *now* in every main level of society for God; yes, if we will dare believe God is still the same! The answer to the second question depends on how rapidly we can carry out the first one. The system needs change. Neither violence nor dropping out of it can help it. No political, educational or scientific answers seem to be forthcoming that will strike deep to the roots of the problem. The system is *people*. People need to be changed. Until that happens, every revolution is doomed to failure. And one thing that God can do very well is change people. That is, *if* His people will obey Him and be the kind of people that everyone else is talking about needing. And that can happen to you!

Christians can promote spiritual awakening in any situation in five major ways:

1. *By evangelism.* Spiritual revolution will be accomplished in this decade only when *every Christian* shoulders the task of evangelism. This is not the task of a few talented religious superstars; it is the mandate for every child of God who loves Him. This will not be easy. Man is *not* looking for God; man is not searching for Him. Lost people may be searching for happiness, or for peace, or maybe even for a religious experience. But they are certainly *not* searching for God. *God is not lost! Man* is, and from the story of the Fall, man has been hiding from God in

works and words while God has been looking for man. He loves people back to himself in order that they may join Him in His search-and-redeem mission. This will not be easy. The gospel is a costly enterprise; it cost God His Son and Christ His life. It may well cost us ours. But there is no other way to make the kind of impact we need.

2. *By confession and restitution.* Sin always hurts. It hurts God; it hurts others; it hurts ourselves. Forgiveness is God's method of dealing with our guilt; confession and restitution is His way of putting back together things sin has helped pull apart. If we have hurt God, let us apologize to Him sincerely and deeply; but if our sin against Him has hurt others, let us not stop there. The Apostle Paul could say, "Herein do I exercise myself, to have always a conscience void of offence toward God and toward men" (Acts 24:16). Confession is admitting wrong done to others and asking for their forgiveness. Restitution is the willingness to make things right with them as far as it is humanly possible to do (Lev. 6:1-6; Prov. 28:13; Ezek. 18:27-28).

3. *By reproof and rebuke.* What can the Christian do to help stop society from sinning? Is there a Christian form of social protest? How do you put a block in the path of wrong that is happening to your world? The answer to this is biblical reproof. Every Christian must realize that true Christian love is not sentimental; it is wise and holy as well as compassionate and caring. We are to be "angry, and sin not" (Eph. 4:26). We must stick up for the truth, whatever the cost to our reputation; we must tell the world in no uncertain terms what sin does to hurt God. The cost of love is the willingness to know the truth about ourselves and tell the truth about others in a way that will honor God. If we love God, we will hate the things He hates. God hates sin. Christians have learned to sit quietly by and let the world rush on to hell without saying a word. And this will not do if we want to be Christ's real friends.

4. *By social reform.* We hear loud cries from the secular world about the uselessness of the church. Many have left it completely out of their thinking as any useful contribution to social change. But the record of history speaks differently. Almost every major change for the better in society has come from a return to the Bible commands concerning man and his world. William Wilburforce worked to get child labor outlawed, and did it. Kier Hardy began the labor movement. William Booth forged into a mighty social force the early Salvation Army. Charles Finney preached strongly for human equality among blacks and whites when slavery was accepted. John Wesley's work created a spiritual awakening that saved England from another bloody revolution like that which

nearly destroyed France. We need more Christians like this.

5. *By prayer and fasting.* Two essential conditions must be met to usher in any spiritual awakening. The first is unity. Common understanding of what God is saying to this generation must be the basis of true unity. We must agree on what the message of Jesus is, and this will happen only with truth. Common unselfishness is the second part of this base unity. We must all be really working for the same Person. We must be right in our motives, and not just *use* God and the gospel for promoting our own name, our own glory and our own ends.

We can call these two facets of unity *reformation* (a return to the true message of the Bible) and *revival* (a return to the true motives of the disciples of Jesus). But both of these can be met, and without prayer there will be no awakening. Prayer and fasting is a means by which we can prove to God that we really mean business, that we really care about what is happening to our world and to His heart. Nations have been under His anger before, and a return to these Bible principles on the part of His people have averted national disaster. His promise has not changed: "If my people, who are called by my name, shall humble themselves, and pray, and seek my face, and turn from their wicked ways, then will I hear from heaven, and will forgive their sin, and will heal their land" (2 Chron. 7:14).

Problem Index